THE APPLAUSE ACTING SERIES

SHAKESCENES

SHAKESPEARE FOR TWO

✠

Edited and presented by

JOHN RUSSELL BROWN

✠

An Ann L. Rhodes Book

D1056079

Library of Congress Cataloging-in-Publication Data

Shakespeare, William, 1564-1616.
    Shakescenes : Shakespeare for two / edited by John Russell Brown.
        p. cm.
    ISBN 1-55783-049-5 : $8.95
    1. Dialogues, English. 2. Acting. I. Brown, John Russell.
II. Title.
PR2771.B68   1992
822.3'3--dc20
                                                                    90-30114
                                                                    CIP

Applause Theatre Book Publishers
211 West 71st Street
New York, NY 10023
(212) 595-4735

First Applause Printing, 1992

" . . . there is an upstart Crow, beautified with our
feathers, that with his 'Tiger's heart wrapped in a
player's hide,' supposes he is as well able to
bombast out a ... the best of you, and
... Johannes Factotum, is in his own
conceit the only Shake-scene in a country."

—Robert Greene, 1592

CONTENTS

✠

SCENES FOR TWO ACTRESSES

SCENES FOR TWO ACTORS

✠

INTRODUCTION

✠

This collection of scenes is presented from an actor's point of view, with various commentaries and other help, so that an actor may learn how to make the most of them in performance. In his own day Shakespeare was known as a dramatist writing as if he were "the only Shake-scene in the country." Each scene to be studied testifies to that unique dynamic which is released in performance and to a vivid sense of actual, individual life.

As in life no person is an island unto himself or herself, so in these plays no role enjoys its true meaning standing alone. The surface of the dialogue will interest a solitary reader easily enough, but its inner life is released only when two or more actors are working together: when they listen as well as speak; play off each other and are aware of a situation that they share.

In private an actor can improve technical ability by exercise, and of course soliloquies can be rehearsed on one's own. But a good play cannot be studied adequately unless interplay between actors is taken into account. Between two actors, it is possible to reach towards the mainsprings of drama: conflict; reconciliation; transformation; pursuit; resolution; watchfulness; interface; withdrawal; and aggression. Speech is no longer an independent element, but part of a performance in which a silent presence may have greater force than a stream of words. Closeness, distance, movement, touching, unease and responsiveness all become crucial, and outstrip the reach of a single imagination. What words themselves accomplish will change as they become part of interacting performances:

outward appearance can deny or modify what is actually said; what a speaker intends words to mean is not the same as what they seem to mean; simultaneously, words reveal both conscious and unconscious thought. Between actors, speaking a text as part of their total and shared performance, drama is experienced as a game, an entertainment, or a celebration. Imagination is stimulated and challenged, and theatre becomes an unexpected experience, open to many kinds of perception, discovery, and stimulation.

Shakespeare was so skillful an inventor that he could endow comparatively short passages of dialogue with a large measure of all these riches, and yet call upon no more than two actors. This book is therefore a collection of duologues, small scenes each lasting about five minutes in performance, each providing two equal but contrasting roles. A few scenes take rather longer to perform, and others rather less; these are included to give a variety of challenges and allow for varying conditions of work—shorter time for preparation, or opportunity to shape a scene of somewhat larger scale. But the majority of scenes may be studied, memorized, rehearsed, and then performed within the same resources of time. None of them call for stage properties or other physical requirements that the two participants cannot readily obtain for themselves at little or no expense. All of them are able to stand on their own, needing neither study of the whole play from which they are taken nor any special explanation to an audience when they are performed.

The scenes are divided into three groups, calling for two actresses, two actors, or one of each. Within these groups they are arranged chronologically in order of composition, so that Shakespeare's simpler writing is encountered before the more deeply-felt and concentrated speech of the great tragedies, or the more involved syntax and subtle phrasing of his last plays.

Before each scene, an introductory note explains the dramatic situation, gives crucial information about the characters and, very briefly, describes the visual setting. A more extensive commentary after each text draws attention to its main crises and indicates a number of ways in which work can start and develop. Several different interpretations of character and action are proposed, so that actors can experiment before choosing which will be best for their own talents and imaginations. The nature of these commentaries differs from one scene to another, so that numerous ways of working are encountered in the course of the book.

All the texts are edited afresh with the needs of actors in mind. Particular care has been taken with punctuation. Most published versions of Shakespeare's plays are liberally supplied with commas, colons and semi-colons in an effort to make them easy to read at first sight. But such heavy punctuation is not what Shakespeare intended: the few pages that have survived in his own handwriting are sparsely and sensitively marked, and scholars believe that, for those plays which were printed from his own manuscripts, the original punctuation was of a similar kind. But even when based on good manuscripts, early printed editions did not reproduce the original punctuation accurately; Elizabethan typesetters felt free to change such details to suit themselves or the convenience of the moment. The profuse and regular punctuation of most modern texts does not appear by virtue of Shakespeare's authority and has most often been introduced to help the solitary reader who has little experience of speaking texts aloud. This imposed punctuation is an impediment to actors, breaking up lines of thought and feeling, suggesting fussy, spiritless rhythms, and encouraging pedantic delivery. Some theatre directors so dislike the intrusive commas and colons of published versions that they have special rehearsal scripts prepared that have almost no punctuation at all. The texts printed here attempt a practical compromise; their light punctuation is sufficient to prevent ambiguities, but not so heavy that it will govern the way in which a text is spoken.

Spelling is modernized, since the many variations of the original printed editions have no more authority than their punctuation and serve only to confuse an actor. But, of course, the language is still essentially that of Shakespeare's day, different from our own and not always clear to a modern reader. For each scene therefore, a glossary is supplied to give meanings for words and phrases no longer current and explain grammatical usages, allusions and references when these are unfamiliar or obscure. It also annotates some familiar words when they are used in obsolete ways, draws attention to puns and ambiguities, and clarifies syntax or offers paraphrases where meanings are particularly complicated or exceptional.

Shakespeare often played with words and double meanings, teasing and forcing language to perform unusual feats, so that even Elizabethan actors may have needed help before understanding fully what they had to speak. Modern plays do not need all this explication, but the difficulties of Shakespeare's language should not be over-emphasized either. The language of his day can be mastered and communicated with much of its original sense intact. When his words are fully understood, actors gain in clarity and force so that audiences enjoy the exhilaration of language well and bravely used.

ADVICE TO ACTORS

✠

There is no such person as a "Shakespearean Actor," if that phrase implies the possession of unique qualifications or unusual gifts. Shakespeare's plays are available to all good actors, no matter what their training or experience may be.

Yet, of course, the texts reprinted here are not like those of twentieth-century plays. Shakespeare does present special problems, and the blunt assurance that his writing is open for anyone to explore will not sound very convincing to a student-actor meeting it for the first time. The following approaches are offered as encouragement to make a start and free imagination to work intelligently on the texts.

Character

First of all, an actor in any play must discover the person behind the words of any particular role. How does he or she move and speak, how think and feel, what does he or she look like, sound like? Where does this individual come from, what know, what want? How could anyone recognize the person who speaks these lines? Why does this particular person *need* to speak these particular words? Such are the basic questions, and some of them should be tackled at the start, even though more satisfactory answers may be found much later.

Of course, an actor must learn how to speak the character's lines clearly and forcefully, but that alone will not bring the play to life. Speech is not all, because Shakespeare did not write for talking heads. He first imagined individual persons in lively interplay with each other and *then* conjured words for them to speak; and that is the best sequence for an actor to follow. A living person has to be brought on to the stage, and then he or she can begin to speak—and become more fully-realized in the process.

In Elizabethan times, plays were performed on a large platform-stage that jutted out into the middle of a crowded audience, many of whom were standing rather than sitting as is the custom today; and in this open arena everything took place by daylight. Some performances were given indoors, but then the audience was illuminated along with the actors. Such conditions were more like those of a public meeting in our day, or of a booth in a fairground. They called for an acting style that was grounded in a basic physical delineation of each character. An actor had to maintain the vibrant outlines of the role, so that his performance could be viewed from all sides and at all times whenever he was on stage.

Of course, we should not try to recreate original performances—we do not know enough to start trying, and our theatres and audiences, and ourselves, are all very different from anything that Shakespeare knew. But what we can deduce about Elizabethan stage practice should encourage present-day actors to seek out distinctive physical characteristics for each role they play in Shakespeare, possess or embody them as fully as possible, and then play the text boldly. This will provide the appropriate dynamic and credibility.

The moment actors walk on to the stage in character, they must be strong and expressive, even before a word has been spoken. Then as each person is drawn into the drama, there must be no loss of definition, but growth, development and surprise. As the play continues, new facets and new resources will be revealed, until each character has become fully present and open to an audience. In performance, actors need to be alert and active, and must possess great reserves of energy. They are like boxers in a ring, who dare not lose concentration or the ability to perform at full power. They have to watch, listen, move and speak, and at the same time embody the persons they represent. It is like levitating, or flying through the air, by a continuous act of will and imagination. Characters must have clarity; actors courage.

But how can an actor find the person to present? Trial and error play no small role in shaping a trained instinct for Shakespeare's people. And this trial begins with a close interrogation of the text.

Normally, private study of the complete play will start the process, but when working on the scenes in this book an actor is not required to read the whole play. An earlier reading may help in a general way, but the task in hand is to act only the lines of one short duologue and to bring those comparatively few words to life in as complete a manner as possible. For such a limited drama, the most efficient help toward performance will arise from the scene on its own. Knowledge of other actors in the same part is, for much the same reasons, best forgotten for present purposes. Emulation and imitation are good spurs to achievement, but they are not very important when discovering how to study a Shakespeare role for oneself for the first time, and how to develop one's own interpretation of it.

An actor should first read the whole scene, several times, to become familiar with the words and gain a general sense of what is happening on stage. Then he or she should concentrate only on the words of the part to be played, asking very basic questions. How old is this person? What physical characteristics are essential for an impersonation? (Shakespeare's plays do not often insist on unusual physiques or facial features, but rely instead on a special use of ordinary characteristics.) What is this person's family situation? What are the political, professional and social conditions of life? Then more difficult questions follow, which help to define personality and consciousness. How does this person "see" and respond to the world around him or her? What does he or she like and dislike, what pursue and what seek to avoid? What conventions, social pressures or political forces influence behavior, either consciously or unconsciously? Clues to these psychological, sociological and political questions are in the character's choice of words and they must be followed up carefully and actively.

For example, in Scene 27, why does King John speak so much about light and dark, about eyes and sight, and about physical actions, often violent and rapid ones? Why is he so aware of faces and bodies, including his own? Answers to such questions should be related to the known facts of John's life and situation: he has succeeded a famous brother to the throne of England; he is unmarried; he has just heard that his mother has died; he is in a perilous political situation, especially while his brother's very young son, the presumptive heir to the throne, is alive. Slowly an actor will discover a sensual and insecure person, both nervous and energized; John is frightened and always seeking assurances, and usually he doubts any success. Is he a guilty man? Or is he a romantic one, who looks for some tenderness and peace beyond what he has found in life?

In a search for the person to bring on stage, first impressions may be deceptive or, rather, limiting. For example, on a first reading, Romeo and Juliet in Scene 2 may appear to be two "typical" romantic lovers who delight in each other's presence and have much in common, including parents who would disapprove very strongly of their love if they were to know of it. All that is true and useful, but if the two actors for these roles were each to make a list of the nouns in their respective speeches, two very different sensibilities and personalities would be revealed. The minds of Romeo and Juliet run in different directions; they have their own sensations and feelings, and distinct views of the world around them.

Having used the text to gain entry into the mind of a character, the actor can then begin to think about how this person walks, talks, behaves, and looks at other people; how he or she dresses, eats and breathes. It helps to look for someone in real life who answers some of the requirements, and then try to imitate this actual person. A good choice is someone from one's own circle of friends or associates, since intimate and precise knowledge can provide interesting clues for performance. But imitation of a person in public life, whom the audience will know as well as the actor, does have the advantage of being instantly recognizable and this may encourage a bolder presentation. However, such experiments do not always provide quick solutions, and so the actor must be ready to go back and scrutinize the words of the text once more, and try out other models. Perhaps two or more persons to imitate will help to satisfy most of the clues.

In none of this exploration is there a single or simple solution. Much depends on the individual actor's imagination and experience, the persons known to him or her, and what the text yields first to study. Lists are often useful: for example, what verbs does the character use? Verbs show most directly what is the "action" going on in a character's mind, the energy which makes speech happen. So in Scene 9, Othello starts with simple verbs—"is . . . is . . . Let . . . name . . . is"—but then equally short but fiercely active ones follow: "shed . . . scar . . . must die . . . betray . . . put out . . . put out . . . quench . . . can . . . restore . . . repent . . . put out . . ." Here repetitions show how Othello is held by the thought of certain activities, while the two verbs beginning with "re-" suggest a quick connection between these two thoughts. Now more delicate verbs follow, but still active ones: "plucked . . . wither . . . smell." When Desdemona wakes, Othello's mind seems to lose confidence: first comes the simplest verb "to be," but then he changes to more considerate activity: praying, thinking, soliciting, forfending. Yet now, for the first time since seeing Desdemona in this scene, he chooses the compact and powerful verb "kill." After that, and after "Amen, with all my heart," verbs disappear for a moment, and "Humh" is a complete speech by itself. Then, once more, slowly and carefully, Othello picks simple verbs, attempting to contain great concepts within each of them. Towards the end of the duologue, violence returns to Othello's verbs, more brutal and coarse than before. But he concludes with the simply phrased and factual, "It is too late."

By looking only at the verbs, an actor can discover the changing quality of Othello's thoughts, of his inner experience. He is direct and yet capable of great shifts of thought and feeling; one sensation yields to another in a moment, and then returns, and yet each sensation is clear in itself. Perhaps the only major ambiguity is in the concluding verb of "It is too late." An actor will need to try various solutions before knowing how this short speech should be spoken, and what is the complete action of which these words are only a part. What happens in Othello's mind and body as he speaks these simple words? And why are they so simple for so complex a moment? Is speech exultant? Or pained . . . hopeless . . . stunned? Or is it firm and resolved . . . satisfied? Or is it hesitant? Are the words spoken to himself or to his wife. Or to Fate, the gods or some other power outside himself? Word-by-word analysis of verbs shows something of how Othello's mind works, but only by playing the part, by finding and creating the sensations and actions step by step, can an actor discover how to act such a line as, "It is too late"—to act, as well as to speak the simple-seeming words. Besides, Othello must interact with his Desdemona before the whole drama comes alive and these words find an appropriate interpretation.

There are many constructive ways of studying Shakespeare's words beyond tracing verb patterns. Preparing lists of adjectives and adverbs may reveal when and where a character is sufficiently thoughtful to qualify an idea, although some speakers in some scenes will never have sufficient command or perception to use a qualifying or descriptive word. Lists of double-meanings, similes, metaphors, references to other realities than the one on-stage—whether the imagined world is distant, intimate, literary, political, religious or historical—can help to show the deeper resources of a character's mind.

For example, in Scene 7, Hamlet refers to brothels, religion, morality, ice and snow, folly, animality; such worlds are readily associated with the dramatic situation as he conceives it. His movement from one image to another charts Hamlet's thought-process in the scene. A further trail of references seems to lead us into the world of learning and debate. The clues here are: "admit no discourse . . . transform . . . translate . . . paradox . . . proof . . . accuse . . . believe none of us . . . wise men know well enough . . . ." In this field of reference, Hamlet concludes as if issuing an edict: "I say we will have no more marriage . . ." To what extent is Hamlet debating his own inner sanity—as if he were before a tribunal? Does Hamlet live in order to understand, or to be secure in his own mind, or to avoid being in two minds? To what extent does he confront Ophelia, and to what extent "affront" her? Hamlet seems to wrestle with his own reactions to her presence. Slowly, by such analysis of the text, a psychological "identikit" can be assembled, marking predominant colors, preconceptions, modes of thought and feeling. Many such separate and small details begin to suggest a more embracing idea about a person.

Another line of enquiry will ask how he or she addresses the other character in the duologue. Do questions, assertions, explanations, answers, excuses, qualifications, elaborations or repetitions predominate? Are sentences long or short, leisured and assured or compact and urgent? Are sentences governed by a single main verb? Or are they supplied with a sequence of phrases each governed by its own subsidiary verb? How does this person refer to others: always in the same way, or with variations? With different names, titles or endearments? Is address intimate or formal, simple or elaborate? Or is contact between two characters assumed and assured, so that names are not required at all? In Scene 7, Hamlet calls Ophelia successively *you*, *thee* and then a generalized *you*, concluding with no word of address at all: "To a nunnery, go." Ophelia uses "My lord . . . your honor . . . My lord . . . you . . . My honored lord, you . . . my lord . . . my lord . . . your lordship . . . my lord . . . my lord, you . . . my lord;" but her last two speeches are not addressed to him at all, although he speaks with increasing urgency directly to her. Hamlet is intimate only with difficulty; Ophelia hardly at all.

Normally such detailed verbal enquiry is a continuous process which goes on throughout a long rehearsal period. But when working on these duologues this scrutiny may be concentrated near the beginning. Lacking the broader perspective of the entire play, actors will need to rely on many small observations and suggestions in order to ground their characters firmly. Besides, a scrutiny of every word in these short scenes will help to develop a sensitivity to words, a facility which can be drawn upon constantly throughout an actor's career in whatever plays he or she may perform.

On the other hand, it would be a mistake to read and analyze for too long; an actor needs to start to act and to speak, just as soon as intuition and imagination are quickened by more deliberate investigations. The actor's own being has to be satisfied and used in performance, as well as the details of the text.

Slowly, a sense of the character's consciousness will emerge and a number of physical traits will become established. One danger is that too many details will attract attention, so that the basic presence is left undeveloped. After making his discoveries, the actor must therefore decide which of his discoveries are truly necessary and which can be discarded.

If the part were King John, for instance, in the scene on page 229, an actor might imitate details in the behavior of some real person who seems, like John, to be isolated and under some kind of restraint. Then as the text is spoken, the actor might notice how this person would be caught, on occasion, looking very intently into someone's eyes, perhaps searching for reassurance. Or he may find that John becomes restless and capable of very swift and abrupt movements, especially when his hand reaches out to touch or grip. Such instinctive impulses will come from within the actor as he works on the text with another actor, and they should be allowed to simplify or perhaps supersede what had earlier been observed and imitated.

So, the stage character should evolve slowly, from within itself, freshly and uniquely created; actions will suit the words, and reveal a sense of being that attracts and repays attention. There is no knowing what may happen; perhaps John's searching eyes will be firmly closed at times, as if light were unbearable, or as if an inner pain or fire made any contact with other people an additional burden which he dare not undertake.

Careful and patient study, analysis, exploration, imitation, quiet impulse, quick imagination, and the luck of adventurous rehearsal all have a contribution to make in the creation of these plays.

Verse, Prose and Language

As an actor begins to speak and act Shakespeare's dialogue, the formal features of the text have to be studied just as carefully. The structure of both verse and prose cannot be neglected for long. While some phrases and short sentences in these duologues might be found in ordinary spoken English today— as they were in sixteenth- and seventeenth-century speech— no one in real life has ever spoken in the blank verse or elaborate prose which are the staples of Shakespearian theatre. Somehow these contrived speeches have to become part of an imitation of life, at one with lively, individual and spontaneous behavior. This may well seem dauntingly difficult, and very few actors have not despaired, at some time or other, of being able to speak verse adequately. Such a reaction is wholly natural, but it has to be overcome; verse and unusual eloquence are in these plays to be used, not to be feared or avoided.

Laurence Olivier in his portrayal of the lead in *Henry the Fifth* decided to be real, rather than phoney, grand, or rhetorical. So he "got underneath the lines," and in rehearsal his acting became so close to natural behavior that the words were sometimes indistinct and difficult to hear. Then one day, Tyrone Guthrie, the director, stopped the rehearsal—he had been away for a while—and insisted that this actor should perform the verse and the rhetoric: "Larry . . . let's have it properly," he called out from the back of the theatre. For a moment, Olivier hesitated, and then did as he was told; and the change, as he tells the story,* was instantaneous and transforming. He had always known that verse and sentence structure, and imagery, were instructing him to speak with confidence, enjoyment and resonance, and that they had a commanding and developing power, but he had held back in distrust. Now he found that artificial verse and grand language fitted his character like necessary and proper clothes, and they gave him the ability to rouse his audience on stage and in the auditorium. (When he came to act the part in the film, they even roused his horse.†) Olivier was still truthful, but now he was also heroic.

Poetry is the natural idiom of Shakespeare's stage, as swimming is for the ocean, singing for opera or musical theatre, controlled and exceptional movement for dance, or solemnity for great occasions. Speaking Shakespeare's verse becomes as instinctive as song, and the actor forgets that he or she is being metrically correct and vocally subtle.

Elizabethan audiences were so convinced by performances in which verse was spoken that a play written wholly in prose would be more likely to seem artificial. Today Shakespeare's plays can become just as real, if actors both use the verse and

* See Laurence Olivier, *On Acting* (New York, 1986), pp. 91-96.

also act with truth to life. Bernard Shaw advised actors in Shakespeare's early plays to treat the verse like a child does a swing, without self-consciousness or hesitation. In later plays the art of verse is more demanding, the pleasure it gives more deep; but both must be similarly instinctive.

Until verse-speaking has become second nature—as it quite quickly does—an actor should study the meter of the lines well in advance of rehearsals, methodically picking out the words to be stressed and finding, by trial and error, the most appropriate phrasing. It is necessary to speak the lines out loud, so that meaning and syntax can be related to the demands of versification and *vice versa.* Breathing and speaking should work together so that the energy of thought and feeling responds to the text and begins to motivate speech. Texture, linked variations of sound, alliteration, assonance, rhyme and rhythm must all be heeded. These concepts cannot be explored fully in the mind. By speaking the words their sounds and visceral impact will reveal different levels of meaning. Phrasing, breathing, tempo, pace, pitch, intonation, silence, have all to be considered. The lines must be spoken aloud again and again, as one way of speaking is tested against another; and then, slowly, by following the clues inherent in the text, a fully responsive delivery can emerge.

Being able to speak finely with an appearance of energy is not the only goal here. The words have to belong to a character, whose speech must be true to the character's inner consciousness as well as his/her presence in action and in interaction with others.

There are three factors in the equation: actor, character and text. The actor has two distinct yet related tasks: the primary one is character; its complement is the use of Shakespeare's cunningly wrought text, whether in prose or verse. The double effort is cumbersome to talk or write about, but much easier to demonstrate and do, because the two activities reinforce and stimulate each other. When reading this book start to "do" whenever doubt arises. Generations of actors will assure you that with practice the acting of Shakespeare's poetry—not merely the speaking of it—becomes instinctive and fluent, pleasurable and, in the context of the play, both true and natural.

The actor should begin by appreciating Shakespeare's preferred medium, the iambic pentameter. Each line should have ten syllables, alternately weak and strong, so that each pair of syllables forms one "foot," and five feet complete a line. While few pentameters are entirely regular—if they were the dialogue would be unbearably wooden and predictable—all follow the on-going pattern to some degree. It is their likeness that links them together, while their irregularity draws attention to particular words, varies rhythm and pace, and lends a forward movement to speech as disturbance of pattern awakens an expectation that pattern will be reasserted and finally satisfied.

An example from an early play gives clear indication of both regularity and irregularity:

(*King Edward speaks to his queen about political enemies.*)

ᵕ — ᵕ — ᵕ — ᵕ ᵕ — —
My love, forbear to fawn upon their frowns.

ᵕ — ᵕ — ᵕ — ᵕ — ᵕ — ᵕ
What danger or what sorrow can befall thee

ᵕ — ᵕ — ᵕ — ᵕ — ᵕ —
So long as Edward is thy constant friend

ᵕ — ᵕ — ᵕ — ᵕ — ᵕ —
And their true sovereign whom they must obey?

— ᵕ ᵕ — ᵕ— ᵕ — — —
Nay, whom they shall obey, and love thee too,   5

ᵕ — ᵕ — ᵕ — ᵕ ᵕ — —
Unless they seek for hatred at my hands—

ᵕ — ᵕ — — ᵕ ᵕ — ᵕ —
Which if they do, yet will I keep thee safe

ᵕ — ᵕ — ᵕ — ᵕ — ᵕ —
And they shall feel the vengeance of my wrath.

(*Henry VI, Part III*, IV.i.75-82)

Some of the strong stresses marked in these lines might be changed, but very few; and all its irregularities are brief. The close of line 5 is most problematical: it is marked here with three consecutive strong syllables as the sense of the parenthesis seems to require, but the final "too" might be unstressed or, possibly, the penultimate "thee." (Three consecutive strong stresses should be used very sparingly, because they doubly disturb the underlying norm.) A similar uncertainty arises at the end of line 2, which is marked here with the final "thee" as an extra unstressed syllable. Alternatively, "can" would not be stressed and "befall" counted as a single strong syllable, so that "thee" could follow with equal stress.

In deciding how to scan a line, some general rules may be applied. Nouns and verbs always need to be stressed in order to make the sense clear—more stressed than adjectives, adverbs, pronouns, prepositions or conjunctions. Moreover the fourth syllable of any line, being the most able to re-establish the normal pattern after irregularities and most in control of each individual line, is nearly always stressed in a regular way. If the end of a line is irregular, the beginning of the following one is likely to be regular, for two, or three, consecutive feet. However the first foot in a line is very frequently irregular, since a reversed foot, with the strong syllable coming first, gives fresh impetus to new thought.

Sense, syntax, speakability and an underlying regularity are the principal guides in scanning a line, but they do not always provide an unequivocal lead. Until well-practiced in verse-speaking, a student should mark the text in pencil, changing the stresses until sure enough to start rehearsals. Still more changes may be made later, before this slow and methodical preparation can be forgotten and taken for granted—that is the last and absolutely necessary part of the process.

All the strong syllables are not equally stressed in speech, and here actors have much more liberty to find the emphasis that suits their own interpretation of a character. Many choices are available. In most iambic pentameters only three syllables take major emphasis, the other stressed syllables being only slightly more prominent than the unstressed ones. So one reading of the same passage might be:

> My love, for*bear* to *fawn* upon their *frowns*.
> What *dan*ger or what *sor*row can be*fall* thee
> So *long* as *Ed*ward is thy constant *friend*
> And their true *sov*ereign whom they *must* o*bey*?
> Nay, whom they *shall* obey, and *love thee* too,
> Unless they *seek* for *hat*red at my *hands*—
> Which if they *do*, yet will I *keep* thee *safe*
> And they shall *feel* the *veng*eance of my *wrath*.

Perhaps the first line should have four major emphases, as Edward presses his argument. In line 3, "constant" may be more significant than "long" and so take the emphasis; but the "f" in *friend* makes that word able to gain strength from the other stressed *f*s in the preceding lines. Choice of stress will also be influenced by words set either in opposition to contrast with each other or in agreement to reinforce each other. Stressing these words can often clarify the logic of what the speaker is saying. For example, in line 4, "their" might be stressed and the penultimate foot reversed, so that "they" is stressed as well for reinforcement, and "must" would count only as a weak syllable. Such a reading would raise the possibility that in line 7, "thee" might be stressed rather than "keep," so that the "they" in line 8 could be a fourth major emphasis in contrast with "thee," to bring a relatively sturdy finish to the whole speech. But, in general, pronouns should not be emphasized, because that takes away prominence from the nouns and verbs, which have to sustain the sense of any speech; those are the elements that form the supporting backbone for strong dialogue and provide its thought-action and forward impetus.

This simple speech of eight lines illustrates how metrical considerations become, very quickly and necessarily, issues of character as well. The same is true when problems of phrasing are introduced. In the early verse plays especially, a brief pause at the end of each line is usual and provides a further guide to phrasing beyond those inherent in sense and syntax. Yet this is not a constant rule, and sometimes only the slightest rise of pitch or marking of a final consonant is sufficient indication of a line-ending; in this way, two consecutive lines will run into each other almost without hesitation or change of impression. In this passage, if Edward pauses slightly after "friend," the last word of line 3, and after "safe" at the end of line 8, his thoughts of "love" will seem more urgent than those concerning political power because, in this reading, the latter will seem to be afterthoughts. But if line 3 runs over into line 4, without the customary pause at the line-ending, the two reactions become almost inseparable; and then the political motivation will outweigh the amorous, because it is expressed in a longer phrase and placed in a climactic position. The relationship between lines 7 and 8 raises similar possibilities.

A pause, or caesura, may also be marked in mid-line. Syntax or sense will sometimes require this to be done (as in line 7 above), but here too a choice is often to be made. The advantage of a mid-line break is that it can give a sense of ongoing thought and quick intelligence. Some critics would argue that every line should have its caesura, but there is good reason not to supply them too strongly or too consistently; such readings encourage a halting delivery and an impression of weakness, and are not always easy to comprehend. In this passage, the final line would clearly be stronger if there were no hint of a pause in mid-line. So might line 2—unless two slight pauses were given, as if commas had been placed after both "danger" and "sorrow," thus giving Edward a very thoughtful and determined manner of speech. Line 6 also seems to run without a break, unless it came after "seek," so giving point to Edward's personal involvement. Seldom should a mid-line pause be placed so that it breaks up a regular iambic foot; normally it should follow, and therefore still further emphasize, a strong syllable. If a caesura is marked in each line of this passage, a general impression of energetic thought might be given, and in some performances this could be useful:

> My love, forbear / to fawn upon their frowns.
> What danger or / what sorrow can befall thee
> So long as Edward is / thy constant friend
> And their true sovereign / whom they must obey?
> Nay, whom they shall obey, / and love thee too,
> Unless they seek / for hatred at my hands—
> Which if they do, / yet will I keep thee safe
> And they shall feel / the vengeance of my wrath.

No decision is solely a technical matter; versification in Shakespeare's mind was an instrument for enhancing a representation of individual characters in lively interplay. Problems of verse-speaking are truly dramatic problems, and so each actor must find solutions which suit his or her own impersonation. While there are many ways of speaking verse that are clearly wrong—too many stressed syllables one after another is a common fault, and too few clear stresses another—there is no one correct way to speak any speech. (For that reason the passage which has just been examined in great detail is not from any of the scenes printed in this book; readers are left free to explore those for themselves.) A respect for versification offers many opportunities to strengthen one's grasp of the play in action and deepen the rendering of a character's very being.

In the later plays there is still more scope for individual speaking of the verse. The iambic pentameter almost disappears at times, or else must make its presence felt by unusual emphases or sudden rushes or flashes of speech. In this passage from *The Winter's Tale* (II.ii 1–25) some lines contain superfluous unstressed syllables and some gain new emphasis in the last foot as a new thought begins strongly and carries impulsively into the next line:

> LEONTES Nor night nor day no rest. It is but weakness
> To bear the matter thus, mere weakness. If
> The cause were not in being—part o' th' cause,
> She, th'adult'ress . . . (For the harlot king
> Is quite beyond mine arm, out of the blank   5
> And level of my brain, plot-proof; but she
> I can hook to me.) Say that she were gone,
> Given to the fire, a moiety of my rest
> Might come to me again. Who's there?
> SERVANT   My lord.
> LEONTES How does the boy?
> SERVANT   He took good rest tonight;   10
> 'Tis hoped his sickness is discharged.
> LEONTES To see his nobleness!
> Conceiving the dishonor of his mother,
> He straight declined, drooped, took it deeply,
> Fastened and fixed the shame on't in himself,   15
> Threw off his spirit, his appetite, his sleep,
> And downright languished. Leave me solely; go
> See how he fares.   *Exit* SERVANT.
>   Fie, fie, no thought of him!
> The very thought of my revenges that way
> Recoil upon me—in himself too mighty,   20
> And in his parties, his alliance; let him be
> Until a time may serve. For present vengeance
> Take it on her. Camillo and Polixenes
> Laugh at me, make their pastime at my sorrow;
> They should not laugh if I could reach them; nor   25
> Shall she within my power.

The incomplete verse lines (11 and 12) indicate a breakdown in speech, with attendant hesitation or insecurity, and with unspoken responses. (Some editors print "his sickness is discharged" as the beginning of a new verse line, so indicating a pause after Leontes's question and a hesitation before the Servant completes his reply.) In contrast, the manner in which two distinct thoughts are contained within a regular iambic pentameter, at lines 9, 17, 18 and 23, shows how the speaker's mind overreaches his words, impelling speech forward without break. By such means, and the new energy at the ends of lines 2, 6, 17 and 25, Shakespeare has ensured that a correct speaking of the verse is never sufficient response to his dialogue; it must be powered by active thoughts and feelings which are only just contained within its form.

As in any lifelike dialogue in prose, the actor must ask why speak at all; that is, he must discover and follow the action of thought and feeling beneath the words, sustaining and shaping them. In other terms, syntax is, in the last analysis, more important than meter. Each complete sentence is a distinct action, requiring breath, physical response and speech, according to its own impulses. In the passage from *The Winter's Tale*, the disruption of ordinary progress within a sentence, at lines 3, 4 and 20, and the piled-up phrases of lines 5-6, 14-17, 20-21 and 24, all mirror and display a fevered and struggling mind; and these syntactical features must influence the speaking of lines that are often remarkably regular metrically. Line 21, however, either has two extra syllables, suggesting a very rapid delivery, or else should be printed as two half-lines, indicating a pause before "let him be" and, possibly, afterwards as well.

The main verb of each sentence—each grammatically complete and separable unit—provides the key to each thought-action, and an actor must follow its prompting. For example, from *Hamlet*, III.iv, marking the separate units of thought-action will show how certain impulses sustain speech while others curtail it.

> HAMLET Look here upon this picture and on this,
> The counterfeit presentment of two brothers. //
> See what grace was seated on this brow:
> Hyperion's curls, the front of Jove himself,
> An eye like Mars, to threaten and command,   5

A station like the herald Mercury
New-lighted on a heaven-kissing hill—
A combination and a form indeed
Where every god did seem to set his seal
To give the world assurance of a man. //   10
This was your husband. // Look you now what follows. //
Here is your husband, like a mildewed ear
Blasting his wholesome brother. // Have you eyes? //
Could you on this fair mountain leave to feed
And batten on this moor? // Ha! // Have you eyes? //   15
You cannot call it love, for at your age
The heyday in the blood is tame, it's humble
And waits upon the judgment, and what judgment
Would step from this to this? // Sense sure you have,
Else could you not have motion, but sure that sense   20
Is apoplexed, for madness would not err,
Nor sense to ecstasy was ne'er so thralled
But it reserved some quantity of choice
To serve in such a difference. // What devil was't
That thus hath cozened you at hoodman-blind? //   25
Eyes without feeling, feeling without sight,
Ears without hands or eyes, smelling sans all,
Or but a sickly part of one true sense
Could not so mope. //
O shame, where is thy blush? // Rebellious hell   30
If thou canst mutine in a matron's bones,
To flaming youth let virtue be as wax
And melt in her own fire. // Proclaim no shame
When the compulsive ardor gives the charge
Since frost itself as actively doth burn   35
And reason panders will.

QUEEN   O Hamlet, speak no more. //
Thou turn'st mine eyes into my very soul
And there I see such black and grained spots
As will not leave their tinct.

HAMLET   Nay, but to live
In the rank sweat of an enseamed bed,   40
Stewed in corruption, honeying and making love
Over the nasty sty—

QUEEN   O speak to me no more. //
    These words like daggers enter in my ears. //
    No more, sweet Hamlet.
HAMLET   A murderer and a villain,
    A slave that is not twentieth part the tithe   45
    Of your precedent lord, a vice of kings,
    A cutpurse of the empire and the rule
    That from a shelf the precious diadem stole
    And put it in his pocket—
QUEEN   No more.

Enter GHOST.

HAMLET   A king of shreds and patches— //   50
    Save me and hover o'er me with your wings,
    You heavenly guards! // What would your gracious figure?
QUEEN   Alas, he's mad.
HAMLET   Do you not come your tardy son to chide,
    That, lapsed in time and passion, lets go by   55
    Th'important acting of your dread command? //
    O, say!

From composed and demonstrative involvement, Hamlet moves forward to speak of his father and then his thoughts lead him into phrases that build one on another's shoulders until a phrase which is sustained for three lines brings him to a full conclusion. At once the rhythm alters, with two short sentences within a single line (11); and at line 15, three separate speeches are contained within a single line, the middle one scarcely expressive. So varying rhythms continue, new ones beginning without pause in the middle of verse lines. Then at lines 26-29, five separate considerations are controlled by a single verb which follows all of them; and a silence follows, indicated by the incomplete verse line in the middle of the speech. The sentence begun at line 39 is never completed. When he is interrupted by his mother, Hamlet speaks again without using a main verb, piling up descriptions of his father's murderer and his mother's new husband until again cut off by his mother—or, possibly, until he sums all up, without needing a verb, and his mother is able to interpose. He starts again only to see the Ghost, and stops with the line incomplete. His mind alternates between prayer, as if in some mortal danger, and respectful questioning, as if assuming a need for obedience.

A start can be made on preparing to act such speeches by examining the meter and then exploring each syntactical unit. In the latter task, the main verbs—and their occasional absence—will indicate the drive and involvement behind each unit; subsidiary verbs will often show a further motivation growing through the first and sometimes superseding it (as at lines 19-24, above). At the same time, this syntactical analysis will provide a useful guide to the rhythms of thought, their speed, force and directness, and the points of climax, conflict and resolution. Moreover verbs suggest physical actions too, not only in the imperatives "Look," "See" or "Proclaim," but also in the more descriptive "seated" (l. 3), "leave to feed And batten" (ll.14-15), and, passing now into a sequence where subsidiary verbs take on a life of their own and almost displace the main verbs, "leave to feed . . . batten . . . is apoplexed . . . err . . . thralled . . . reserved . . . serve . . . cozened . . . mope . . . mutine . . . melt . . . burn . . . pander . . . ." In prose dialogue, sentence structure is the principal means whereby Shakespeare controls and so strengthens an actor's speaking of his text. Often the formal arrangement is very elaborate and sustained. Moreover its effect is reinforced by the use of a series of parallel phrases and by wordplay; these both hold the subsections together and provide a sense of growth and climax. Almost any lengthy speech in prose is so clearly articulated that its form can be represented typographically. An actor may find it helpful to write out his or her own part in this way and so gain a visual idea of how to shape the words. So, for example, Benedick soliloquizes in *Much Ado About Nothing*, II.iii:

> I do much wonder
>> that *one man* seeing how much *another man* is a *fool*
>>> when he dedicates his behaviors to LOVE.
>>> will
>>> after he hath laughed at such shallow *follies* in *others*,
>>> become
>>> the argument of his *own* scorn by falling in LOVE;
>> and such a *man* is Claudio.

> I have known WHEN
>> there was no music with him but the *drum* and the *fife*
>> and NOW
>> had he rather hear the *tabor* and the *pipe*.

> I have known WHEN
>> he would have *walked ten mile afoot* to see a *good armor*
>> and NOW
>> will he *lie ten nights awake* carving the fashion of a *new
>>> doublet.*

And so on . . . the actor's task is to act this speech so that the *shape* of Benedick's thoughts is clear, as well as their sense; the varying weight and force of each phrase, the verbal repetitions, developments, uncertainties, emphases, conclusions. Exploring how the words play off each other in these ways can reveal the character's intentions. Stressing key words, puns and affirmations is not enough; the flow and energy of the language have to be represented in performance, giving a sense of exploration, energy, struggle, attainment, frustration. Sentence structure and wordplay define this music and this drama; and the actor must respond to both and transmit both through performance.

In the comedies, wordplay is often dismissed as mere wit, and of trifling and purely verbal interest; but for Shakespeare, sentence-structure and verbal variation are at one with his deepest dramatic imagination. Here is a soliloquy from *Ham-*

let which shows the same means at work in a moment of obvious gravity as well as wit:

> I have of late
>> but wherefore I know not,
>>> lost all my mirth,
>>> forgone all custom of exercises;
>
> and indeed it goes so heavily with my disposition that
>> this goodly frame,
>> the earth,
>>> seems to me a sterile promontory;
>> this most excellent canopy,
>> the air,
>>> look you,
>> this brave o'er hanging firmament,
>> this majestical roof fretted with golden fire
>> why it
>>> appeareth nothing to me but a foul and pestilent
>>>> congregation of vapors.

The wordplay here is both more subtle and more pervasive, so that typographically it can hardly be expressed as the shape of the thought should be. But a moment's reflection will discover the play on "know . . . seems . . . look . . . appeareth," on "sterile . . . foul and pestilent," "goodly . . . excellent . . . brave . . . majestical . . . golden," "custom . . . frame . . . canopy . . . congregation," "heavily . . . o'erhanging . . . fretted," "all . . . all . . . nothing," and so on. Another link between the separate phrases of this speech is not so clear in the words, but rather lies behind them: "lost" and "forgone," at the beginning of early phrases, suggest a sense of isolation and emptiness which is taken up at the end of later phrases, in "promontory" and, more hauntingly, in "vapors"—this last word concluding the entire line of thought. After this, Hamlet changes tack, perhaps returning to himself as seen from a new perspective: "What a piece of work is a man, . . ."

When two or more speakers are engaged in dialogue, sentence structure and words are echoed and varied between the speakers. But here individual minds have their own ways of shaping speech, turning words and phrases around, and introducing new ones, to bend the interchanges in their own ways. So Hamlet encounters Rosencrantz and Guildenstern, earlier in the same scene:

> HAMLET   . . . What have you,
>   my *good* friends,
>   deserved at the hands of Fortune
>   that she sends you to *prison* hither?
> GUILDENSTERN *Prison*,
>   my lord?
> HAMLET   Denmark's a *prison*.
> ROSENCRANTZ Then is the world *one*.
> HAMLET   A *goodly one*,
>   in which there are many confines,
>   wards, and dungeons
>   Denmark being *one* o' th' *worst*.

Hamlet's "worst" concludes ironically the play on "good," and now Rosencrantz responds by trying a stronger rebuttal: "We *think* NOT so, my lord." This is sufficient to change Hamlet's direction again and also the rhythms of his speech—but "good" and "one" stay with him still and "not" leads to "none" and "nothing":

> HAMLET   *Why then*
>   'tis NONE to you,
>   for there is NOTHING either *good* or bad
>   but *thinking* makes it so.
>   To me it is a *prison*.
> ROSENCRANTZ *Why then*,
>   your ambition makes it *one*;
>   'tis too narrow for your *mind*.

Here "narrow" continues the idea of "prison," and "mind" of "thinking," while "makes it" directly echoes Hamlet; typography cannot easily show these developments. This last short speech has sufficient energy to detonate a thought within Hamlet's consciousness:

> O God!
>> I could be bounded in a nutshell
>> and
>> count myself king of infinite space,
>>> were it not that I have had bad dreams.

"Prison" and "thinking" stay within his mind in "bounded" and "count myself," and so does the antithesis of *good* and *bad*. But the notion of "thinking" is now developed to yield the new idea of "dreams." The change to "dreams" is so notable that Guildenstern picks it up immediately, and Hamlet too. But soon the prince draws talk to an end, for he can no longer "reason"—another development from "thinking":

GUILDENSTERN Which dreams indeed are ambition, for the very substance of the ambitious is merely the shadow of a dream.

HAMLET A dream itself is but a shadow.

ROSENCRANTZ Truly, and I hold ambition of so airy and light a quality that it is but a shadow's shadow.

HAMLET Then are our beggars bodies, and our monarchs and outstretched heroes the beggar's shadows. Shall we to th'court? For, by my fay, I cannot reason.

Wordplay and the changing shape of sentences have shown how Hamlet is now able to contemplate his whole life and motivation, his impoverished needs, and the heroic role that he has been directed to play: "Our monarchs and outstretched heroes [are] the beggar's shadows." Almost certainly, this is a moment of stillness or quiet, which is then broken by shorter phrases of avoidance and apology.

Clearly the demands of this passage of prose dialogue can be met only in a full performance of the play, so astutely is one speech reflective of another and so deeply does Hamlet draw upon his inner consciousness. As in all the verse dialogue that has been examined in these notes, each actor must make his own distinctive response to the challenge of the text. No teacher or director can provide ready-made and sufficient solutions here, and this realization may help to understand something fundamental about the acting of Shakespeare: no instruction can take responsibility away from the actors. Sometimes students are recommended to speak Shakespeare's lines with a certain quality or tone of voice, or a certain accent, and for some exercises or some productions this may be useful. But following such a prescription is likely to do more harm than good, because the actor is distracted from a pursuit of verisimilitude, and from the primary task of finding a voice and being for each character and then responding to the text in his or her own manner. Of course, efficient breathing and voice production are needed to respond to so demanding a text, but technical expertise must always be at the service of the specific demands of character, situation and speech, as these are discovered by each individual actor.

In so far as Shakespeare's language is more demanding than that of other writers, more time will be needed to possess its words and images, ready for performance. Memory and sense perception have to be awoken truly and sensitively, so that they inform speech naturally, and this requires private reflection, exploration, experiment and preparation. When Shakespeare wrote "Or to take arms against a sea of troubles," his mind was alive with visual images, physical activity and past sensations. What for him was a "sea"? How did he imagine the action implied in "take arms"? How did he imagine Hamlet's experience which lies behind these words he uses? In some measure, the actor of Hamlet has to summon similar sensations from his own experience and memories, whether of his own life and observation, or from theatre performances, books, films, paintings, sculptures, architecture, music—

anything which helps to reenact the moment of discovery which provides the character with the necessity for speaking these particular words. Such mental preparation can seldom be done during active rehearsals; it needs peace and quiet, an open mind and steady rumination. But this private study may show little result until, in a late rehearsal or actual performance, unconscious connections are made, and sensations are fused into revelatory speech and action.

Some words and phrases in the plays seem to cry out for a great deal of preparatory work, but it may be only a small exaggeration to say that every word, phrase, sentence and speech may repay in some measure a similar investment. An actor can have an endless adventure when acting Shakespeare, as step by step he or she gets closer to a fully responsive, individual and necessary (and therefore convincing) way of turning text into performance.

The most obviously poetic speeches may be easier to prepare than some of the simplest lines in the plays when those are at points of great tension. In *Much Ado About Nothing*, the actress of Beatrice will have to find what lies behind "Oh that I were a man, I would *eat his heart* in the *market place*." Metaphor, activity, context, energy of syntax must all be considered. But it is even more demanding to use the two words "Kill Claudio," coming a little before this; they carry fewer clues and have a shorter time in which to make their effect. In exploring this speech, it will be useful to ask why Beatrice uses these words and not others. Why "Kill," and not *challenge* or *denounce*, or *slay* or *answer*? None of these alternatives is as strong, but considering them will heighten an understanding of the effectiveness of "kill." Why not *Defend Hero* or *Revenge Hero*, rather than "Kill *Claudio*"? Why not *Right the wrong*? In the context, any of these might serve, but "Kill Claudio" are the two necessary words. How, then, will they be spoken? With what simplicity, what violence, ease or difficulty, with what speed or slowness? With how much expectation that the command will be heeded? With what conviction does Beatrice speak, and why in such a brief imperative? Is there much else that she might say at this point? So many options exist that no one way of speaking these two words can be right. The scene is printed in this book, number 5, and various possibilities may be explored; some ways will draw forth laughter, others will be spoken with tears.

Such highly critical and dramatic speeches are exceptional in their demands, but however fluent and easy the language or however relaxed the character, Shakespeare's text is so finely judged that whole lifetimes of experience may be drawn upon to help in its performance. An actor's mind and body need to be more than usually alert and energized to answer the challenge. What starts as patient and complicated exploration can end, however, in a marvelous extension of an actor's powers of thought, feeling and being, as the poetry comes to fresh and brilliant life. That is why Shakespeare's plays are so rewarding to perform. By making each word sound as if it is necessary to his or her character, an actor will claim attention with amazing ease.

Towards Performance

All kinds of exercises can help inexperienced actors. Very slow rehearsals encourage full awareness of what is thought and felt, as the words are spoken easily without thought of projecting or shaping them. Silent rehearsals, with someone else speaking the text, improvised explorations of moments of encounter or retreat, improvised paraphrasing of Shakespeare's text, or sessions in which the actors sit back-to-back and only speak the words, trying to communicate fully—all these devices may help performers to become more free, adventurous and true. Variations in positions, so that the two actors are at first close and then far apart, quite still and then always on the move, looking at each other or refusing to do so, paying attention to nothing but the sound of words or engaged on other business—all these explorations may find new means of expression or more physical enactments for a scene. Questions should be asked, as for any play, to encourage a fuller sense of what is afoot in a scene: what do they expect from each other? how secure or insecure are they? — many of the questions that were first asked in individual preparation. None of these ordinary ways of working is foreign to Shakespeare's plays.

All the examples of dialogue which have been described in these notes will be revalued when two actors start to work on them together. The speech from *Henry VI, Part Three*, for example, which was discussed several times when considering meter and phrasing, will be far more vital when spoken by King Edward to his queen. Perhaps he will hold her in his arms, or draw her close as he is speaking. Perhaps she responds, without saying a word, more in joy than in "sorrow" or "danger"; but perhaps she weeps, or pretends to weep. What movements does she make and how does her heart beat? And how much of her response does Edward notice? She has nothing more to say in the scene, but her presence remains a key factor in its drama. Much will depend on the "chemistry" between the two persons involved, how they react instinctively to each other, sexually, intellectually, emotionally. As in life, every meeting includes much that is unsaid and remains subtextual for the present; but in the course of a play by Shakespeare, all the important issues do at last come to be expressed in words.

When performing twentieth-century plays, actors have extensive stage directions in the text to guide them: descriptions of activity, unspoken reactions, movements, pauses, silences, and so on. But in Shakespeare's plays there is little of this, and what is printed in modern editions is often the invention of editors and not what Shakespeare wrote. In the versions of scenes printed in this book, stage directions are very scarce and minimal, but the commentary will often point out activity, movement and responses which *may* be required for acting the text.

Actors must learn to read Shakespeare's stage directions implicit in the dialogue: clues for tempo, rhythm-change, breathing, for closeness or distance between the characters, and so on. Very important, because usually unambiguous, is Shakespeare's use of incomplete verse lines to indicate a pause or silence in the middle of speech, or in the interchange between two people. When two characters share a single verse line, each speaking one half of a regular iambic pentameter, the opposite is true; there should be no pause or hesitation here, the dialogue continuing without break and the new speaker responsive to the phrasing, rhythm and pitch of the person he or she follows.

So much can be discovered while working together on a text that simplification must become part of the ongoing process. Actors must identify those elements which are truest and most revealing, and develop those at the cost of losing others. This does not mean that actors should try to become more forceful, finding those punches which can land with greatest power. Rather they should seek clarity, and the elimination of confusing hints and statements. The process is rather like that of thinning trees in a young plantation or choosing one color to emphasize in a visual composition. The aim is to find what can grow from within the character by strength of imaginative life, and then to free that element from what might hide or retard it. Rehearsals before a very small and known audience may help to make the right choices. And actors should meet, between rehearsals, to discuss what is happening between them and to reappraise their grasp on the play's characters. The essential part of this process is to recognize what is particularly alive and new in the work, and take the necessary steps to allow this to grow.

It is here that an experienced director can be most helpful, because he or she functions, in part, as an unusually articulate and sensitive audience. When working on a production, the director will usually make a decision about which elements in the play will be given most prominence and state this theme or concept when meeting with the cast for the first time; this is done to save time and effort when the rehearsal period is limited, and to ensure that casting, design, music, lights and all the other elements of a production work together towards the same end. But for students working on the duologues in this book, whose first concern is to develop their awareness of Shakespeare's text and to stretch their own abilities, such directives will be too limiting if applied too early. Selection is necessary at some stage, and even a short scene should be directed towards achieving particular ends, but before this stage actors should be free to search widely and test many discoveries.

There is a paradox at the heart of what can be said about the task of acting Shakespeare's plays. Imaginatively the performers need to be exceptionally free, and yet the most liberating work will be found by paying strict attention to the minutest details of the text and using them as spurs to invention and exploration. Shakespeare's imagination seems always to be ahead of ours, beckoning us; and so, if the actor is patient and adventurous, he or she will find within the text whatever suits his or her individual abilities and point of view. The text can be ever new, and even the most experienced actor or playgoer is liable to be amazed at what is achieved for the first time with any new production.

Of course actors develop particular ways of working, and their interpretations of a number of roles will have much in common, but it is wise to beware of drawing the possibilities of a Shakespeare text down to the level of performance that a particular actor has found to be reliable. Shakespeare's kings are all different from each other, and so are his fools; and each one is liable to have a different life from scene to scene, sometimes even moment by moment. Even such clear distinctions as that between comedy and drama should be treated with reserve: in important ways, there are no comic and no serious roles in Shakespeare. As we have seen when examining a passage from *Hamlet* alongside one from *Much Ado About Nothing*, the same stylistic devices and the same imaginative sense of minds working below and beyond the interchange of words are found in both tragedy and comedy. Numerous scenes presented in this book will make the same point. Portia and Nerissa talking about suitors in Scene 20 are setting out to make jokes, but underlying the obvious jesting is a deeper and very "serious" sense of these women's predicaments, and this is a drama which calls upon the performers to be more than wittily entertaining. Shakespeare's characters are persons in an illusion of life, rather than vehicles for the exploitation of established comedic personalities;by respecting this priority however, both purposes can be served.

The two Clowns in *Hamlet* (scene 31) are entertainers, as their names in the stage directions and speech prefixes denote. But the categorization must not restrict the actors. Not only do they talk about a possible suicide and the privileges of powerful people, but they are also engaged in a slow and unresolved struggle for power between themselves. Their scene together is not resolved simply by one of them having the last laugh. The older one remains on stage and meets prince Hamlet, and before that he sings a solo about lost youth and its mistakes. In his comic misuse of words here, and throughout the scene, he seems to grasp at some fugitive sense that is beyond usual language.

Perhaps Falstaff is the part which most clearly demonstrates that Shakespeare's comedy is also imaginative drama that calls on more than comedic technique. He is the fat man, the braggart soldier, the Lord of Misrule, the old fool—all comic stereotypes—but actors who have been supremely funny and successful in this role have also, in their time, been famous interpreters of Othello, Lear, Hamlet and Prince Hal. Ralph Richardson has been the most admired of Falstaffs within living memory, and his other Shakespeare roles have included Othello, Iago, Brutus, Mercutio, Prince Hal and Henry V. And the reverse is true; Richardson's sense of comedy was part of his performances in the so-called "serious" roles.

Hamlet or Prince Hal, Romeo or Juliet—as scenes in this book demonstrate—all need to raise laughter and act the fool, drawing on skills which are sometimes considered to be appropriate to comedy. Lady Macbeth and Macbeth in Scenes 11 and 12 of this book are deeply involved in a terrible action, but their minds move with swiftness and fantasy, so that they play with words, very like witty persons in a comedy. In all Shakespeare's roles, villain or hero, lover or fool, an actor must be ready to respond outside conventional limitations.

When Shakespeare's Prince Hamlet tried to instruct the players who arrived in the court of Elsinore, he was concerned with their technique and their attention to the text, but "their special observance," he said, should be with "nature":

> for anything so o'erdone is from the purpose of playing, whose end, both at the first and now, was and is to hold, as 'twere, the mirror up to nature. . . .
>
> (*Hamlet*, III.ii.1ff.)

The key phrase, "hold the mirror up to nature," sounds like a generalized instruction—show everyone what they look like—but in context it is precise. Hamlet is in the process of castigating actors' faults and he continues in the same vein:

> O there be players that I have seen play—and heard others praise, and that highly—not to speak it profanely, that, neither having th'accent of Christians, nor the gait of Christian, pagan nor man, have so strutted and bellowed that I have thought some of Nature's journeymen had made men, and not made them well, they imitated humanity so abominably.
>
> (*Op. cit.*)

The actors have to "make men"; they have to be highly skilled craftspersons, not ordinary workmen ("journeymen"). Characters have to move and speak, and function, as we do: they have been individually crafted and must be alive with individuality. Slowly, skillfully and adventurously, an actor must build an illusion of a living being, one for whom Shakespeare's text is a necessary extension of existence. Hamlet does not speak for Shakespeare, but in creating this character the dramatist wrote with such freedom, precision and obvious pleasure that he must have drawn more deeply than usual on his own ideas and reactions. Lacking Shakespeare's advice to the players, Hamlet's is a good substitute.

SCENES
FOR ONE
ACTOR
AND ONE
ACTRESS

1

Henry VI, Part Two

Act III, Scene ii

QUEEN MARGARET and the DUKE OF SUFFOLK

✠

Suffolk had organized the courtship and marriage of King Henry VI with Margaret, the daughter of the impoverished King of Naples. Margaret, now Queen of England, manages her husband and takes an active role in the politics of the realm. Prior to this scene, Henry has realized how Suffolk uses his influence with the Queen to build up his own power and eliminate those who stand in his way. After Henry's uncle dies suddenly while under arrest in Suffolk's charge, public outcry and his own suspicions cause Henry to pronounce Suffolk's banishment.

Henry leaves the stage with the Earl of Warwick, Suffolk's chief opponent. The Queen stays behind with Suffolk, the man who had brought her to England and became her accomplice and lover.

✠

QUEEN
    Mischance and sorrow go along with you!
    Heart's discontent and sour affliction
    Be playfellows to keep you company!
    There's two of you: the devil make a third
    And threefold vengeance tend upon your steps!   5
SUFFOLK
    Cease, gentle queen, these execrations
    And let thy Suffolk take his heavy leave.
QUEEN
    Fie, coward woman and softhearted wretch!
    Hast thou not spirit to curse thine enemy?
SUFFOLK
    A plague upon them! Wherefore should I curse them?   10

    7 **heavy** sorrowful/slow, reluctant

Would curses kill, as doth the mandrake's groan,
I would invent as bitter searching terms
As curst, as harsh and horrible to hear,
Delivered strongly through my fixèd teeth,
With full as many signs of deadly hate   15
As lean-faced Envy in her loathsome cave.
My tongue should stumble in mine earnest words;
Mine eyes should sparkle like the beaten flint;
Mine hair be fixed an end, as one distract;
Ay, every joint should seem to curse and ban: 20
And even now my burdened heart would break,
Should I not curse them. Poison be their drink,
Gall, worse than gall, the daintiest that they taste,
Their sweetest shade a grove of cypress trees,
Their chiefest prospect murd'ring basilisks,   25
Their softest touch as smart as lizards' stings,
Their music frightful as the serpent's hiss,
And boding screech owls make the consort full!
All the foul terrors in dark-seated hell—

QUEEN

Enough, sweet Suffolk; thou torment'st thyself   30
And these dread curses, like the sun 'gainst glass
Or like an overchargèd gun, recoil
And turn the force of them upon thyself.

SUFFOLK

You bade me ban, and will you bid me leave?
Now, by the ground that I am banished from,   35
Well could I curse away a winter's night,
Though standing naked on a mountain top
Where biting cold would never let grass grow,

---

11 **mandrake's groan** (the **man-drake** is a poisonous plant, its root forked; when pulled from the ground it was fabled to utter a human shriek boding death or sending its hearer mad)

12 **searching** penetrating

19 **an** on; **distract** mad

20 **ban** pronounce damnation

23 **Gall** bile

24 **cypress** (symbol of mourning; often planted beside graves)

25 **basilisks** (fabulous reptile said to kill by its look)

26 **lizards** (used of large reptiles, as well as the small **lizard**)

28 **consort** music/company

And think it but a minute spent in sport.

QUEEN

    O, let me entreat thee cease. Give me thy hand,   40
    That I may dew it with my mournful tears;
    Nor let the rain of heaven wet this place,
    To wash away my woeful monuments.
    O could this kiss be printed in thy hand
    That thou mightst think upon these by the seal,   45
    Through whom a thousand sighs are breathed for thee!
    So get thee gone, that I may know my grief;
    'Tis but surmised whiles thou art standing by,
    As one that surfeits thinking on a want.
    I will repeal thee or, be well assured,   50
    Adventure to be banishèd myself:
    And banishèd I am, if but from thee.
    Go, speak not to me; even now be gone.
    O go not yet! Even thus two friends condemned
    Embrace and kiss and take ten thousand leaves,   55
    Loather a hundred times to part than die.
    Yet now farewell, and farewell life with thee!

SUFFOLK

    Thus is poor Suffolk ten times banishèd,
    Once by the king and three times thrice by thee.
    'Tis not the land I care for, wert thou thence;   60
    A wilderness is populous enough,
    So Suffolk had thy heavenly company,
    For where thou art, there is the world itself
    With every several pleasure in the world;
    And where thou art not, desolation.   65
    I can no more: live thou to joy thy life;
    Myself to joy in nought but that thou liv'st.

QUEEN

    Away! Though parting be a fretful corrosive,

43 **monuments** i.e., the evidence of my tears	54 **condemned** i.e., to death
45 **these** i.e., these lips	64 **several** different
51 **Adventure** risk	66 **joy** enjoy
52 **but** only	68 **fretful corrosive** medicine that eats away the flesh

It is applièd to a deathful wound.
To France, sweet Suffolk; let me hear from thee,　　70
For whereso'er thou art in this world's globe
I'll have an Iris that shall find thee out.
SUFFOLK　I go.
QUEEN
And take my heart with thee.　　　*She kisseth him.*
SUFFOLK
A jewel, locked into the woefull'st cask
That ever did contain a thing of worth.　　75
Even as a splitted bark, so sunder we:
This way fall I to death.　　　　*Exit* SUFFOLK.
QUEEN　　　　　　　This way for me.
　　　　　　　　　　　Exit QUEEN.

69　**deathful** mortal
72　**Iris** messenger of the gods
76　**bark** small ship

✠

Rehearsing the Scene

The Queen curses her husband and her political enemy as soon as they have left the stage; her lover stops her to take his leave only to be accused of being weak and woman-like. Suffolk responds by describing how he might have cursed. The actor has an important choice here: does he speak about violent cursing while staying cool himself, only switching to a full physical involvement when his "burdened heart" overcomes his reason (l. 21); or is his speech as "harsh" and "horrible" as he proposes, becoming controlled (and therefore more dangerously powerful) for the elaborate curse of lines 22-29? Another possibility is that he answers the Queen's criticism by imitating the vigor and bitterness of her own "execrations." When the Queen now interrupts Suffolk, both their speeches suggest an underlying sympathy and a delicacy of feeling. A new quietness may be established as Suffolk imagines the long darkness of a "winter's night" and a mountaintop barren even of grass, or as they hold hands (see l. 40) and the Queen likens her tears to the soundless "dew."

How does the Queen find the new energy and drive with which she urges Suffolk to leave (ll. 47 and 53)? And what prompts her suddenly to bid him to stay (at l. 54)? Are Suffolk's words those of an ardent lover or of a defeated politician? Does the Queen represent to him his personal "heaven" (l. 62) or is she his means to be in charge of a populous and pleasurable "world" (l. 64)? Line 67 is a climax which can support either reading.

In the play their duologue is interrupted here by a messenger on his way to the King with news that Cardinal Beaufort, his great uncle, is on his deathbed. This incident is necessary to carry the story of play forward, but the encounter of Suffolk and Margaret can conclude without it: both were prepared already to imagine their own deaths.

The parting is delicate and subtle. How strong in each is feeling or intelligence, fear or love, fatalism or the will to survive? The Queen's "deathful wound" may cause her to be racked by its pain, so that Suffolk tries to quiet her by saying as little as possible.

When she kisses him, he may reveal a hitherto half-hidden covetousness in the image of a "thing of worth." Much will depend on how she kisses him: is this managed with some composure or, even, formality, or does the kiss show a shared and spontaneous desire for intimacy? Or is the kiss a last-minute act of panic? Is she weeping at any time? Is he?

Even if Suffolk suffers as much as the Queen, the last words are hers and they can be interpreted many ways. She may, for instance, be resigned to follow her own way to death at court. The interplay between these two characters is not complete until both have made their separate exits. Perhaps they should be very similar, or very dissimilar.

A particular challenge of this scene is the imagery. The Queen's mind, in her first speech, must move from affliction to playfellows and good company; and then immediately think of multiple devils and vengeance, together with humble service ("tend upon your steps"). Even if there is little physical movement to be seen, mental activity is ceaseless and demanding. Suffolk's account of how he might curse is a catalogue not only of theatrical effects, but also of physical effects: "searching" terms, teeth "fixed" together with tension, the "lean" face of envy, the "sparkle" of beaten flints, hair also "fixed", and bodily " joints" totally involved in "stumbling" speech. To pile up these impressions in one's mind is part of the actors' task, but he and she must also order them as the text dictates. Hard mental work must prepare for the acting of these lines with full and natural-seeming effect.

2

Romeo and Juliet

Act II, Scene ii

ROMEO and JULIET

✠

In disguise among a party of young men, Romeo has gate-crashed a festive ball given by the Capulets, his family's most hated enemies. All other guests have gone and in the darkness Romeo has given his friends the slip, climbed over the garden wall and stands, now, hoping to catch sight of the girl with whom he had danced. They had talked together and kissed. Romeo is obsessed by Juliet, as previously he had been with Rosaline, only more completely and still more devotedly.

For Juliet, the meeting has been her first experience of love, and now she leans out of her bedroom window, or comes out onto its balcony, to collect her thoughts and enjoy new and thronging sensations.

Throughout the scene the lovers remain at a distance from each other (although by stretching they may just touch fingers), and both are in danger of discovery.

The noise offstage at line 135 and the Nurse's cries can be supplied easily, but it would be sufficient for an audience if Juliet were to imagine that she hears these disturbances.

This duologue is the longest in this collection; it may be shortened by stopping after line 141 or line 156.

✠

Enter ROMEO.

ROMEO
He jests at scars that never felt a wound.

Enter JULIET *at a window, above.*

But soft! What light through yonder window breaks?

2 **soft** stop

It is the East, and Juliet is the sun!
Arise, fair sun, and kill the envious moon
Who is already sick and pale with grief   5
That thou her maid art far more fair than she.
Be not her maid since she is envious:
Her vestal livery is but sick and green
And none but fools do wear it. Cast it off.
It is my lady! O it is my love!   10
O that she knew she were!
She speaks yet she says nothing. What of that?
Her eye discourses; I will answer it.
I am too bold; 'tis not to me she speaks.
Two of the fairest stars in all the heaven,   15
Having some business, do entreat her eyes
To twinkle in their spheres till they return.
What if her eyes were there, they in her head?
The brightness of her cheek would shame those stars
As daylight doth a lamp; her eyes in heaven   20
Would through the airy region stream so bright
That birds would sing and think it were not night.
See how she leans her cheek upon her hand!
O that I were a glove upon that hand
That I might touch that cheek!
JULIET   Ay me!
ROMEO   She speaks.   25
O speak again bright angel, for thou art
As glorious to this night, being o'er my head,
As is a wingèd messenger of heaven
Unto the white-upturnèd wond'ring eyes
Of mortals that fall back to gaze on him   30
When he bestrides the lazy puffing clouds
And sails upon the bosom of the air.

6 maid (virgins were the maids of
   Diana, the moon goddess)
8 vestal virgin
   green anemic (wordplay on the
   motley green dress of court fools)
13 discourses speaks

17 spheres orbits
21 region (of the sky)
29 white-upturned looking up, so
   that the whites only are seen on
   earth

JULIET

    O Romeo, Romeo! Wherefore art thou Romeo?
    Deny thy father and refuse thy name
    Or, if thou wilt not, be but sworn my love   35
    And I'll no longer be a Capulet.

ROMEO (*Aside.*)

    Shall I hear more or shall I speak at this?

JULIET

    'Tis but thy name that is my enemy.
    Thou art thyself, though not a Montague.
    What's a Montague? It is nor hand, nor foot,   40
    Nor arm, nor face, nor any other part
    Belonging to a man. O be some other name!
    What's in a name? That which we call a rose
    By any other word would smell as sweet.
    So Romeo would, were he not Romeo called,   45
    Retain that dear perfection which he owes
    Without that title. Romeo doff thy name,
    And for thy name which is no part of thee
    Take all myself.

ROMEO   I take thee at thy word.
    Call me but love and I'll be new baptized;   50
    Henceforth I never will be Romeo.

JULIET

    What man art thou that, thus bescreened in night,
    So stumblest on my counsel?

ROMEO   By a name
    I know not how to tell thee who I am.
    My name, dear saint, is hateful to myself   55
    Because it is an enemy to thee.
    Had I it written, I would tear the word.

JULIET

    My ears have yet not drunk a hundred words

---

34 **Deny** disown
    refuse renounce
39 **though not** even if you were not
46 **owes** owns
47 **doff** put off, thrust aside

48 **for** in exchange for
49 **at thy word** at once/as you offer
    yourself
53 **counsel** secret, private thoughts

Of thy tongue's uttering yet I know the sound.
Art thou not Romeo and a Montague?   60

ROMEO

Neither, fair maid, if either thee dislike.

JULIET

How camest thou hither, tell me, and wherefore?
The orchard walls are high and hard to climb
And the place death, considering who thou art,
If any of my kinsmen find thee here.   65

ROMEO

With love's light wings did I o'erperch these walls
For stony limits cannot hold love out,
And what love can do that dares love attempt,
Therefore thy kinsmen are no stop to me.

JULIET

If they do see thee, they will murder thee.   70

ROMEO

Alack, there lies more peril in thine eye
Than twenty of their swords! Look thou but sweet
And I am proof against their enmity.

JULIET

I would not for the world they saw thee here.

ROMEO

I have night's cloak to hide me from their eyes,   75
And but thou love me, let them find me here.
My life were better ended by their hate
Than death proroguèd, wanting of thy love.

JULIET

By whose direction found'st thou out this place?

ROMEO

By Love that first did prompt me to inquire: 80
He lent me counsel and I lent him eyes.
I am no pilot, yet wert thou as far

61 **dislike** displease	76 **but** if only
62 **wherefore** why	78 **prorogued** deferred
66 **o'erperch** surmount	81 **I . . . eyes** (because Love is blin-
73 **proof against** invulnerable to	folded)

As that vast shore washed with the farthest sea,
I should adventure for such merchandise.

JULIET

Thou knowest the mask of night is on my face   85
Else would a maiden blush bepaint my cheek
For that which thou hast heard me speak tonight.
Fain would I dwell on form—fain, fain deny
What I have spoke. But farewell compliment!
Dost thou love me? I know thou wilt say "Ay"   90
And I will take thy word. Yet if thou swear'st,
Thou mayst prove false. At lovers' perjuries,
They say Jove laughs. O gentle Romeo,
If thou dost love, pronounce it faithfully.
Or if thou thinkest I am too quickly won,   95
I'll frown and be perverse and say thee nay
So thou wilt woo; but else, not for the world.
In truth, fair Montague, I am too fond
And therefore thou mayst think my havior light,
But trust me, gentleman, I'll prove more true   100
Than those that have more cunning to be strange.
I should have been more strange, I must confess,
But that thou overheard'st, ere I was ware,
My truelove passion. Therefore pardon me
And not impute this yielding to light love   105
Which the dark night hath so discoverèd.

ROMEO

Lady, by yonder blessèd moon I vow,
That tips with silver all these fruit-tree tops—

83 **that . . . sea** (alluding to the journey toward Death's kingdom)
84 **adventure** risk all/journey
88 **Fain** gladly
   dwell on form keep within limits of conventional behavior
89 **compliment** etiquette
94 **pronounce** declare
97 **So** if only
98 **fond** affectionate/foolish
99 **havior** behavior
   light lightheaded/immodest
101 **strange** distant, reserved
103 **ware** aware
104 **passion** outburst, expression of deep feeling
105 **light** easy/wanton
106 **discovered** revealed

JULIET

O swear not by the moon, th' inconstant moon
That monthly changes in her circled orb,   110
Lest that thy love prove likewise variable.

ROMEO

What shall I swear by?

JULIET   Do not swear at all;
Or if thou wilt, swear by thy gracious self
Which is the god of my idolatry,
And I'll believe thee.

ROMEO   If my heart's dear love—   115

JULIET

Well, do not swear. Although I joy in thee,
I have no joy of this contract tonight.
It is too rash, too unadvised, too sudden,
Too like the lightning which doth cease to be
Ere one can say it lightens. Sweet, good night!   120
This bud of love, by summer's ripening breath,
May prove a beauteous flow'r when next we meet.
Good night, good night! As sweet repose and rest
Come to thy heart as that within my breast!

ROMEO

O wilt thou leave me so unsatisfied?   125

JULIET

What satisfaction canst thou have tonight?

ROMEO

Th' exchange of thy love's faithful vow for mine.

JULIET

I gave thee mine before thou didst request it;
And yet I would it were to give again.

ROMEO

Wouldst thou withdraw it? For what purpose, love?   130

JULIET

But to be frank and give it thee again.
And yet I wish but for the thing I have:

117 **contract** exchange of vows

124 **as that** as to that heart which is
131 **frank** free, generous

My bounty is as boundless as the sea,
My love as deep; the more I give to thee,
The more I have, for both are infinite.   135
I hear some noise within. Dear love, adieu!
(NURSE *calls from within.*)
Anon, good nurse! Sweet Montague, be true
Stay but a little, I will come again.   *Exit.*

ROMEO
O blessèd, blessèd night! I am afeard,
Being in night, all this is but a dream,   140
Too flattering-sweet to be substantial.

Enter JULIET *again.*

JULIET
Three words, dear Romeo, and good night indeed.
If that thy bent of love be honorable,
Thy purpose marriage, send me word tomorrow,
By one that I'll procure to come to thee,   145
Where and what time thou wilt perform the rite
And all my fortunes at thy foot I'll lay
And follow thee my lord throughout the world.
(NURSE *Within.* Madam!)
JULIET
I come anon.—But if thou meanest not well,
I do beseech thee—
(NURSE *Within.* Madam!)
JULIET   By and by I come.—   150
To cease thy strife and leave me to my grief.
Tomorrow will I send.
ROMEO   So thrive my soul—

133 **bounty** kindness/liberality/gift
137 **Anon** coming
141 **substantial** real
143 **bent** aim, force (as of a **bent** bow)
145 **procure** arrange

147 **fortunes** possessions/fortune
149 **anon** at once
150 **By and by** immediately
151 **strife** striving
152 **So . . . soul** as I hope to be saved

JULIET

A thousand times good night!   *Exit.*

ROMEO

A thousand times the worse, to want thy light!
Love goes toward love as schoolboys from their books   155
But love from love, toward school with heavy looks.

Enter JULIET *again.*

JULIET

Hist! Romeo, hist! O for a falc'ner's voice
To lure this tassel gentle back again!
Bondage is hoarse and may not speak aloud,
Else would I tear the cave where Echo lies   160
And make her airy tongue more hoarse than mine
With repetition of "My Romeo!"

ROMEO

It is my soul that calls upon my name.
How silver-sweet sound lovers' tongues by night,
Like softest music to attending ears!   165

JULIET

Romeo!

ROMEO   My sweet?

JULIET   What o'clock tomorrow
Shall I send to thee?

ROMEO   By the hour of nine.

JULIET

I will not fail. 'Tis twenty years till then.
I have forgot why I did call thee back.

ROMEO

Let me stand here till thou remember it.   170

JULIET

I shall forget, to have thee still stand there,
Rememb'ring how I love thy company.

152 **So . . . soul** as I hope to be saved
154 **want** lack
158 **lure** recall (a term of falconry)
     tassel gentle male peregrine falcon
159 **Bondage is hoarse** I am watched and can only whisper
160 **tear the cave** pierce the air; **Echo** (a nymph who pined for Narcissus until only her voice was left)
165 **attending** attentive
171 **still** always

ROMEO

And I'll still stay to have thee still forget,
Forgetting any other home but this.

JULIET

'Tis almost morning: I would have thee gone—   175
And yet no farther than a wanton's bird,
That lets it hop a little from his hand
Like a poor prisoner in his twisted gyves,
And with a silken thread plucks it back again,
So loving-jealous of his liberty.   180

ROMEO

I would I were thy bird.

JULIET   Sweet, so would I,
Yet I should kill thee with much cherishing.
Good night, good night! Parting is such sweet sorrow
That I shall say good night till it be morrow.   *Exit.*

ROMEO

Sleep dwell upon thine eyes, peace in thy breast!   185
Would I were sleep and peace, so sweet to rest!
Hence will I to my ghostly friar's close cell,
His help to crave and my dear hap to tell.   *Exit.*

---

176 **wanton's** playful child's
178 **gyves** fetters
179 **thread** (tied to its leg)
184 **morrow** morning

187 **ghostly** spiritual (i.e., he is her confessor)
   close secluded, private
188 **dear hap** good fortune

✠

Rehearsing the Scene

Romeo's first line is said either to his friends who have laughed at him for being in love, or to himself, thoughts of Juliet making everything else seem trivial.

Before Juliet speaks a word, it should be clear that she is wrapped up in her first love. Romeo's opening speech supplies some stage directions for her, but these are not all that is required: the actress has to ensure that every movement and breath comes from a continuous and ardent involvement in a totally new experience.

Some short verse lines (11, 42, 153) suggest silences during this scene, but there can be many more, especially when a verse line concludes with a full stop. Full stops in the middle of lines should not be allowed to break the strong drive forward provided by the full lines of verse; they indicate no more than a slight pause, for the start of a new idea and new breath.

Both actors need to keep their thoughts racing and their sensations exceptionally rich and exploratory in order to provide the motivations for speaking so many words. Imaginary sights have to be created in their minds. Romeo envisions the whole night sky and the next moment seems to hear birds singing endlessly (ll. 20-22) ; then his thoughts are of angels, revelation, worshipping mortals and levitation (ll. 26-32). Juliet is more practical in her thoughts, until Romeo's oath makes her think of the "inconstant moon" (l. 109); and then her fear, or her urgent desire to understand and so possess new experiences, must be checked by amazement, impatience, sheer pleasure; towards the end of the scene her mind is alive with images of the hunt, imprisonment and cries for help.

Romeo and Juliet are both so excited that even their most serious thoughts are enlivened by a keen sense of humor, as if they find their wonder almost absurd, or as if they have to laugh in order to avoid crying or to avoid being simply speechless. For example, Romeo seeing Juliet rest her face in her hand, suddenly wants to be a glove upon that hand (l. 24); is this self-mockery, making light of an unfulfilled desire to be close to Juliet, or an excited recognition of sexual drive and physical awareness?

They also have a sharp sense of immediate reality. Short sentences represent thoughts which stab their consciousness: Romeo's "But soft . . . Cast it off. . . . it is my lady . . . What of that? . . . She speaks"; and Juliet's thoughts, more weighty than his, "Dost thou love me? . . . Do not swear at all. . . . Well, do not swear. . . . Romeo . . . I will not fail." However, Juliet's first encounters with Romeo are speeches which run fully and strongly within single verse lines (see ll. 60, 62, 70, 74 and 79).

Their struggle towards mutual understanding and security comes to a momentary crisis with Romeo's line "O wilt thou leave me so unsatisfied?" (l. 125). This is developed further after a momentary fear of being discovered, by Juliet, with "If that thy bent of love be honorable. . . ." (l. 143). Still it becomes increasingly obvious that they must for now part immediately. Yet the two lovers instinctively hold back (see ll. 169-74): shared silences can now be lengthy or brief; movement almost nil, or nervous and almost incessant.

3

A Midsummer Nights Dream

Act II, Scene i

DEMETRIUS and HELENA

✠

It is a moonlit night in an enchanted wood outside Athens.

Demetrius is the young man whom Egeus has chosen as husband for his only daughter, Hermia. But she loves, and is loved by, Lysander. So the day before this scene, Egeus had brought all three before the Duke of Athens and begged him to enforce the "ancient privilege of Athens" which gives a father the right to "dispose" of his daughter (I.i.42-45): if Hermia will not marry Demetrius, he wants her to be put to death.

The duke has offered Hermia the further choice of becoming a nun and has given her until the next new moon to make a decision. During this public hearing, Demetrius had asked Hermia to relent and told Lysander to yield to him. Neither would do so and, in refusing, Lysander accused Demetrius of having:

> Made love to Nedar's daughter, Helena,
> And won her soul; and she, sweet lady, dotes,
> Devoutly dotes, dotes in idolatory,
> Upon this spotted and inconstant man.   (I.i.107-110)

As soon as Lysander and Hermia are alone, they agree to meet in the wood the following night, and then to elope. But they share their secret with Helena and she, in turn, tells Demetrius. She hopes Demetrius will follow Hermia to the wood so that she may intercept and confront him. According to plan, Demetrius appears with Helena in pursuit.

✠

DEMETRIUS
> I love thee not, therefore pursue me not.
> Where is Lysander and fair Hermia?
> The one I'll slay, the other slayeth me.

Thou told'st me they were stol'n unto this wood;
And here am I and wood within this wood   5
Because I cannot meet my Hermia.
Hence, get thee gone and follow me no more!

HELENA

You draw me, you hardhearted adamant,
But yet you draw not iron, for my heart
Is true as steel. Leave you your power to draw   10
And I shall have no power to follow you.

DEMETRIUS

Do I entice you? Do I speak you fair?
Or rather do I not in plainest truth
Tell you I do not nor I cannot love you?

HELENA

And even for that, do I love you the more.   15
I am your spaniel and, Demetrius,
The more you beat me I will fawn on you.
Use me but as your spaniel, spurn me, strike me,
Neglect me, lose me; only give me leave,
Unworthy as I am, to follow you.   20
What worser place can I beg in your love—
And yet a place of high respect with me—
Than to be used as you use your dog?

DEMETRIUS

Tempt not too much the hatred of my spirit
For I am sick when I do look on thee.   25

HELENA

And I am sick when I look not on you.

DEMETRIUS

You do impeach your modesty too much,
To leave the city and commit yourself
Into the hands of one that loves you not,

5 **and wood** and mad, frantic
8 **adamant** (1) mineral of great hardness, (2) lodestone, magnet
9 **iron** (of much less value than **steel**)

12 **speak** call, proclaim/speak with
fair beautiful/politely
25 **sick** nauseated
26 **sick** faint, longing
27 **impeach** discredit, call in question

To trust the opportunity of night   30
And the ill counsel of a desert place
With the rich worth of your virginity.

HELENA

Your virtue is my privilege. For that
It is not night when I do see your face,
Therefore I think I am not in the night;   35
Nor doth this wood lack worlds of company
For you in my respect are all the world.
Then how can it be said I am alone
When all the world is here to look on me?

DEMETRIUS

I'll run from thee and hide me in the brakes   40
And leave thee to the mercy of wild beasts.

HELENA

The wildest hath not such a heart as you.
Run when you will, the story shall be changed:
Apollo flies and Daphne holds the chase,
The dove pursues the griffin, the mild hind   45
Makes speed to catch the tiger—bootless speed
When cowardice pursues and valor flies.

DEMETRIUS

I will not stay thy questions. Let me go!
O if thou follow me, do not believe
But I shall do thee mischief in the wood.   50

HELENA

Ay in the temple, in the town, the field,
You do me mischief. Fie Demetrius!
Your wrongs do set a scandal on my sex:
We cannot fight for love as men may do;

31 **desert** deserted
33 **virtue** merit, strength
   privilege authority
37 **respect** esteem, opinion
40 **brakes** thickets
44 **Daphne** (the nymph who was pursued by the god Apollo and, at her own entreaty, was changed into a laurel tree)
   holds persists in
45 **griffin** (fabulous beast, with the upper part an eagle, the lower a lion)
   hind female deer
46 **bootless** unavailing
48 **stay** wait for

We should be wooed and were not made to woo.   55

                             Exit DEMETRIUS.

I'll follow thee and make a heaven of hell
To die upon the hand I love so well.   *Exit.*

57 **upon** by means of

⊞

Rehearsing the Scene

Actors might start rehearsals together by placing a number of objects about the acting area to represent trees and bushes. They could improvise their entrances into this unknowable and possibly dangerous environment. Music might be helpful.

Demetrius enters searching for Hermia, and Helena pursues him. Does she call after him? Does she catch up because he takes a moment's rest, or does he turn and wait for her? Might he have to fight her off, literally perhaps? Do they both show signs—pantings, loosened clothes, unruly hair—of a long chase?

A lot may be learned about this scene by studying its rhythms, syntax and meter. His rhythms are variable and emphatic, hers more calm and sustained. His lines are often broken into two phrases, hers tend to run to their full length without break, line 9 running over without pause into the following line. He jumps from one idea to another, or repeats a statement that was already emphatic at first speaking: "And here am I / and wood within this wood," or "Hence, / get thee gone / and follow me no more!" He may seem half crazy ("wood") with frustration, she settled and resolute.

One way of playing the scene is to make Helena the stronger. She develops what she wishes to say, rather than making a number of short thrusts in her speech. Helena's "spaniel" metaphor, for instance, grows step by step in declaring at once the subservience and vehemence of her love. Possibly she is holding him by this time, having trapped him in some way. When Demetrius tries sober respect as another tactic to get rid of Helena—or perhaps this is the result of fear—she replies at line 33 with an ardent affirmation of the "rich worth" of her love for him, not of her virginity. Here again she overreaches him, delight in his presence sustaining her rhythms and phrasing, confidence enabling her to use very simple language (three out of six lines are all monosyllables) to offer a grand image of radiance and fulfillment. Perhaps at lines 40 and 48, Demetrius can say only that he "will" escape being unable to do so at that moment, so securely has Helena trapped him; in which case "cowardice" of line 47 and "we cannot fight for love" of line 54 will be highly ironic. She could make a conscious decision to let him go at lines 54-55, which is when she remembers that capturing him is not enough.

Another way of playing the scene (and one more equally balanced between the two roles) is for Demetrius to exert a stronger physical force over Helena from the beginning, on line 7 turning her away irresistibly. She would give chase at once and he would elude her. He might take hold of her to deliver the more sustained reproach of lines 27-32. (The speech has more polysyllables than any other in the scene and more sustained rhythms; it could be spoken rather pompously.) So Helena would speak most ardently while still imprisoned, and at lines 40-41 Demetrius might relinquish hold of her heartlessly. At that point Helena might be able to grasp some part of him or of his clothing, having become desperate while using the outrageous analogues of lines 45-47. This would lead Demetrius into exerting all his strength and becoming very obviously able to do her "mischief" in a fight with no holds barred. He might leave because he does not want to kill her—as he easily could (see line 57).

But a trial of strength between these two can give very equal results, first one and then the other appearing the stronger. In rehearsal many variations can be discovered, given time, trust and invention, both physically and in speech.

Of course, the scene is also very funny. But its humor does not depend on the actors being conscious of this and timing their speeches like gags in a comedy routine. If each actor provides clear and independent intentions for every word and action, and plays each moment only for what is true in that moment, what they do will often be funny, as well as affecting. They will find that their performances go beyond what they intended and that they become a little moonstruck in consequence.

4

The Merchant of Venice

Act III, Scene ii

PORTIA and BASSANIO

✠

When Portia's father died, his will specified that his rich and beautiful daughter should marry only that man who made the correct choice of three caskets. Two princes have just failed this test, and so the audience knows that the preferred casket is the lead one, not the gold or silver.

Bassanio is a young Venetian, "a scholar and a soldier," who had visited Belmont when Portia's father was still alive. To the eyes of Portia and her maid he is "the best deserving a fair lady" of all the men they have ever seen (I.i.108-115). For his part, Bassanio remembers Portia as both "rich" and "fair," and "of wondrous virtues" (I.i161-63). Besides, he believes that she had taken very particular notice of him: he would be "fortunate," if only he had the money to furnish himself as an acceptable suitor. He has told this to his friend, the merchant Antonio, who straightway had borrowed three thousand ducats on Bassanio's behalf, for which he gave as security a pound of his own flesh.

In new clothes and with servants in fresh liveries, Bassanio arrives at Belmont to make his choice of the caskets. If he fails in this test, he must swear

> Never to speak to lady afterward
> In way of marriage. (II.i41-42)

✠

PORTIA

I pray you tarry; pause a day or two
Before you hazard for in choosing wrong
I lose your company, therefore forbear awhile—
There's something tells me (but it is not love)
I would not lose you and you know yourself

5

Hate counsels not in such a quality;
But lest you should not understand me well
(And yet a maiden hath no tongue but thought)
I would detain you here some month or two
Before you venture for me. I could teach you   10
How to choose right but then I am forsworn;
So will I never be—so may you miss me.
But if you do, you'll make me wish a sin
That I had been forsworn. Beshrew your eyes!
They have o'erlooked me and divided me;   15
One half of me is yours, the other half yours—
Mine own I would say, but if mine then yours
And so all yours. O these naughty times
Put bars between the owners and their rights!
And so, though yours, not yours. Prove it so,   20
Let Fortune go to hell for it, not I.
I speak too long, but 'tis to peize the time,
To eche it and to draw it out in length
To stay you from election.

BASSANIO   Let me choose,
For as I am, I live upon the rack.   25

PORTIA

Upon the rack, Bassanio? Then confess
What treason there is mingled with your love.

BASSANIO

None but that ugly treason of mistrust
Which makes me fear th' enjoying of my love.
There may as well be amity and life   30

---

6 **quality** manner

8 **And . . . thought** (cf. *As You Like It*, III.ii: "Do you not know I am a woman? When I think, I must speak": the idea was proverbial and, probably, to be laughed at)

14 **Beshrew** evil befall (usually meant lightheartedly)

15 **o'erlooked** bewitched

18 **naughty** wicked, worthless

20 **though . . . not yours** yours in my very being, not yours in fact **Prove it so** if it prove so

22 **peize** piece out, extend

23 **eche** eke out

25 **rack** instrument of torture which stretched the body until joints broke   used to extract confessions of treason

29 **fear** doubt

'Tween snow and fire, as treason and my love.

PORTIA

Ay, but I fear you speak upon the rack
Where men enforced do speak anything.

BASSANIO

Promise me life and I'll confess the truth.

PORTIA

Well then, confess and live.

BASSANIO   Confess and love   35

Had been the very sum of my confession.
O happy torment when my torturer
Doth teach me answers for deliverance!
But let me to my fortune and the caskets.

PORTIA

Away then! I am locked in one of them;   40
If you do love me, you will find me out.
Nerissa and the rest, stand all aloof.
Let music sound while he doth make his choice,
Then if he lose he makes a swanlike end,
Fading in music. That the comparison   45
May stand more proper, my eye shall be the stream
And wat'ry deathbed for him. He may win
And what is music then? Then music is
Even as the flourish when true subjects bow
To a new-crowned monarch; such it is   50
As are those dulcet sounds in break of day
That creep into the dreaming bridegroom's ear
And summon him to marriage. Now he goes
With no less presence but with much more love
Than young Alcides when he did redeem   55
The virgin tribute paid by howling Troy

---

33 **enforced** under torture
38 **for deliverance** which will free me
44 **swanlike end** (in fable, swans sang when they foresaw their death)
49 **flourish** fanfare
54 **presence** commanding dignity

55 **Alcides** Hercules (he rescued Hesione, not for love, but for the reward of a team of horses)
56 **virgin tribute** (unless a virgin was offered for it to devour, the monster would continue to threaten Troy)

To the sea monster. I stand for sacrifice;
The rest aloof are the Dardanian wives
With bleared visages come forth to view
The issue of th' exploit. Go, Hercules!   60
Live thou, I live. With much, much more dismay
I view the fight than thou that mak'st the fray.

(A song the whilst BASSANIO *comments on the caskets to himself.)*

> *Tell me where is fancy bred,*
> *Or in the heart or in the head?*
> *How begot, how nourishèd?*   65

CHORUS   *Reply, reply.*

> *It is engend'red in the eyes,*
> *With gazing fed, and fancy dies*
> *In the cradle where it lies.*
> *Let us all ring fancy's knell.*   70
> *I'll begin it—Ding, dong, bell.*

CHORUS   *Ding, dong, bell.*

BASSANIO

So may the outward shows be least themselves;
The world is still deceived with ornament:
In law, what plea so tainted and corrupt   75
But being seasoned with a gracious voice
Obscures the show of evil? In religion,
What damned error but some sober brow
Will bless it and approve it with a text,

58 **Dardanian** Trojan
59 **bleared** i.e., with weeping eyes
61 **Live thou** if you live
  dismay loss of courage
62 **fray** attack
63 **fancy** sexual attraction
64 **Or** either
67 **engend'red . . . eyes** (Portia and Bassanio are both aware that they have kindled each other's "fancy"; the song warns that only a deeper love will endure)
73 **So** (Bassanio continues from his private thoughts)
  least themselves least what they really are
74 **still** continually
79 **approve . . . text** confirm it with a biblical text

Hiding the grossness with fair ornament? 80
There is no vice so simple but assumes
Some mark of virtue on his outward parts.
How many cowards whose hearts are all as false
As stairs of sand, wear yet upon their chins
The beards of Hercules and frowning Mars, 85
Who inward searched, have livers white as milk—
And these assume but valor's excrement
To render them redoubted. Look on beauty
And you shall see 'tis purchased by the weight
Which therein works a miracle in nature, 90
Making them lightest that wear most of it:
So are those crisped snaky golden locks
Which maketh such wanton gambols with the wind
Upon supposèd fairness, often known
To be the dowry of a second head, 95
The skull that bred them in the sepulcher.
Thus ornament is but the guiled shore
To a most dangerous sea, the beauteous scarf
Veiling an Indian beauty; in a word,
The seeming truth which cunning times put on 100
To entrap the wisest. Therefore then, thou gaudy gold,
Hard food for Midas, I will none of thee,
Nor none of thee, thou pale and common drudge
'Tween man and man. But thou, thou meager lead

86 **searched** probed
livers . . . milk (when the blood was cold, the liver was supposed to be pale: a sign of cowardice)
87 **excrement** outgrowth (i.e., beards)
88 **redoubted** dreaded (used of monarchs and men of great power); **Look on** i.e., judge by outward show
89 **purchased . . . weight** i.e., it is cosmetic, bought at so much per ounce
91 **lightest** most unchaste (pun on light=weighing little)
92 **crisped** curled
snaky long and sinuous (with allusion to a snake's poison and deceit)
93 **wanton** playful, seductive
95-96 **dowry . . . sepulcher** i.e., wig made from hair of a dead person
97 **guiled** treacherous, guileful
102 **Midas** legendary king of Phrygia; all he touched turned to gold
103 **pale . . . drudge** (silver is much used in everyday, unglamorous-trade)

Which rather threaten'st than dost promise aught,   105
Thy paleness moves me more than eloquence,
And here choose I—joy be the consequence!

PORTIA
How all the other passions fleet to air,
As doubtful thoughts and rash-embraced despair,
And shudd'ring fear and green-eyed jealousy.   110
O love, be moderate, allay thy ecstasy,
In measure rain thy joy, scant this excess!
I feel too much thy blessing, make it less
For fear I surfeit.

BASSANIO   What find I here?
He opens the leaden casket.

Fair Portia's counterfeit! What demigod   115
Hath come so near creation? Move these eyes?
Or whether, riding on the balls of mine,
Seem they in motion? Here are severed lips
Parted with sugar breath—so sweet a bar
Should sunder such sweet friends. Here in her hairs   120
The painter plays the spider and hath woven
A golden mesh t' entrap the hearts of men
Faster than gnats in cobwebs. But her eyes!
How could he see to do them? Having made one,
Methinks it should have power to steal both his   125
And leave itself unfurnished. Yet look how far
The substance of my praise doth wrong this shadow
In underprizing it, so far this shadow
Doth limp behind the substance. Here's the scroll,
The continent and summary of my fortune.   130

Reads.

---

106 **Thy** (in contrast to silver's)
109 **As** such as
112 **scant** lessen
114 **surfeit** sicken with too much
115 **counterfeit** likeness, portrait
    demigod near-divine painter
117 **Or whether** or
    balls of mine my eyeballs
119 **bar** i.e., Portia's breath

120 **friends** i.e., Portia's lips
123 **Faster** more securely
126 **unfurnished** i.e. without the other eye
127 **substance** meaning, contents
    this shadow the portrait
129 **the substance** Portia herself
130 **continent** receptacle

You that choose not by the view
Chance as fair, and choose as true.
Since this fortune falls to you,
Be content and seek no new.
If you be well pleased with this   135
And hold your fortune for your bliss,
Turn you where your lady is,
And claim her with a loving kiss.

A gentle scroll. Fair lady, by your leave,
I come by note to give and to receive,   140
Like one of two contending in a prize
That thinks he hath done well in people's eyes,
Hearing applause and universal shout,
Giddy in spirit, still gazing in a doubt
Whether those peals of praise be his or no,   145
So, thrice-fair lady, stand I even so,
As doubtful whether what I see be true
Until confirmed, signed, ratified by you.

PORTIA

You see me, Lord Bassanio, where I stand,
Such as I am. Though for myself alone   150
I would not be ambitious in my wish
To wish myself much better, yet for you
I would be trebled twenty times myself,
A thousand times more fair, ten thousand times more rich,
That only to stand high in your account   155
I might in virtues, beauties, livings, friends,
Exceed account. But the full sum of me
Is sum of something—which, to term in gross,
Is an unlessoned girl, unschooled, unpracticed;
Happy in this, she is not yet so old   160
But she may learn; happier than this,

---

139 **gentle** courteous	155 **account** esteem/financial reckoning
140 **by note** according to the account rendered	156 **livings** possessions
141 **prize** prize fight	158 **sum of something** (a variation of the common phrase "sum of all")
145 **his** intended for him	

She is not bred so dull but she can learn;
Happiest of all, is that her gentle spirit
Commits itself to yours to be directed
As from her lord, her governor, her king.   165
Myself, and what is mine, to you and yours
Is now converted. But now I was the lord
Of this fair mansion, master of my servants,
Queen o'er myself; and even now, but now,
This house, these servants and this same myself   170
Are yours—my lord's!—I give them with this ring,
Which when you part from, lose or give away,
Let it presage the ruin of your love
And be my vantage to exclaim on you.

BASSANIO

Madam, you have bereft me of all words,   175
Only my blood speaks to you in my veins
And there is such confusion in my powers
As after some oration fairly spoke
By a beloved prince there doth appear
Among the buzzing pleasèd multitude,   180
Where every something being blent together
Turns to a wild of nothing save of joy
Expressed and not expressed. But when this ring
Parts from this finger, then parts life from hence—
O then be bold to say Bassanio's dead!   185

167 **converted** transformed, changed	173 **presage** foretell
But now just now	174 **vantage . . . you** opportunity to accuse/protest against you

✠

Rehearsing the Scene

This scene is longer than most in this collection. It also contains
five longer-than-usual speeches and, in consequence, the quick

verbal interchanges common in the comedies are much reduced. So two actors can do a great deal of their study independently and their rehearsals together need be no longer than those for much shorter texts. A certain power comes in performance by the mastery and use of long speeches that are rich in imagery, sustained in rhythm, and strong in syntax and structure. Shakespeare makes this scene particularly vital and vivid by numerous sharp, idiomatic and seemingly spontaneous phrases. No real-life persons would or could so hold the stage, but Shakespeare has given to the long utterances of this scene an impression of actual thought and feeling, with varying pulse and confidence, underlying their more measured verbal progress.

Although both characters spend much time speaking with elaborate eloquence about their own thoughts, interplay between them is crucial almost all the time: after all they are meeting in order to be together for life—from the first word the scene is about their hoped-for marriage. Moreover this happens in a place where they are watched all the time by nameless attendants, mostly female for Portia, mostly male for Bassanio. These two characters perform for three audiences—themselves, each other and their attendants. (The actors will have a fourth audience in the theatre.)

When the scene is performed in class, it would be helpful if half the audience were asked to stand within the acting area and become partisans for one or other of the characters, active in expressing concern, bewilderment or pleasure, as they wish. The actors need to be aware constantly of which audience is appropriate. When either of them speaks entirely for him or herself (and for the theatre audience), this should be clearly defined and achieved by appropriate concentration and shift of attention.

Some further arrangements will be needed. Three boxes or other objects representing the caskets must be placed on a table or stand so that Bassanio can address each in turn without stooping. Within the lead casket should be something representing the portrait of Portia and a paper on which its message is written. The song and its chorus can be recorded on tape, together with the music called for at line 43; the song could be spoken on tape, if appropriate music cannot be found. If need be, Portia could turn the tape on at line 45.

Two textual problems must be considered before work can proceed far. Firstly, does Portia introduce the song in order to guide Bassanio in his choice of caskets? Its message is that "Fancy," a response to outward beauty, would be attracted to the gold and silver caskets; it implies that a true lover would ignore appearances for a greater wealth which lies within, and so would choose the lead. However, Portia has said that she would never "teach" Bassanio how to choose, because this would be a "sin" (ll. 10-13). Is the choice of song an accident then, or the contribution of some well-intentioned servant? And does Bassanio pay no attention to it anyway, as the stage direction printed here suggests? Actors can experiment with these possibilities and then choose for themselves. But the odds must be on the stage direction being a true indication of the answer because it was probably written in the printer's copy in Shakespeare's own hand, or was printed from a manuscript copied from Shakespeare's. It is unusual in form and therefore less likely to be the introduction of some scribe or prompter working in the playhouse. Perhaps the song is intended for the audience on stage who could join in the chorus. Certainly its occurrence is mysterious, as its words are mysterious and riddle-like. It allows Bassanio time in which to face his dilemma and so ensure that his following words do not appear too glib to represent deep consideration. Together with the silent caskets it also helps to establish the imaginary world of fairy tale, in which moral choices are simply right or wrong and yet are encountered in enigmatic form.

The second major problem is Portia's speech in which she submits to Bassanio as if he were her absolute lord and master (ll. 149-171). How can this servile attitude be the right response from the independently-minded Portia? The answer must lie in how this speech is spoken. The submission raises still more questions about both Portia and Bassanio. Almost in the same breath, Portia proceeds to give Bassanio a ring and in doing so takes the bridegroom's rather than the bride's initiative. This alone might give the impression that she both gives and takes away; but the questions raised by her submissive words reach still further, to her own character and to her upbringing. Since the death of her father, she has been used to the privileges of great wealth; what marriage offers her is a release from all this responsibility and a chance to commit her entire self to the man who had won her affections on his first visit. Her speech of submission shows that she cares for neither gold nor silver, nor, indeed, for anything in her life, com-

pared with her love for Bassanio. By her submission she has
pledged away all the security her father had arranged for her. In
a sense, it is a rebellious speech. Indeed the rhythms in what she
says will instruct an actress to speak with delight and perhaps
laughter; it is a joyous fantasy, sharpened by a sense of danger
and lightened by the realization that in Bassanio she has won
everything she had ever dreamed of. The huddling together of potent words at lines 14-21 show a mind leaping forwards and back-
wards in exciting and perilous anticipation. When Bassanio has
chosen correctly, a thrillingly sensitive soliloquy reveals Portia's almost unbearable confusion of emotions.

On the surface, this is one of those rare scenes in which Shakespeare seems to deny what Lysander says in A Midsummer Night's
Dream:

The course of true love never did run smooth.(I.i.134)

But both actors should look for uncertainties and dangers. Portia's first speech is full of sudden breaks and modifications. Then
they share the quick and perhaps uneasy word games of lines 24-
36. She remembers "howling Troy" as Bassanio approaches the
caskets (ll. 55-62), and, having chosen rightly, he is held in wonder gazing at Portia's portrait and at Portia. All of Bassanio's finery
and servants are borrowed: he might well then view the reality of
his great fortune at first as an illusion. Most editions of the play
have a stage direction requiring him to kiss Portia at line 139, but
this has no authority; the text itself suggests that he should remain
"in a doubt" (l. 144) until Portia speaks. When she has done so, he
is at first "bereft" of all words and his thoughts are in "a wild of
nothing" (ll. 175-83). Not until his vow of lines 183-85, does Bassanio stand on steady ground; perhaps this is when he kisses Portia as the scroll had instructed (see l. 138).

The undercurrents can give vitality and credibility to the scene
and help both actors and audience to entertain the fiction of Belmont, the beautiful mountain which is remote from the pressures
of city life.

5

Much Ado About Nothing

Act IV, Scene i

BENEDICK and BEATRICE

✠

The scene takes place in summer, in a church at Messina, Sicily. The wedding of Count Claudio and Hero has been violently disrupted by the groom, who denounced his bride as a "wanton," more intemperate than animals that "rage in savage sensuality" (IV.i.44 and 59-61).

Claudio has been visiting Hero's father Leonato, after taking part in a military expedition. Don Pedro, Prince of Arragon, had conducted the campaign against the revolt of his bastard brother, Don John. This villain, wishing to revenge himself by making trouble—any trouble—for Don Pedro, has encouraged a ruffian in his pay to talk to Hero's young waiting-woman as she leaned "out at a window", disguised in the clothes of her mistress and answering as if she were indeed Hero. He also arranged for Claudio and Don Pedro to see this assignation and afterwards to hear the ruffian confess to other secret encounters with Hero. The evidence convinced the two onlookers, against all appearance of modesty and loving affection in Hero, that she had been unfaithful. The most that can be said for Claudio is that he scarcely knew his young bride and had wooed her only through the good offices of his friend, Don Pedro.

Now to the two characters in our scene: Benedick, who is also a soldier and a close friend of Claudio, has been tricked into thinking that Beatrice, Hero's orphaned cousin, has fallen in love with him. Beatrice has meanwhile been tricked into thinking that Benedick has fallen for her. Each has decided that despite all their emphatic and witty talk against matrimony, and their public disapproval of each other, they should each return the love which appears to have been given unsought.

✠

BENEDICK Lady Beatrice have you wept all this while?

BEATRICE Yea and I will weep a while longer.

BENEDICK I will not desire that.

BEATRICE You have no reason; I do it freely. 5

BENEDICK Surely I do believe your fair cousin is
wronged.

BEATRICE Ah how much might the man deserve of me
that would right her!

BENEDICK Is there any way to show such friendship? 10

BEATRICE A very even way but no such friend.

BENEDICK May a man do it?

BEATRICE It is a man's office but not yours.

BENEDICK I do love nothing in the world so well as
you. Is not that strange? 15

BEATRICE As strange as the thing I know not. It were
as possible for me to say I loved nothing so well as
you. But believe me not. And yet I lie not: I confess
nothing nor I deny nothing. I am sorry for my cousin.

BENEDICK By my sword Beatrice, thou lovest me. 20

BEATRICE Do not swear and eat it.

BENEDICK I will swear by it that you love me and I will
make him eat it that says I love not you.

BEATRICE Will you not eat your word?

BENEDICK With no sauce that can be devised to it. I 25
protest I love thee.

BEATRICE Why then, God forgive me!

BENEDICK What offense, sweet Beatrice?

BEATRICE You have stayed me in a happy hour: I was
about to protest I loved you. 30

BENEDICK And do it with all thy heart.

BEATRICE I love you with so much of my heart that
none is left to protest.

BENEDICK Come bid me do anything for thee.

BEATRICE Kill Claudio. 35

BENEDICK Ha, not for the wide world!

11 **even** straightforward
13 **office** duty, function
21 **eat it** i.e., eat your words
26 **protest** affirm solemnly

BEATRICE You kill me to deny it. Farewell.

BENEDICK Tarry sweet Beatrice.

BEATRICE I am gone, though I am here; there is no
love in you. Nay, I pray you let me go!   40

BENEDICK Beatrice—

BEATRICE In faith I will go!

BENEDICK We'll be friends first.

BEATRICE You dare easier be friends with me than
fight with mine enemy.   45

BENEDICK Is Claudio thine enemy?

BEATRICE Is he not approved in the height a villain
that hath slandered, scorned, dishonored my kins-
woman? O that I were a man! What, bear her in hand
until they come to take hands and then with public   50
accusation, uncovered slander, unmitigated rancor—
O God that I were a man! I would eat his heart in the
market place!

BENEDICK Hear me Beatrice—

BEATRICE Talk with a man out at a window! A proper   55
saying!

BENEDICK Nay but Beatrice—

BEATRICE Sweet Hero, she is wronged, she is slandered,
she is undone.

BENEDICK Beat—   60

BEATRICE Princes and counties! Surely a princely
testimony, a goodly count, Count Comfect; a sweet
gallant surely! O that I were a man for his sake or
that I had any friend would be a man for my sake!
But manhood is melted into curtsies, valor into com-   65
pliment and men are only turned into tongue, and
trim ones too. He is now as valiant as Hercules that

37 **to deny it** i.e., by refusing to do
so
47 **approved** proved, convicted to
be
49 **bear . . . hand** lead her on with
false hopes
51 **uncovered** barefaced

55 **proper** fine (ironical)
61 **counties** counts
62 **count** (1) story, (2) item in an in-
dictment
Count Comfect sugar-plum count
65 **curtsies** courtesies, ceremony
67 **trim** fine, nice (ironical)

only tells a lie and swears it. I cannot be a man with
wishing therefore I will die a woman with grieving.
BENEDICK Tarry good Beatrice. By this hand, I love   70
thee.
BEATRICE Use it for my love some other way than
swearing by it.
BENEDICK Think you in your soul the Count Claudio
hath wronged Hero?   75
BEATRICE Yea, as sure as I have a thought or a soul.
BENEDICK Enough, I am engaged. I will challenge
him. I will kiss your hand and so I leave you. By this
hand, Claudio shall render me a dear account. As
you hear of me, so think of me. Go comfort your   80
cousin. I must say she is dead. And so farewell.

✠

Rehearsing the Scene

The scene starts quietly with Beatrice weeping and Benedick
making polite enquiries. Already, however, their attitudes are in
conflict: he cannot avoid a patronizing tone; she cannot avoid
confrontation. Soon they are quarrelling with bitterness and passion. The challenge to actors is to play the differences strongly and
yet to achieve a true meeting between the two characters which
reconciles them.

Mixed with Beatrice's fierce anger are feelings of the tenderest
kind. At Hero's wedding, she was "about to protest" (that is to
proclaim) that she loved Benedick. Her equivocations ("I confess
nothing nor I deny nothing") finally give way to her boldest proclamation of love (see ll. 32-33). Now, Benedick, who had earlier
side-stepped Beatrice's wish that some man would "right" her cousin (ll. 8-9), is moved to offer to "do anything" for her. Agreement
between them seems possible already, but Beatrice replies "Kill
Claudio," and Benedick steps back with "Ha, not for the wide
world!" He is Claudio's friend and comrade in arms. Benedick and
Beatrice are further apart now than ever.

There are several possible motivations for Beatrice's unequivo-

cal demand. Her pent-up feelings may now give vent to brutal exaggeration as she attempts to shock Benedick into action. Or she
may use this command as a test of Benedick's love, so that she
speaks very quietly and deliberately. Beatrice's "let me go" and "In
faith I will go!" (ll. 40 and 42) suggest that Benedick takes hold of
her at this point and struggles physically to detain or persuade
her. But the lines work just as well if he is merely standing in the
way of her exit and she refuses to struggle.

Here again, Beatrice's anger flares up unmistakably. Perhaps
Benedick's blunt question "Is Claudio thine enemy?" (l. 46) so
clearly marks the distance between their thoughts, that she breaks
free from his grasp and returns to attack him with words. Perhaps
her accusation that he is afraid to fight (ll. 44-45) has so taken
Benedick by surprise that tension is broken.

But the greatest change in Beatrice is yet to come: now she
wishes "O that I were a man!" Earlier in the play she had scorned
men and their ways constantly, but now, three times over, she
wishes to have a man's strength so that she could take the action
which was regarded universally to be man's prerogative. Benedick
cannot stem the tide of her passion, although he tries three times
(ll. 54, 57, and 60). "I would eat his heart in the market place" (ll.
52-53) is a gruesome cry, but almost certainly she means it. Anger
at Claudio and impatience with mankind, including Benedick, makes
her respond with the instinctive force and speed of a wild animal.

Yet she is not wholly savage. A moment later she recovers sufficiently to castigate the hypocrisy and pretension of men. Her energy is expressed now in exclamations, repetitions, ironies and mock-
eries. For all her bitter passion, she is also more tender and more
practical than any man she knows: Leonato and Benedick, and
other guests at the wedding, had neither taken initiative to stand
up unequivocally for Hero, nor wept helplessly as she had done. In
the end, however, it is her realism that takes over: "I cannot be a
man with wishing therefore I will die a woman with grieving" (ll. 68-
69).

Here lies Benedick's second chance of being reconciled with
Beatrice and he tries to take it. First he reiterates his love, very sim-
ply. When Beatrice implies that this is only talk, he is drawn on to
take her position more seriously and to ask the critical question:
"Think you in your soul that the Count Claudio hath wronged
Hero?" Beatrice issues her verdict with judicial solemnity. Both

know how much is at stake: perhaps they look each other in the eye during a long silence. Every word now may be quiet, slow, almost dispassionate; underneath may be sensed the mutual love and respect, coexisting with and motivating the acceptance of the duel. Yet, possibly, the two are only beginning to sense the awakening of mutual trust.

It may be useful to break down the emotional elements of the scene individually and try out various physical equivalents. To explore their emotional modulation between intimacy and hostility, the actors may wish to maintain a greater than usual physical distance from each other. Some run-throughs might be very slow indeed, followed perhaps by one that goes very fast. One rehearsal might be played so that every exchange is a self-conscious trial of strength, the scene becoming a passionate and at times ugly conflict, a weary, almost hopeless struggle which neither truly wins; both may be tormented by their inability to respond trustingly to each other. Another rehearsal might be played with a sense of the absurdity of the rapid transitions and numerous repetitions: Beatrice might laugh so that she does not weep; Benedick so that he does not admit his impotence.

One thing is certain about the end of the scene: Beatrice is now silent. Perhaps as she confesses that she "cannot be a man with wishing," Benedick holds her in his arms, so that he can then quieten her and lead her towards a trust in him. When they part at the end of the scene, after he has kissed her hand (see l. 78), her silence might then speak for a new intimacy, peace and strength. Although Benedick seems to be in charge, he has accepted all that she has wished.

[Note on line 81: "I must say she is dead." In playing this scene on its own, this brief sentence is best omitted. In the play it refers to the ruse of announcing Hero's death after her emotional swoon at the accusation of unfaithfulness.]

6

As You Like It

Act III, Scene ii

ROSALIND and ORLANDO

✠

Rosalind and Orlando had briefly met at court, fallen in love and were then separately banished. Both independently sought refuge in the Forest of Arden. Rosalind, in order to avoid being robbed or terrorized, has taken on the disguise of a swashbuckling young man named Ganymede. She and Orlando now meet in the Forest, where Orlando has been hanging poems in praise of Rosalind on trees. Rosalind had escaped to the Forest with her cousin Celia, who observes this scene but takes no active part. Rosalind's first line is addressed to her.

✠

ROSALIND I will speak to him like a saucy lackey and
    under that habit play the knave with him. Do you
    hear, forester?

ORLANDO Very well. What would you?

ROSALIND I pray you, what is't o'clock?   5

ORLANDO You should ask me what time o' day; there's
    no clock in the forest.

ROSALIND Then there is no true lover in the forest,
    else sighing every minute and groaning every hour
    would detect the lazy foot of Time as well as a clock.   10

ORLANDO And why not the swift foot of Time? Had
    not that been as proper?

ROSALIND By no means, sir. Time travels in divers paces
    with divers persons. I'll tell you who Time ambles
    withal, who Time trots withal, who Time gallops   15
    withal and who he stands still withal.

2 **habit** guise, behavior   10 **detect** reveal
   play the knave trick him/pretend
   to be a young man

ORLANDO I prithee, who doth he trot withal?

ROSALIND Marry, he trots hard with a young maid
between the contract of her marriage and the day it
is solemnized. If the interim be but a se'nnight,   20
Time's pace is so hard that it seems the length of
seven year.

ORLANDO Who ambles Time withal?

ROSALIND With a priest that lacks Latin and a rich man
that hath not the gout; for the one sleeps easily   25
because he cannot study and the other lives merrily
because he feels no pain; the one lacking the burden
of lean and wasteful learning, the other knowing no
burden of heavy tedious penury. These Time ambles
withal.   30

ORLANDO Who doth he gallop withal?

ROSALIND With a thief to the gallows, for though he
go as softly as foot can fall, he thinks himself too soon
there.

ORLANDO Who stays it still withal?   35

ROSALIND With lawyers in the vacation, for they sleep
between term and term and then they perceive not
how time moves.

ORLANDO Where dwell you, pretty youth?

ROSALIND With this shepherdess my sister, here in   40
the skirts of the forest, like fringe upon a petticoat.

ORLANDO Are you native of this place?

ROSALIND As the cony that you see dwell where she
is kindled.

ORLANDO Your accent is something finer than you   45
could purchase in so removed a dwelling.

ROSALIND I have been told so of many. But indeed an

19 **contract . . . marriage** betrothal
20 **se'nnight** seven days, week
21 **hard** (trotting hard is an uncom-
fortable ride on a horse)
28 **wasteful** causing (the scholar's
body) to waste away

33 **softly** slowly
37 **term** session of the courts
43 **cony** rabbit
44 **kindled** littered, born
46 **purchase** acquire; **removed** remote

old religious uncle of mine taught me to speak who
was in his youth an inland man, one that knew
courtship too well for there he fell in love. I have   50
heard him read many lectures against it and I thank
God I am not a woman, to be touched with so many
giddy offenses as he hath generally taxed their whole
sex withal.

ORLANDO   Can you remember any of the principal   55
evils that he laid to the charge of women?

ROSALIND   There were none principal. They were all
like one another as halfpence are, every one fault
seeming monstrous till his fellow fault came to
match it.   60

ORLANDO   I prithee recount some of them.

ROSALIND   No, I will not cast away my physic but on
those that are sick. There is a man haunts the forest
that abuses our young plants with carving "Rosalind"
on their barks, hangs odes upon hawthorns and   65
elegies on brambles, all, forsooth, deifying the name
of Rosalind. If I could meet that fancy-monger, I
would give him some good counsel for he seems to
have the quotidian of love upon him.

ORLANDO   I am he that is so love-shaked. I pray you   70
tell me your remedy.

ROSALIND   There is none of my uncle's marks upon
you. He taught me how to know a man in love, in
which cage of rushes I am sure you are not prisoner.

ORLANDO   What were his marks?   75

ROSALIND   A lean cheek which you have not, a blue

---

48   **religious** i.e., a hermit or member
of a monastic order
49   **inland** living close to the center
of affairs
50   **courtship** high society/wooing
52   **touched** tainted
53   **taxed** accused
62   **physic** healing arts
67   **fancy-monger** dealer in love/in

fanciful verses
69   **quotidian** fever of daily recur-
rence accompanied with shivering
(see **shaked**, l. 70)
74   **cage of rushes** i.e., a prison easy
to break out from (rings of rushes
were exchanged by rural lovers)
76   **blue** with dark rings indicating
sleeplessness

eye and sunken which you have not, an unquestionable spirit which you have not, a beard neglected
which you have not—but I pardon you for that, for
simply your having in beard is a younger brother's   80
revenue. Then your hose should be ungartered, your
bonnet unbanded, your sleeve unbuttoned, your shoe
untied and everything about you demonstrating a
careless desolation. But you are no such man: you are
rather point-device in your accouterments, as loving   85
yourself than seeming the lover of any other.

ORLANDO   Fair youth, I would I could make thee
believe I love.

ROSALIND   Me believe it? You may as soon make her
that you love believe it, which I warrant she is apter   90
to do than to confess she does; that is one of the points
in the which women still give the lie to their consciences. But in good sooth, are you he that hangs the
verses on the trees wherein Rosalind is so admired?

ORLANDO   I swear to thee, youth, by the white hand of   95
Rosalind, I am that he, that unfortunate he.

ROSALIND   But are you so much in love as your rhymes
speak?

ORLANDO   Neither rhyme nor reason can express how
much.   100

ROSALIND   Love is merely a madness and, I tell you,
deserves as well a dark house and a whip as madmen
do, and the reason why they are not so punished and
cured is that the lunacy is so ordinary that the whippers
are in love too. Yet I profess curing it by counsel.   105

ORLANDO   Did you ever cure any so?

ROSALIND   Yes, one, and in this manner: he was to
imagine me his love, his mistress, and I set him every

77-78 **unquestionable** i.e., not to be
       spoken with
   80 **simply** obviously
80-81 **younger . . . revenue** small por-
       tion
   84 **careless** uncared for

   85 **point-device** in perfect order
   92 **still** always
   93 **sooth** truth
  101 **merely** purely, entirely
  102 **dark . . . whip** (the usual treat-
       ment for the violently insane)

day to woo me. At which time would I, being but a
moonish youth, grieve, be effeminate, changeable,   110
longing and liking, proud, fantastical, apish, shallow,
inconstant, full of tears, full of smiles; for every
passion something and for no passion truly anything,
as boys and women are for the most part cattle of this
color; would now like him, now loathe him; then   115
entertain him, then forswear him; now weep for him,
then spit at him; that I drave my suitor from his mad
humor of love to a living humor of madness which
was to forswear the full stream of the world and to
live in a nook merely monastic and thus I cured him   120
and this way will I take upon me to wash your liver
as clean as a sound sheep's heart, that there shall
not be one spot of love in't.

ORLANDO   I would not be cured, youth.

ROSALIND   I would cure you if you would but call   125
me Rosalind and come every day to my cote and
woo me.

ORLANDO   Now by the faith of my love, I will. Tell
me where it is.

ROSALIND   Go with me to it and I'll show it you, and   130
by the way you shall tell me where in the forest you
live. Will you go?

ORLANDO   With all my heart, good youth.

ROSALIND   Nay, you must call me Rosalind.

Exeunt.

110   **moonish** changeable
116   **entertain** welcome
117-18   **mad humor . . . of madness**
(metaphorical) madness of love to
clinical madness

121   **liver** (supposed seat of the passions)
126   **cote** cottage
131   **by** along

⊞

Rehearsing the Scene

Rosalind, prepared for Orlando's entrance, certainly appears to be in charge of the scene that follows; in fact, one might say that she directs the action. Yet, Rosalind also becomes susceptible to its action once in motion—and she must occasionally yield control to Orlando's response and initiative. And while she may exert greater control over the logistics of the scene, she is not entirely in control of her new identity. Rosalind's meeting with Orlando is, after all, the first serious sustained test of her performance as Ganymede.

One might note, for example, that her broad stereotypical characterization of a young man gives way to a more sensitive portrayal as it progresses. And while she may control the external action, the actress must be aware of Rosalind's inner drama which runs parallel to it. There she is, after all, with the man with whom she's very much smitten, but unable to respond as a woman.

The actor of Orlando is free to experiment with how much his character knows or guesses, or intuits, of the truth behind Rosalind's performance. Her first words to Orlando may overplay a masculine brusqueness and so his "Very well" (l. 4) can be an easy put-down. This would lead Rosalind to take refuge in a conventional enquiry about time, but she is put down once more for forgetting where she is: she has to be more bold, and so starts to talk about lovers. Perhaps she is relieved to be led from this greater openness into an enumeration of the various paces of Time. Now Orlando does seem to be held by the attractions of her mind; perhaps so much so that by the end of her recital his questions irritate her.

Rosalind might well be proud of her verbal swordplay with Orlando on the subject of time. Her victory is marked by Orlando's new domestic line of inquiry "Where dwell you pretty youth?" (l. 39). But relaxing a little, she lets slip the very female simile of a petticoat's fringe, which could wreck her pretense to be a man. She recovers her poise with the quick invention of a hermit-uncle. Orlando's enquiry, however, about the "principal evils that he laid to the charge of women" may seek to discover the true nature of this "pretty youth," as much as the uncle's wisdom about women.

When Orlando acknowledges that he is the "love-shaked" man and asks for a remedy for love, the tone changes; with a single compelling image, he has taken the lead from Rosalind by daring to be serious. It might well be that by now he knows that he is talking to Rosalind. Such knowledge is against the usual conventions of disguise in Elizabethan drama, but not entirely against Shakespeare's use of it for presenting Portia, Nerissa and Jessica as males in *The Merchant of Venice*, or for Viola as Cesario in *Twelfth Night*, where a half-knowledge of the reality under the disguise hovers in the minds of those who are closest to them.

Whether Orlando is conscious of Rosalind's presence or not, his later speeches ring with true feeling. The strength of his "Fair youth, I would I could make thee believe I love"—the first time he uses *thee* in preference to *you*—could well take Rosalind by surprise. When he swears by "the white hand of Rosalind," he may well look into her eyes and take Ganymede's hand without self-consciousness. At line 101, Rosalind acknowledges the madness and contagion of love in a wholly new image—dangerously true and developed step by step as if she is realizing its truth for the first time as she speaks.

Orlando's response—"Did you ever cure any so?" which is either incredulous or taunting—spurs Rosalind to invent a new wooing-game. She remembers again to "play the knave" as seriously as she can, castigating the role of women in love as well as men's. When Orlando declines the charade, this triggers something more: without any eloquence or elaboration, Rosalind promises to cure Orlando. This is the moment when they are closest to each other. For her to "cure" him is to love him, not to argue him out of his love. Orlando responds by forgetting that he is addressing a boy and speaking of the "faith of his love" with a simple, unequivocal "I will." She says nothing in reply to this and, probably after a pause, it is Orlando who must be practical now, asking where the cottage is located.

As the two leave the stage, Orlando may go ahead, to be reproved for not letting the "lady" go first. Or Rosalind can leave ahead of him, as he stands still, wondering what can have happened; so "Will you go?" is spoken to urge him on. Or they may be laughing together, happy as they agree to see each other again; in which case, Rosalind's last rejoinder serves to keep that happiness afloat.

This encounter can be played in several ways. Is Rosalind in charge or trapped by her disguise and Orlando's presence? Is Orlando a reluctant victim or a delighted lover who permits and enjoys the masquerade?

Attention to several contrasting aspects of the characters will help the actors to play both the comedy and the depth of feeling. Orlando is at home in the country, whereas to Rosalind it is unfamiliar territory. Orlando has proved himself a powerful wrestler in an earlier scene; Rosalind is dressed in unfamiliar clothes and can only pretend to the toughness of a "saucy lackey." Orlando may discover the force behind the relative economy of his speech. He can speak directly of his love; Rosalind must talk first about many other things, and when love is her subject she must spend most of her time mocking and denigrating a woman's part in its affairs.

The question which most concerns Rosalind, "But are you so much in love as your rhymes speak?" (ll. 97-98), will be almost impossible to pose as the "saucy lackey" whom she has chosen to hide behind. An actress might try to say it this way, even if she discards it for performance in favor of being much more exposed in feeling. The attempt will help her to understand the contrary impulses at work within Rosalind. The actor of Orlando should experiment by remaining silent for a time, before replying; so he will discover the power he can wield over Rosalind.

7

Hamlet

Act III, Scene i

HAMLET and OPHELIA

✠

Ophelia meets Hamlet in order that his behavior may be observed in secret by Polonius, her father, and Claudius, the king. Claudius wishes to judge whether the melancholy or madness of Hamlet is due to his thwarted love of Ophelia, who has been told to avoid his company, or perhaps to the death of Hamlet's father and/or his mother's subsequent marriage to Claudius.

The audience knows, but the king and others do not, that Hamlet has a mission of his own: to discover the truth of his father's death, for which he suspects Claudius. Hamlet acts mad in order to keep his mission secret and give himself freedom of maneuver. But by this time, the audience may not be sure how much the madness is pretense and how much it is real.

Hamlet now notices Ophelia, who has been told by Polonius to walk in the "lobby" of the palace at Elsinore (see II.**i**.160-61).

✠

HAMLET
  The fair Ophelia!—Nymph in thy orisons
  Be all my sins remembered.
OPHELIA   Good my lord,
  How does your honor for this many a day?
HAMLET
  I humbly thank you, well.
OPHELIA
  My lord, I have remembrances of yours   5

---

1 **orisons** prayers (poetic; Ophelia had been given a prayer book to read as she awaited Hamlet)

4 **I . . . well** (as if speaking to a stranger)

That I have longed long to redeliver.
I pray you now receive them.

HAMLET   No, not I.
I never gave you aught.

OPHELIA
My honored lord, you know right well you did
And with them words of so sweet breath composed   10
As made the things more rich. Their perfume lost,
Take these again, for to the noble mind
Rich gifts wax poor when givers prove unkind.
There, my lord.

HAMLET Ha, ha! Are you honest?   15

OPHELIA My lord?

HAMLET Are you fair?

OPHELIA What means your lordship?

HAMLET That if you be honest and fair, your honesty
should admit no discourse to your beauty.   20

OPHELIA Could beauty, my lord, have better commerce
than with honesty?

HAMLET Ay, truly; for the power of beauty will sooner
transform honesty from what it is to a bawd than the
force of honesty can translate beauty into his likeness.   25
This was sometime a paradox but now the time gives
it proof. I did love you once.

OPHELIA Indeed my lord, you made me believe so.

HAMLET You should not have believed me for virtue
cannot so inoculate our old stock but we shall relish   30
of it. I loved you not.

OPHELIA I was the more deceived.

HAMLET Get thee to a nunnery. Why wouldst thou be

---

15 **honest** (1) truthful (2) chaste
20 **admit . . . to** (1) permit no one to
   converse with (2) keep apart from
21 **commerce** dealings/intercourse
   (taken in sexual sense by Hamlet)
24 **bawd** pimp, procurer
26 **paradox** idea contrary to received
   opinion

26-27 **now . . . proof** (e.g., the example of
   his mother)
30 **inoculate** graft on to
   old stock i.e., original sinful nature
   relish taste
33 **nunnery** (to preserve her chastity;
   very occasionally = brothel)

a breeder of sinners? I am myself indifferent honest
but yet I could accuse me of such things that it were   35
better my mother had not borne me. I am very proud,
revengeful, ambitious, with more offenses at my beck
than I have thoughts to put them in, imagination to
give them shape or time to act them in. What should
such fellows as I do crawling between earth and   40
heaven? We are arrant knaves all; believe none of us.
Go thy ways to a nunnery. Where's your father?
OPHELIA At home, my lord.
HAMLET Let the doors be shut upon him that he may
play the fool nowhere but in's own house. Farewell.   45
OPHELIA O help him, you sweet heavens!
HAMLET If thou dost marry, I'll give thee this plague for
thy dowry: be thou as chaste as ice, as pure as snow,
thou shalt not escape calumny. Get thee to a nunnery,
farewell. Or if thou wilt needs marry, marry a fool   50
for wise men know well enough what monsters you
make of them. To a nunnery go and quickly too.
Farewell.
OPHELIA Heavenly powers, restore him!
HAMLET I have heard of your paintings well enough. God   55
hath given you one face and you make yourselves
another. You jig and amble, and you lisp; you nickname
God's creatures and make your wantonness your
ignorance. Go to, I'll no more on't; it hath made me
mad. I say we will have no more marriage. Those   60
that are married already—all but one—shall live. The
rest shall keep as they are. To a nunnery go.   *Exit*.
OPHELIA
O what a noble mind is here o'erthrown!
The courtier's, soldier's, scholar's, eye, tongue, sword,

34 **indifferent** moderately
37 **beck** call
51 **monsters** horned beasts, cuckolds
57 **nickname** find new names for
58-59 **make . . . ignorance** excuse your wanton affectation by pretending you do not know better

Th'expectancy and rose of the fair state,   65
The glass of fashion and the mold of form,
Th' observed of all observers quite, quite down!
And I, of ladies most deject and wretched
That sucked the honey of his music vows,
Now see that noble and most sovereign reason   70
Like sweet bells jangled, out of time and harsh,
That unmatched form and feature of blown youth
Blasted with ecstasy. O woe is me
T' have seen what I have seen, see what I see!

65 **expectancy and rose** hope of
youthful perfection
66 **glass** mirror
   mold of form pattern for excellent
   behavior/order
67 **observed** honored

69 **music** like music
70 **sovereign** having the right to rule
   (over other faculties)
72 **feature** shapeliness
   blown in full flower
73 **ecstasy** madness

☒

Rehearsing the Scene

Hamlet, of all Shakespeare's plays, is most open to different interpretations. Its dialogue bristles and beckons with words of multiple meanings and syntax of subtle force; its central character has a tirelessly resourceful mind. When Hamlet claims that he does not know why he acts as he does, actors, directors and scholars have never been at a loss to supply possible reasons.

Two major uncertainties affect the playing of this scene. First, when Hamlet asks Ophelia where her father is and she replies "At home, my lord" (ll. 42-43), does she know that her father and the king are hiding nearby? On the one hand Ophelia may be innocently unaware; she agreed to meet Hamlet in order to help him and "bring him to his wonted way again" (III.i.41-42). On the other hand, if she has heard the King and her father arranging to hide so that they may trap Hamlet, then the most obvious lie about her father (l. 43) may well ring false. In this interpretation, Ophelia is a traitress, and Hamlet may be expected to see through her. Everything he says after her lie may be an "antic disposition" (I.v.180), a pretended madness used deliberately to conceal his plan to revenge his father's murder.

The first interpretation, in which Ophelia's "At home, my lord" represents the truth as she believes it, will make this duologue a painful love scene. Hamlet's tenderness towards Ophelia and his horror at the out-of-joint world fight for supremacy, the one infecting the other. The second interpretation, in which the same words are a deliberate lie by Ophelia and recognized as such by Hamlet, turns the scene into a corrosive attack by Hamlet on his enemies; he leaves Ophelia to express her wonder and woe for what she has witnessed, without hope of forgiveness.

A third interpretation may prove the most savage of all. Ophelia is, in fact, unaware of her father's presence. But Hamlet, in his legitimately suspicious state, senses Polonius' proximity and damns the innocent Ophelia for her complicity in the general collusion against him. The abruptness of "Where's your father?" (l. 42) must raise question about what Hamlet is not saying, what subtextual pressures drive his mind forward to ask this question.

The second, still more inescapable, problem is represented by Hamlet's contradictory avowals: "I did love you once" and "I loved you not" (ll. 27 and 31). Does he deny his love in order to protect her from what he feels will be his own fate? Does he fear that his true feelings, once pronounced, will distract him from his plan for revenge? Or does he now learn that he never truly loved Ophelia?

Hamlet's involvement with Ophelia keeps the energy of his mind racing until the very last command "To a nunnery go." But the sexual passion of these speeches may also come in part from his feelings towards his mother, whose presence should then be felt throughout the scene, in talk of wantonness and ignorance, honesty and beauty, "playing the fool" and marriage.

These uncertainties in the play should not inhibit actors. Instead the ambiguities might well inspire actors to different interpretations and opportunities to explore them in rehearsal. Actors might, for example, choose two distinct interpretations and try them one after another in early rehearsals.

Actors will discover stage directions woven into the dialogue: the silences marked by incomplete verse lines in the earlier part of the scene; Ophelia's attempt to give back Hamlet's letters and other keepsakes (this goes beyond her father's instructions, which shows her to be independent and persistent, not merely a dutiful daughter); Hamlet's repeated attempts to get Ophelia to leave, or to leave himself (which may start as early as line 33 and continue until the end of the scene); and Ophelia's attempt to pray to the heavens and heavenly powers (does she kneel to do so?). In some interpretations, Hamlet might kiss Ophelia or be about to do so. In some rehearsals one of them might speak very slowly or very quickly. Violence of speech and action will come very readily; yet a full blown shouting match will certainly obscure the subtleties of the text.

A variety of approaches will reveal many fascinating possibilities, but about halfway through the rehearsal time, firm decisions should be made about the two main issues which have been discussed here. Otherwise too much will remain tentative and the scene will not gather its necessary force.

All's Well That Ends Well

Act IV, Scene ii

BERTRAM and DIANA

✠

Bertram, young and born to privilege, has inherited great estates on the death of his father, but has continued to live with his mother until leaving to go the king's court. There he was married against his will by the king's command to Helena, a poor physician's daughter from his hometown who has loved him, from a distance, for many years. Immediately after the ceremony he vowed never to consummate the union except on almost impossible conditions. He then volunteered for military service in Florence and left France for Italy. There he has excelled as a brave and successful soldier.

In Florence he catches sight of Diana, a girl renowned for her beauty. He falls in love with her, despite her own humble origins.

The situation is, however, more complicated than Bertram knows. Helena has also come to Florence disguised as a pilgrim and is staying in the house of Diana's widowed mother. So Bertram's new love knows all about his marriage. When she invites him to her bedroom, it is to allow Helena to take her conjugal place.

✠

BERTRAM
    They told me that your name was Fontibell.
DIANA
    No my good lord, Diana.
BERTRAM   Titled goddess
    And worth it with addition. But fair soul,
    In your fine frame hath love no quality?
    If the quick fire of youth light not your mind,   5
    You are no maiden but a monument.

---

2 **Diana** (virgin goddess of hunting)   4 **frame** body; **quality** place, rank
3 **addition** further honor

When you are dead you should be such a one
As you are now, for you are cold and stern
And now you should be as your mother was
When your sweet self was got.   10

DIANA
She then was honest.

BERTRAM   So should you be.

DIANA   No.
My mother did but duty, such my lord,
As you owe to your wife.

BERTRAM   No more o' that!
I prithee do not strive against my vows.
I was compelled to her, but I love thee   15
By love's own sweet constraint and will forever
Do thee all rights of service.

DIANA   Ay so you serve us
Till we serve you. But when you have our roses,
You barely leave our thorns to prick ourselves
And mock us with our bareness.

BERTRAM   How have I sworn!   20

DIANA
'Tis not the many oaths that makes the truth
But the plain single vow that is vowed true.
What is not holy that we swear not by,
But take the High'st to witness. Then pray you tell me:
If I should swear by Jove's great attributes   25
I loved you dearly, would you believe my oaths
When I did love you ill? This has no holding,
To swear by Him whom I protest to love
That I will work against Him. Therefore your oaths
Are words and poor conditions but unsealed,   30
At least in my opinion.

BERTRAM   Change it, change it.

18 **serve you** (in a sexual sense)
19 **barely** only just, scarcely
20 **bareness** nakedness/destitution, loss
27 **ill** i.e., not at all

30 **conditions but unsealed** legal stipulations without any force, being uncertified
31 **opinion** expectation (pun on legal usage)

Be not so holy-cruel: Love is holy
And my integrity ne'er knew the crafts
That you do charge men with. Stand no more off
But give thyself unto my sick desires,   35
Who then recovers. Say thou art mine and ever
My love as it begins shall so persever.

DIANA

I see that men may rope's in such a snare,
That we'll forsake ourselves. Give me that ring.

BERTRAM

I'll lend it thee my dear, but have no power   40
To give it from me.

DIANA   Will you not my lord?

BERTRAM

It is an honor 'longing to our house,
Bequeathed down from many ancestors,
Which were the greatest obloquy i' th' world
In me to lose.

DIANA   Mine honor's such a ring: 45
My chastity's the jewel of our house,
Bequeathed down from many ancestors,
Which were the greatest obloquy i' th' world
In me to lose. Thus your own proper wisdom
Brings in the champion Honor on my part   50
Against your vain assault.

BERTRAM   Here, take my ring.
My house, mine honor, yea, my life be thine
And I'll be bid by thee.

DIANA

When midnight comes, knock at my chamber-window:
I'll order take my mother shall not hear.   55
Now will I charge you in the band of truth,
When you have conquered my yet maiden bed,

---

38 **may . . . snare** i.e., may tie us in
   such a trap (Folio ed. reads **make .
   . . scarre** for which no satisfactory sense has been found)
39 **forsake** surrender

44 **obloquy** disgrace
49 **proper** fine (ironical)/personal, peculiar
53 **bid** commanded
56 **band** bond

Remain there but an hour, nor speak to me.
My reasons are most strong and you shall know them
When back again this ring shall be delivered.   60
And on your finger in the night I'll put
Another ring, that what in time proceeds
May token to the future our past deeds.
Adieu till then; then fail not. You have won
A wife of me though there my hope be done.   65

BERTRAM

A heaven on earth I have won by wooing thee.

DIANA

For which live long to thank both heaven and me—
You may so in the end.   *Exit* BERTRAM.
My mother told me just how he would woo,
As if she sat in's heart. She says all men   70
Have the like oaths. He had sworn to marry me
When his wife's dead therefore I'll lie with him
When I am buried. Since Frenchmen are so braid,
Marry that will; I live and die a maid.
Only in this disguise, I think't no sin   75
To cozen him that would unjustly win.   *Exit*.

---

73 **braid** twisted, cunning (?)   76 **cozen** cheat

✠

Rehearsing the Scene

The balance of power seems to be wholly on Diana's side. Five
times she takes Bertram's words and uses them against him: his arguments about her "mother" (ll. 9-13); about "service" (ll 16-18);
"oaths" (ll. 20-31); possession (ll. 36-39); and, most devastatingly,
about "honor" (ll. 42-51). Besides, whereas his words show a
mind running on melodramatic, or even apocalyptic issues—
goddess, soul and body, fire, light, monumental stone, striving,
compulsion, rights, service, holiness and cruelty—her language is

varied, practical and witty. Diana's images are taken from flowers, legal processes, hunting, treasure and chivalry. His thought runs according to extravagant male stereotypes; hers is much more surprising, and free to play with whatever is offered to her. Diana is also concerned with warfare, but she does not talk of this until the conclusion of their engagement, when Bertram has nothing to say and she has a number of practical instructions to give; and then she speaks of conquering her "maiden bed" (l. 57) in male, not female terms, giving him the impression that she has yielded to his entreaties—something she had decided to do from the outset, but on her own terms and for her own purposes.

Diana can be played as a cold and calculating person, but Shakespeare has given her a parting thought for Bertram which could be used to show a different, warmer attitude towards the defeated man. Besides, her closing soliloquy can express a sense of fun and adventure—"My mother told me just how he would woo" is an almost certain laugh line—which an actress can maintain underneath the words throughout the encounter. At line 38 Diana can either learn something new or show that she had been waiting for just this moment before putting her crucial demand (because she must get the ring to catch Bertram in Helena's trap). The silence, indicated by an incomplete verse line (53), which Diana holds before proceeding with her instructions, may also be played in a number of ways: does she show pleasure in her own success, or amusement at his defeat? Or could her hesitation reveal a fear, or a concern for how much is at stake?

The actor may well ask how Bertram's integrity can survive when he is outclassed at every turn. Yet Bertram acts with completely genuine feeling over against Diana, who is only pretending most of the time. His truth can outshine her artifice; and in this sense, he is the stronger of the two. There is also progression in Bertram's character. He starts on the wrong foot, getting Diana's name wrong and at the same time showing that he has had to make enquiries at a distance. He reveals his narrow and possessive instincts ("say thou art mine") without any sense that love could be a self-giving (compare Juliet's "My bounty is as boundless as the sea, My love as deep," Romeo and Juliet, II.ii.133-34). Yet he does move to a more generous position when he bestows on Diana the impossible gift of his family ring.

How does Bertram effect this change? When he gives the ring, the rhythm of his speech changes and he enumerates, very simply, all that he gives with it. The moment can be played with a deeply affecting directness and quietness, Bertram caught up with total belief in this unprecedented encounter and finding a new sense of himself. Or it can be played rashly or desperately, as if he were a gambler, or an angry and naturally violent person, forced to do what he still does not want to do. Whatever way is chosen to play this moment, it can be developed as Bertram listens speechless to Diana's following speech, not even reacting verbally to its concluding reference to a "wife"—perhaps not even hearing it. He has one last line to sum up his response. Most editions print it as an exit line, but the scene will be more finely balanced if Diana hears and responds verbally to him: she might give and receive a kiss, or some other token of their agreement. The two actors must find the right moment and the right manner for their parting. Some Dianas will be able to speak only after Bertram has left.

The actor of Bertram may have one other option. This young wooer could be acting the strength of his "sick desires" (1. 35) and only pretending to each variety of feeling—as Diana herself is doing. Everything he says and does is according to the book (as Diana's mother knows it, see 1. 69) and he may be doing it by the book, for the fun of it and for his own self-esteem. So he would say nothing to Diana's apparent capitulation except an aside on his exit, a line which then becomes a flash of triumph when his mission is completed.

The scene, which looks very simple and one-sided on first reading, is capable of many interpretations because both characters can be conscious of using words as a means to other ends: Bertram for his own sexual or mental satisfaction; Diana to effect a good turn for someone else and to have fun on the way. The strongest way of acting the scene may well be for Bertram to be totally sincere and unaware of anything but his own needs; but this may not be the funniest or most exciting.

Perhaps the most important single moment to consider is when Bertram gives the ring and action takes over, for a moment, from words. Here the two characters are bound to make physical contact. Bertram has the crucial move and can make it gently, solemnly, rashly, violently or with cold calculation. Has he kept at a distance until now, or has Diana had to escape his advances? At line

39, they must have been close enough for her to see but not to touch the ring (she says "that ring," not "this ring"). Then, with "I'll lend it thee my dear" (he has not used such an intimate form of address before), he may move still nearer towards her. To some extent this is a "chase and capture" scene, and many movements to-and-fro can be given to it. It might be possible to make Diana the pursuer and Bertram the helpless prey: as she parries his verbal moves, she may draw closer, trapping him and leading him to ever more extreme avowals and closer physical contact. This would not be an obvious way to play the scene, but at least it would be instructive to rehearse once or twice with these movements. On the other hand, they might start seated at some distance from each other, and Bertram attempt several times to sit with Diana, or move his chair closer. This version of the chase could be used in rehearsal to explore the comic potentials of the text.

9

Othello

Act V, Scene ii

OTHELLO and DESDEMONA

✠

Othello, the distinguished Moor, has just been relieved of his post as commander of the Venetian troops in Cyprus. He is ordered to return to Venice, and his second-in-command, Cassio, has now been named his successor. But dominating Othello's mind is his belief that Cassio is the secret lover of his own young bride, Desdemona. Iago, Othello's personal adjutant, has incited the sparks of sexual jealousy in Othello, so that he now doubts that Desdemona could ever have loved him:

> Haply for I am black
> And have not those soft parts of conversation
> That chamberers have, or for I am declined
> Into the vale of years—yet that's not much—
> She's gone. I am abused and my relief
> Must be to loathe her. O curse of Marriage
> That we can call these delicate creatures ours
> And not their appetites!   (III.iii.262-69)

The doubt flares up into accusation and violence as Othello strikes and humiliates Desdemona in public, and orders her to bed. The audience has last seen him exulting in the revenge Iago has promised to take on Cassio's life. As he goes to Desdemona, he calls out:

> Minion, your dear lies dead
> And your unblest fate hies. Strumpet, I come:
> Forth of my heart those charms, thine eyes, are blotted.
> Thy bed, lust-stained, shall with lust's blood be spotted.
>   (V.i.33-36)

Desdemona is asleep when he enters the bedroom.

✠

Enter OTHELLO, *with a light:* DESDEMONA *in her bed.*

OTHELLO

It is the cause. It is the cause, my soul.
Let me not name it to you, you chaste stars.
It is the cause. Yet I'll not shed her blood
Nor scar that whiter skin of hers than snow
And smooth as monumental alabaster.   5
Yet she must die, else she'll betray more men.
Put out the light and then put out the light.
If I quench thee, thou flaming minister,
I can again thy former light restore,
Should I repent me, but once put out thy light,   10
Thou cunning'st pattern of excelling nature,
I know not where is that Promethean heat
That can thy light relume.
When I have plucked the rose,
I cannot give it vital growth again;   15
It needs must wither. I'll smell thee on the tree.

He kisses her.

O balmy breath, that dost almost persuade
Justice to break her sword. One more, one more!
Be thus when thou art dead, and I will kill thee
And love thee after. One more and that's the last!   20
So sweet was ne'er so fatal. I must weep
But they are cruel tears. This sorrow's heavenly;

---

1 **cause** grounds for action (i.e., adultery)/agent (causing disaster)
4 **whiter . . . snow** her skin whiter than snow
7 **light . . . light** (i.e., the torch . . . Desdemona's life)
8 **minister** servant, agent (i.e., the torch; but also biblical ref.; cf. *Psalms*, civ. 4: the Lord "maketh his angels spirits, his ministers a flaming fire")
11 **cunning'st . . . nature** most skillfully wrought example of Nature excelling herself
12 **Promethean heat** divine fire (Prometheus, a Titan, stole fire from heaven to give it to mankind)
13 **relume** rekindle
22 **heavenly** (biblical; cf. *Hebrews*, xii. 6: "whom the Lord loveth, he chasteneth")

It strikes where it doth love. She wakes.

DESDEMONA
Who's there? Othello?

OTHELLO   Ay, Desdemona.

DESDEMONA
Will you come to bed, my lord?   25

OTHELLO
Have you prayed tonight, Desdemon?

DESDEMONA   Ay, my lord.

OTHELLO
If you bethink yourself of any crime
Unreconciled as yet to heaven and grace,
Solicit for it straight.

DESDEMONA
Alack, my lord, what may you mean by that?   30

OTHELLO
Well do it, and be brief; I will walk by.
I would not kill thy unpreparèd spirit.
No, heavens forfend! I would not kill thy soul.

DESDEMONA
Talk you of killing?

OTHELLO   Ay, I do.

DESDEMONA   Then heaven
Have mercy on me!

OTHELLO   Amen, with all my heart.   35

DESDEMONA
If you say so, I hope you will not kill me.

OTHELLO
Humh.

DESDEMONA
And yet I fear you, for you're fatal then
When your eyes roll so. Why I should fear I know not
Since guiltiness I know not. But yet I feel I fear.   40

OTHELLO
Think on thy sins.

31 **by** nearby
38 **fatal** fateful, deadly

DESDEMONA   They are loves I bear to you.

OTHELLO

Ay, and for that thou diest.

DESDEMONA

That death's unnatural that kills for loving.
Alas why gnaw you so your nether lip?
Some bloody passion shakes your very frame.   45
These are portents, but yet I hope, I hope,
They do not point on me.

OTHELLO   Peace and be still.

DESDEMONA

I will so. What's the matter?

OTHELLO

That handkerchief which I so loved and gave thee,
Thou gav'st to Cassio.

DESDEMONA   No, by my life and soul!   50
Send for the man and ask him.

OTHELLO   Sweet soul, take heed,
Take heed of perjury; thou art on thy deathbed.

DESDEMONA

Ay, but not yet to die.

OTHELLO   Presently.
Therefore confess thee freely of thy sin,
For to deny each article with oath   55
Cannot remove nor choke the strong conception
That I do groan withal. Thou art to die.

DESDEMONA

Then Lord have mercy on me.

OTHELLO   I say, amen.

DESDEMONA

And have you mercy too. I never did
Offend you in my life, never loved Cassio   60
But with such general warranty of heaven
As I might love. I never gave him token.

---

41 **loves . . . you** (for which she deceived her father)
53 **Presently** immediately
55 **article** item (of the charge; legal)
56 **conception** belief/plan (pun: **conception** = giving birth)
60 **Offend** harm, sin against
61 **warranty** allowance

OTHELLO

By heaven, I saw my handkerchief in's hand!
O perjured woman, thou dost stone my heart
And mak'st me call what I intend to do   65
A murder, which I thought a sacrifice.
I saw the handkerchief.

DESDEMONA   He found it then.

I never gave it him. Send for him hither;
Let him confess a truth.

OTHELLO   He hath confessed.

DESDEMONA What, my lord?   70

OTHELLO

That he hath used thee.

DESDEMONA   How? Unlawfully?

OTHELLO   Ay.

DESDEMONA

He will not say so.

OTHELLO   No, his mouth is stopped.
Honest Iago hath ta'en order for't.

DESDEMONA

O my fear interprets! What, is he dead?

OTHELLO

Had all his hairs been lives, my great revenge   75
Had stomach for them all.

DESDEMONA

Alas, he is betrayed and I undone!

OTHELLO

Out strumpet! Weep'st thou for him to my face?

DESDEMONA

O banish me, my lord, but kill me not!

OTHELLO

Down, strumpet!   80

DESDEMONA

Kill me tomorrow; let me live tonight!

---

64 **stone** turn to stone   76 **stomach** appetite
73 **ta'en order for't** arranged it

OTHELLO
   Nay, if you strive . . .
DESDEMONA
   But half an hour!
OTHELLO   Being done, there is no pause.
DESDEMONA
   But while I say one prayer!
OTHELLO   It is too late.

   Smothers her. A call from within.

   What noise is this? Not dead? Not yet quite dead?   85
   I that am cruel am yet merciful;
   I would not have thee linger in thy pain.
   So, so.

---

83 **Being . . . pause** now that the
     deed is begun, I cannot stop

⌘

Rehearsing the Scene

   The slow killing of Desdemona, in full view of the audience, is without parallel in Shakespeare's plays: Juliet kills herself quickly; Portia (in *Julius Caesar*), Ophelia, Lady Macbeth and Cordelia all die offstage; Gertrude has only two lines as she dies, and those are an urgent call to warn her son of treachery; Cleopatra is almost serene as she chooses suicide. From line 30 onwards, however, defenseless Desdemona can have little doubt of Othello's intentions and the audience will share her horror and suffering.

   The protracted confrontation flows partly from his concern for Desdemona's soul. The language, however, takes on the quality of a contentious trial with phrases like "perjury,", "confess," "article," "oath," "mercy," "warranty," "unlawfully" and "matter," asserting themselves throughout. Othello offers Desde-

mona the opportunity to defend herself, but when passion over-
whelms him, he denies her even his initial favor of a final prayer.

The text offers many implicit stage directions for the actor of
Othello. He starts tenderly: he thinks of chaste stars, white snow,
smooth alabaster and a withering rose; he responds to "balmy
breath" and kisses her so gently that he does not wake the sleeping Desdemona—she wakes only after he "must weep." (At some
point he will have put down the light he carries; or possibly he
will have extinguished it.) Othello offers time for Desdemona to
pray (see l. 30), but then, after an inarticulate cry (l. 37), his
"eyes roll," his face is contorted and passion "shakes" his whole
body. He controls himself sufficiently to order Desdemona
"peace and be still" (l. 47) and her unexpected compliance stops
him in his tracks leaving Desdemona now to take up the initiative: "I will so. What's the matter?" (l. 48) has fewer than the expected ten syllables, which suggests a faltering in the action.

The verse is often irregular. For Desdemona's lines 39 and
40, extra syllables are crushed into the frame of iambic pentameters, the pace of speech seeming to forbid four successive half-
lines. Elsewhere, half-lines indicate highly charged pauses, at
lines 25, 29, 37, 42, 70 and 76. Towards the end of the scene,
half-lines probably indicate where physical violence takes over
from words (80 and 82). At other times, single verse lines are
split between two or three speeches, as Desdemona and Othello
respond to each other almost intuitively, without missing a beat
(ll. 34-35, 41, 47, 51-53, etc.).

After Othello has confronted Desdemona with what he considers irrefutable evidence of her infidelity, all his tenderness disappears. From "sweet soul" (l. 51), she becomes "perjured woman" (l. 64) and, soon afterwards, "strumpet." At line 72, he
makes a harsh joke about Cassio's death and then glories in his
own insatiable "revenge" (l. 75). Violence follows almost at once.
When he hears Emilia calling from offstage, Othello makes a final
reference to "mercy" (l. 86), but the actor can play this in different ways: it could be either a last tenderness or a brutally ironic
comment on his need to finish the murder.

A textual crux illustrates the extreme interpretations to which
Desdemona's role is open. In the Quarto edition of 1622, after
Othello's "It is too late" (l. 84), Desdemona says "O Lord, Lord,
Lord," which is usually taken to be the beginning of the prayer

she has begged time to make. But this short speech is missing from the Folio text of 1623, so that in this version Desdemona may never have intended to pray; she may have been making one more desperate plea for time only so that her death may be delayed. Because Othello responds to all her other cries as he struggles to kill her, the Folio text has been printed in the scene as reproduced here.

If Desdemona does pray, her sense of her own sins and of her need for God's mercy (see line 58) will seem stronger than her fear of Othello and her love of him. If she does not pray, her dying moments will all be spent trying to postpone the murder, even for the shortest moment, in the hope that Othello's pity will stay his hand; or perhaps fear prompts the call for delay.

Another puzzle comes earlier. Why does Desdemona speak of Cassio in such a way that Othello's suspicions will be strengthened? Why does she start to weep only after she has realized that Cassio is "betrayed," and why does she answer Othello's most direct charge with only "He will not say so" (l. 72). Does a stubborn will to be truthful or an impulsive generosity of spirit make her admit that she

> loved Cassio
> But with such general warranty of heaven
> As I might love;   (ll. 60-62)

could she not have said this less provocatively, without using the dangerous word "love"? Even Desdemona's assertion that her sins are "loves I bear to you" (l. 41) is readily interpreted by Othello as an admission of adultery.

Desdemona can be played in many ways, depending on how the actress answers these questions. How scrupulously truthful is Desdemona, how impulsive and unthinking? How tense is she with fear, how gripped by fatalism, how determined not to die without physical as well as emotional struggle? Is she so strong in assurance of her own love for Othello and in knowledge of the true facts, that she is simply incredulous until the last possible moment? What strength can her love give to her?

One further question should also be asked. Why does it take so long for the powerful Othello to kill Desdemona? It could hardly be that she is especially strong physically. Is he so shattered by the truth as he sees and feels it, that he is incapable of exerting any great strength? Or is he frightened of what he does?

10

Measure for Measure

Act III, Scene i

CLAUDIO and ISABELLA

✠

Claudio is in prison condemned to death for fornication, a punishment prescribed by an old law which has recently been newly enforced by Angelo, the duke's deputy during his absence abroad. Claudio has been prepared for death by a Friar who has reminded him that no pleasure in life is permanent or perfect.

Claudio's sister, Isabella, arrives with at best a paradoxical comfort. She has taken special leave from the convent where she is a novice to appeal to Lord Angelo for her brother's life. Her plea is granted, but only on conditions which she cannot accept—as she explains in this scene.

✠

CLAUDIO

Now sister, what's the comfort?

ISABELLA

                                   Why

As all comforts are, most good—most good indeed.
Lord Angelo, having affairs to heaven,
Intends you for his swift ambassador
Where you shall be an everlasting leiger,   5
Therefore your best appointment make with speed,
Tomorrow you set on.

CLAUDIO   Is there no remedy?

ISABELLA

None but such remedy as, to save a head,
To cleave a heart in twain.

CLAUDIO   But is there any?

5 **leiger** resident ambassador   6 **appointment** preparations

ISABELLA

Yes, brother, you may live.   10
There is a devilish mercy in the judge
If you'll implore it, that will free your life
But fetter you till death.

CLAUDIO   Perpetual durance?

ISABELLA

Ay, just: perpetual durance, a restraint,
Though all the world's vastidity you had,   15
To a determined scope.

CLAUDIO   But in what nature?

ISABELLA

In such a one as, you consenting to't,
Would bark your honor from that trunk you bear
And leave you naked.

CLAUDIO   Let me know the point.

ISABELLA

O I do fear thee Claudio, and I quake   20
Lest thou a feverous life shouldst entertain
And six or seven winters more respect
Than a perpetual honor. Dar'st thou die?
The sense of death is most in apprehension
And the poor beetle that we tread upon   25
In corporal sufferance finds a pang as great
As when a giant dies.

CLAUDIO   Why give you me this shame?
Think you I can a resolution fetch
From flow'ry tenderness? If I must die,
I will encounter darkness as a bride   30
And hug it in mine arms.

ISABELLA

There spake my brother, there my father's grave

---

13 **durance** imprisonment
15 **vastidity** vastness
16 **determined scope** fixed limits/
   space
18 **bark** strip

21 **entertain** cherish/welcome
24 **sense** feeling
   apprehension anticipation/ imagination
28 **fetch** derive

Did utter forth a voice. Yes thou must die,
Thou art too noble to conserve a life
In base appliances. This outward-sainted deputy   35
Whose settled visage and deliberate word
Nips youth i' th' head and follies doth enmew
As falcon doth the fowl, is yet a devil.
His filth within being cast, he would appear
A pond as deep as hell.

CLAUDIO   The precise Angelo!   40

ISABELLA

O 'tis the cunning livery of hell,
The damned'st body to invest and cover
In precise guards. Dost thou think Claudio,
If I would yield him my virginity,
Thou mightst be freed?

CLAUDIO   O heavens, it cannot be.   45

ISABELLA

Yes, he would give't thee, from this rank offense,
So to offend him still. This night's the time
That I should do what I abhor to name
Or else thou diest tomorrow.

CLAUDIO   Thou shalt not do't.

ISABELLA   O were it but my life   50
I'd throw it down for your deliverance
As frankly as a pin.

CLAUDIO   Thanks, dear Isabel.

ISABELLA

Be ready Claudio, for your death tomorrow.

CLAUDIO

Yes. Has he affections in him
That thus can make him bite the law by th' nose   55

---

35 **appliances** expedients, remedies
37 **enmew** drive into the water
39 **cast** scoured away
40-43 **precise** puritanical (Folio edition
     reads **prenzie**, a word otherwise
     unknown; some editors emend

to **princely**)
42 **invest** furnish
43 **guards** trimmings
46 **give't** i.e., grant freedom
54 **affections** feelings, passions

When he would force it? Sure it is no sin,
Or of the deadly seven it is the least.

ISABELLA
Which is the least?

CLAUDIO
If it were damnable, he being so wise,
Why would he for the momentary trick   60
Be perdurably fined? O Isabel!

ISABELLA
What says my brother?

CLAUDIO   Death is a fearful thing.

ISABELLA
And shamed life a hateful.

CLAUDIO
Ay, but to die and go we know not where,
To lie in cold obstruction and to rot;   65
This sensible warm motion to become
A kneaded clod and the delighted spirit
To bathe in fiery floods or to reside
In thrilling region of thick-ribbed ice,
To be imprisoned in the viewless winds   70
And blown with restless violence round about
The pendent world; or to be worse than worst
Of those that lawless and incertain thought
Imagine howling—'tis too horrible!
The weariest and most loathed worldly life   75
That age, ache, penury and imprisonment
Can lay on nature is a paradise
To what we fear of death.

ISABELLA   Alas, alas!

56 **force** enforce
57 **deadly** seven i.e., pride, envy,
   wrath, sloth, avarice, gluttony,
   lechery
60 **trick** folly, trifle (of sexual inter-
   course)/ruse
61 **perdurably fined** eternally punished
65 **obstruction** stillness (*rigor mor-
   tis*)

66 **sensible** sensitive
   motion mechanism, impulse (to
   move)
67 **delighted** delightful
69 **thrilling** piercing
70 **viewless** invisible
72 **pendent** hanging in space
73 **lawless** unbridled
   incertain uncertain, restless

CLAUDIO Sweet sister let me live.
    What sin you do to save a brother's life,   80
    Nature dispenses with the deed so far
    That it becomes a virtue.
ISABELLA   O you beast!
    O faithless coward! O dishonest wretch!
    Wilt thou be made a man out of my vice?
    Is't not a kind of incest, to take life   85
    From thine own sister's shame? What should I think?
    Heaven shield my mother played my father fair
    For such a warped slip of wilderness
    Ne'er issued from his blood. Take my defiance,
    Die, perish! Might but my bending down   90
    Reprieve thee from thy fate, it should proceed.
    I'll pray a thousand prayers for thy death,
    No word to save thee.
CLAUDIO
    Nay, hear me Isabel.
ISABELLA   O, fie, fie, fie!
    Thy sin's not accidental but a trade.   95
    Mercy to thee would prove itself a bawd,
    'Tis best that thou diest quickly,
CLAUDIO   O hear me, Isabella!

81 **dispenses with** grants pardon for
87 **shield** grant that
88 **wilderness** wildness, worthless-
    ness
89 **defiance** contempt, rejection

90 **bending down** i.e., wordless
    prayer
96 **bawd** pander (i.e., bringing un-
    lawful freedom)

✠

Rehearsing the Scene

Lord Angelo's conditional reprieve condemns Claudio and Isabella to further misery. Rather than a solution to their predicament, Angelo's proposal offers fresh confusion and despair. For both characters, feelings ultimately overwhelm careful, measured thoughts.

The law prescribing death for fornication is accepted by both characters, although no one in Shakespeare's world or in our own would do so. The action takes place in a surreal world where this monstrous law is enforced: sex outside marriage is a matter of life and death. Actor's should try to imagine the consequences of this: fear of sexuality, fear of one's own thoughts and of being found out.

The underlying fears of these two young people are, perhaps, most apparent and communicable in their silences. In her own mind, Isabella knows what she must do, but she fears that Claudio may not be strong enough to uphold her principles (see ll. 20-23). But she also fears what she will do: she is silent at first, saying nothing on entry; subsequently her evasive speeches are interrupted by his simple urgent questions; his sixth speech begs her to come to "the point." Even then she takes refuge in metaphors and images in order to avoid the ultimate test of her brother's honor. She stops in her own tracks at least twice (see the incomplete verse-line 10 and lines 19-20); when he asserts his "resolution," she pauses before continuing (see the incomplete line 31).

Once Isabella has delivered her message, the silences are probably all Claudio's, as he struggles to avoid the consequences of the law and remain alive: see lines 49, 54, 63, 79, 93. The pause at line 58 might be Isabella's expressing her incredulity and fear at what Claudio is suggesting; but once she has cried "Alas, alas!", her condemnation and his fear are both expressed with sustained and passionate energy, and with no more silences. At line 93, she may start to leave, halting only to condemn Claudio once more and to assure him (or herself) that mercy is no longer possible. The scene ends with Claudio's demand to be heard: he may try to hold her back; or he may be shackled to the floor of the prison so that he can only cry out as she stands transfixed at a distance from him.

Two moments in this confrontation require special attention. The first can become almost absurd. Isabella tries to speak of herself, in self-defense, at the very moment when Claudio agrees that she cannot agree to Angelo's conditions. But Isabella overstates what she might do if it were her life which would redeem him:

> O were it but my life
> I'd throw it down for your deliverance
> As frankly as a pin.   (ll. 50-52).

The hypothetical courage is, inevitably, cheapened by the image she uses: the visual and physical reality behind "a pin" is laughably casual. If incredulity is part of the audience's response, Claudio's reply may well tip that over into laughter: "Thanks, dear Isabel." But both speeches are deadly serious: under Claudio's everyday politeness, his search to escape punishment begins, as the next incomplete and broken verse line shows.

Actors will find many ways to stop the audience's laughter: he may embrace his sister, or speak with tense and quiet voice; she may be so afraid and so impulsively selfless that, when she speaks with such violence, shock is communicated rather than the triviality of the image. Or she could understand very well the impact of the image, and press it on his attention with a steady, challenging voice.

Another interpretation of the entire scene may use this moment to reveal Isabella's fear of her own awakened sexuality. Bodily images and physical activity have been present in all but her earliest speech; although reluctant to come to the "point," everything she says has a sustaining rhythm and sensual evocation. She may see fear in Claudio because she has become afraid of herself. Angelo's suggestion, made outside the safety of the convent, could have forced her to recognize her own sensual nature, so that now it colors all she says and does. Either she is cruelly objective, in searching for an appropriate image to pronounce "Mercy to thee would prove itself a bawd" (l. 96), or her mind is helplessly aflame with sexuality.

A second crucial moment concerns Claudio's "speech on death," as it might be called, lines 64-78. It is in starkest contrast to his earlier stoicism: "I will encounter darkness as a bride / And hug it in mine arms" (ll. 30-31). But both are highly sensual speeches, and in both Claudio imagines strong physical activity: the same consciousness is at work. If the actor, like the player in *Hamlet*, can express a "dream of passion" and "force his soul . . . to his own conceit" so that the audience sees:

> Tears in his eyes, distraction in his aspect,
> A broken voice and his whole function suiting

> With forms to his conceit,   (*Hamlet*, II.ii.557-62)

the cumulative effect of this speech is almost monstrous, a vision of a carnal purgatory that appalls or confounds its audience. Some actors may wish to speak it objectively without the realism of the player in *Hamlet*, but his way is enormously rewarding, and few actors will want to resist it. But then another question remains: does Claudio speak for himself, absorbed in the horror of his predicament, or does he say it to Isabella, so that she is drawn into his nightmare? Actors should try it both ways. As so frequently at a moment of such power, Shakespeare allows the interplay to use whatever the actors can bring. Isabella's verbal, "Alas, alas!", is able to enforce many different reactions.

11

Macbeth

Act II, Scene ii

LADY MACBETH and MACBETH

✠

Macbeth has earlier this evening feasted Duncan, King of Scotland, at a banquet in his honor. After the King goes to bed, Macbeth kills him in his sleep.

Lady Macbeth, is an accomplice; she has drugged the men who guard the King's bedchamber and urged her husband to be "so much more the man" by committing the murder which promises to make them King and Queen of Scotland. She had staked their marriage on his success:

> From this time
> Such I account thy love . . .   (I.vii.38-39)

and had shamed him into action with the assurance that she would have dashed out the brains of her own infant at her breast:

> had I so sworn as you
> Have done to this.   (I.vii.54-59)

Two daggers and some blood will be needed to perform this scene, and someone to knock at a door some distance offstage.

✠

Enter LADY MACBETH.

LADY MACBETH

That which hath made them drunk hath made me bold;
What hath quenched them hath given me fire.—Hark!
    Peace!
It was the owl that shrieked, the fatal bellman
Which gives the stern'st good-night. He is about it.

3 **bellman** (the owl, bird of death, is compared to the bellman sent to warn a condemned prisoner the night before his execution)

The doors are open and the surfeited grooms   5
Do mock their charge with snores. I have drugged
     their possets,
That death and nature do contend about them
Whether they live or die.

MACBETH   (*Within.*) Who's there? What ho?

LADY MACBETH

Alack, I am afraid they have awaked
And 'tis not done! Th' attempt and not the deed   10
Confounds us. Hark! I laid their daggers ready;
He could not miss 'em. Had he not resembled
My father as he slept, I had done't.

Enter MACBETH.

                              My husband!

MACBETH

I have done the deed. Didst thou not hear a noise?

LADY MACBETH

I heard the owl scream and the crickets cry.   15
Did not you speak?

MACBETH   When?

LADY MACBETH   Now.

MACBETH   As I descended?

LADY MACBETH   Ay.

MACBETH   Hark!
Who lies i' th' second chamber?

LADY MACBETH   Donalbain.

MACBETH   This is a sorry sight.   20

LADY MACBETH

A foolish thought, to say a sorry sight.

MACBETH

There's one did laugh in's sleep and one cried
     "Murder!"

---

5 **grooms** household servants
6 **mock . . . snores** make a mockery of their duty to guard the
king by sleeping
possets bed-time drinks

7 **nature** natural life
11 **Confounds** destroys
20 **sorry** painful/wretched, worthless

That they did wake each other. I stood and heard them.
But they did say their prayers and addressed them
Again to sleep.

LADY MACBETH   There are two lodged together   25

MACBETH

One cried "God bless us!" and "Amen" the other,
As they had seen me with these hangman's hands.
List'ning their fear, I could not say "Amen,"
When they did say "God bless us!"

LADY MACBETH   Consider it not so deeply.

MACBETH

But wherefore could not I pronounce "Amen"?   30
I had most need of blessing and "Amen"
Stuck in my throat.

LADY MACBETH   These deeds must not be thought
After these ways; so it will make us mad.

MACBETH

Methought I heard a voice cry "Sleep no more!
Macbeth does murder sleep"—the innocent sleep,   35
Sleep that knits up the raveled sleave of care,
The death of each day's life, sore labor's bath,
Balm of hurt minds, great nature's second course,
Chief nourisher in life's feast—

LADY MACBETH   What do you mean?

MACBETH

Still it cried "Sleep no more!" to all the house: 40
"Glamis hath murdered sleep and therefore Cawdor
Shall sleep no more: Macbeth shall sleep no more."

LADY MACBETH

Who was it that thus cried? Why, worthy thane,
You do unbend your noble strength, to think
So brainsickly of things. Go get some water   45
And wash this filthy witness from your hand.

---

27 **hangman's** i.e., bloody (he dis-
  membered as well as hanged)
36 **raveled sleave** tangled skein
38 **course** dish (in a feast)/way of

living (compared with waking
life)
44 **unbend** undo (unstring a bow)
46 **witness** evidence

Why did you bring these daggers from the place?
They must lie there: go carry them and smear
The sleepy grooms with blood.

MACBETH   I'll go no more.
I am afraid to think what I have done;   50
Look on't again I dare not.

LADY MACBETH   Infirm of purpose!
Give me the daggers. The sleeping and the dead
Are but as pictures. 'Tis the eye of childhood
That fears a painted devil. If he do bleed,
I'll gild the faces of the grooms withal   55
For it must seem their guilt.   *Exit. Knock within.*

MACBETH   Whence is that knocking?
How is't with me when every noise appalls me?
What hands are here? Ha—they pluck out mine eyes!
Will all great Neptune's ocean wash this blood
Clean from my hand? No, this my hand will rather   60
The multitudinous seas incarnadine,
Making the green one red.

        Enter LADY MACBETH.

LADY MACBETH

My hands are of your color but I shame
To wear a heart so white (*Knock.*) I hear a knocking
At the south entry. Retire we to our chamber.   65
A little water clears us of this deed:
How easy is it then! Your constancy
Hath left you unattended. (*Knock.*) Hark! More
    knocking.
Get on your nightgown, lest occasion call us
And show us to be watchers. Be not lost   70
So poorly in your thoughts.

---

54 **painted** i.e., unreal
55 **gild** paint
61 **incarnadine** redden
62 **green one red** green-one (i.e.,
   the ocean) red/green totally red
67 **constancy** fortitude, faithfulness

68 **left you unattended** deserted
   you
69 **nightgown** dressing gown
70 **watchers** i.e., awake late
71 **poorly** unworthily

MACBETH

To know my deed, 'twere best not know myself.

(*Knock.*)

Wake Duncan with thy knocking! I would thou
    couldst!
                                 Exeunt.

73 **To . . . myself** i.e., having done
what I have done, I had rather
not be myself

✠

Rehearsing the Scene

This scene should be played as if in near darkness. One or both of the characters might carry a light. The scene is set after everyone has gone to bed, so Lady Macbeth should be dressed ready for bed, but Macbeth is fully clothed. Macbeth's cry from offstage should be strained or indistinct so that his wife's elation changes at once to fear. She sees again, in her mind's eye, the old King lying asleep at the scene of the crime. The impact of the murder is so powerful that it goes beyond Duncan's death to a vision of her own father: "Had he not resembled my father. . . ." Is she voicing her compassion or her horror? Or self-reproach for not being able to commit the crime herself? All her words have seemed to come involuntarily, but these must have sufficient compulsion or purpose to obliterate other concerns about the details of the plot. Then, at this very moment, Macbeth enters with bloody hands, holding two daggers. She turns to him and, either involuntarily or with careful reassurance, says simply, "My husband."

This opening sets the level and tone for the whole scene: it is alive with immediate awareness; sharp with wordplay and double-think which reach out to hold violent images in place; and quick with shifting feelings which, in a brief moment, can send consciousness lurching forward or backward in time, and reaching upward or plummeting down to other modes of consciousness.

Actors must be patient in unraveling the movements within

these characters' consciousnesses. The scene is rich with clues to physical actions which reveal the characters' inner struggles. For example, neither of them mentions the blood on Macbeth's hands until line 20. Does Lady Macbeth notice it before then? What is it which awakens Macbeth's consciousness to speak of the "sorry sight"—but not to speak of the blood itself until line 27? Why does Macbeth fasten on the simple prayer, belonging to ordinary and peaceful existence, in much the same way as Lady Macbeth remembered the image of her father? Why does he repeat the simple words, even though they torture him? While his wife recalls him to practical business, why does Macbeth become haunted by fantasy and then by a lingering memory of the blessings of gentle sleep? When he, like an unstrung bow (see l. 44), stands "brainsick" and perhaps almost "mad" (ll. 45 and 33), Lady Macbeth takes the initiative, her hands clutching the daggers and so becoming red like his: is her action carefully considered or impulsive? Does she remember the "eye of childhood" because he is so obviously terrified of the blood, or to reassure herself?

At line 56 a knock is heard from some distance off stage. This intrusive sound almost represents another character, at least a reminder of a world other than the nightmarish one which they both inhabit. The sound quickens Macbeth's private horror; it "appalls" him (l. 57). He sees the blood on his hands again, but now as if those hands belong to someone else and are about to attack him. Then, with an extended, dreamlike image, his words ring out with an impulse that seems both to engulf and strengthen him. After a brief silence, Lady Macbeth reenters, reproves him and, when repeated knockings signal danger, gathers strength.

These characters live in the distant past, in the moment just past, in the burning, terrifying present, and in the future. Depending on how they have travelled on their individual journeys through the scene, meeting on the way only for brief and intense passages, they will leave the stage together or separately. She may support him, leading him; so his final words, as he begins to move off, are a confession of guilt after he has relinquished initiative to his wife. Or she may have to draw him, almost pull him, offstage, so that his last words are a defiance of her as well as the cry of a defeated man. Or he may now accept his own guilt and grief, using these words as a way of resisting his wife's judgment. In this case they may leave at the same time, but in distinctly different ways; he asserts his own sense of doom, she deals with practical and tangible matters. He may, however, leave before she does, hurrying at the sound of the knocking and paying little or no heed to what she has said. He may have become more frenzied and a little mad. Although she manages to cope with the situation, is there something in her assurance that all is "easy" (l. 67) which shows that she is also dealing with thoughts which threaten her sanity so that she overstates her case recklessly?

Although no one is present with them on stage, both characters are aware of others offstage, and both know that they must leave as soon as possible. The scene should therefore drive forward, even though actors may want to speak slowly and may choose sometimes to speak in a half-whisper. There are very few half verse lines to indicate pauses, except at the initial meeting when they listen in silence to know whether they are overheard or likely to be discovered. From this moment on, they follow close on each other's words, no matter how dissimilar their intentions or their thoughts.

12

Macbeth

Act III, Scene ii

LADY MACBETH and MACBETH

✠

It is late in the day and Lady Macbeth has sent to tell her husband that she attends his "leisure" for a few words. But as soon as she is alone she speaks.

Together they have killed Duncan, King of Scotland, making it seem that his servants had been responsible. Macbeth has in turn killed the servants. The king's two sons have fled the land, and Macbeth has been "named" and "invested" as king (II.iv.31-32).

When all the thanes were called to a "solemn supper" (III.i.11-15) to celebrate the accession, Banquo was prepared to leave court with his son and so Macbeth had questioned his intentions. Banquo is his most dangerous rival: the witches who had prophesied that he would be king had also told Banquo that he would be "greater" and "more happy" than Macbeth:

> Thou shalt get kings, though thou be none

> (I.iii.64-66)

As Banquo rode from court promising to return for the feast in the evening, Macbeth had arranged to assassinate him and his son. Lady Macbeth does not know that he has done this.

✠

LADY MACBETH   Nought's had, all's spent,
Where our desire is got without content.
'Tis safer to be that which we destroy
Than by destruction dwell in doubtful joy.

Enter MACBETH.

---

1 **Nought's . . . spent** i.e., we have
achieved nothing and spent
everything

4 **doubtful** apprehensive, fearful/
uncertain

How now, my lord! Why do you keep alone,   5
Of sorriest fancies your companions making,
Using those thoughts which should indeed have died
With them they think on? Things without all remedy
Should be without regard: what's done is done.

MACBETH

We have scorched the snake, not killed it: 10
She'll close and be herself, whilst our poor malice
Remains in danger of her former tooth.
But let the frame of things disjoint, both the worlds
     suffer,
Ere we will eat our meal in fear and sleep
In the affliction of these terrible dreams   15
That shake us nightly. Better be with the dead,
Whom we, to gain our peace, have sent to peace,
Than on the torture of the mind to lie
In restless ecstasy. Duncan is in his grave;
After life's fitful fever he sleeps well.   20
Treason has done his worst: nor steel, nor poison,
Malice domestic, foreign levy, nothing,
Can touch him further.

LADY MACBETH   Come on,
Gentle my lord, sleek o'er your rugged looks;
Be bright and jovial among your guests tonight.   25

MACBETH

So shall I, love; and so I pray be you:

6 **sorriest** most wretched
7 **Using** being familiar with
8 **without** beyond the reach of
10 **scorched** slashed (with a knife)
11 **close** heal
   malice power to do harm
12 **former tooth** i.e., her fangs, as
   dangerous as before
13 **frame . . . disjoint** structure of
   the universe falls apart
   both the worlds terrestial and
   celestial worlds, heaven and
   earth
   suffer perish

17 **to gain. . . . to peace** to put our
   minds at peace, have sent to the
   peace of death
18 **torture of the mind** (the bed is
   a rack, an instrument of torture)
19 **restless ecstasy** sleepless/
   unceasing frenzy, delirium
20 **fitful** violent, full of fits
21 **his** its
22 **Malice domestic** civil war
   levy army
23 **touch** wound
24 **sleek** smoothe
   rugged furrowed, harsh

Let your remembrance apply to Banquo,
Present him eminence both with eye and tongue.
Unsafe the while that we
Must lave our honors in these flattering streams   30
And make our faces vizards to our hearts,
Disguising what they are.

LADY MACBETH   You must leave this.

MACBETH

O full of scorpions is my mind, dear wife!
Thou know'st that Banquo and his Fleance lives.

LADY MACBETH

But in them nature's copy's not eterne.   35

MACBETH

There's comfort yet! They are assailable.
Then be thou jocund: ere the bat hath flown
His cloistered flight, ere to black Hecate's summons
The shard-borne beetle with his drowsy hums
Hath run night's yawning peal, there shall be done   40
A deed of dreadful note.

LADY MACBETH   What's to be done?

MACBETH

Be innocent of the knowledge, dearest chuck,
Till thou applaud the deed. Come, seeling night,
Scarf up the tender eye of pitiful day
And with thy bloody and invisible hand   45

27 **apply** attend
28 **Present him eminence** pay him
   special honor
29-30 **Unsafe . . . streams** we are so insecure at this time that we clean
   (ironic) our royal dignities with
   endless flattery
31 **vizards** masks
33 **scorpions** (the sting of this reptile was proverbially intensely
   painful; also = whips, used as in-
   struments of torture)
35 **copy** form/lease
   eterne eternal

38 **cloistered** (bats fly in and
   around buildings, rather than in
   open spaces)
   Hecate's summons (the Greek
   goddess commanded witches
   and presided over magical rites)
39 **shard-borne** born in dung/borne
   in the air by its wing-cases
42 **chuck** chick (term of endear-
   ment)
43 **seeling** eye-closing (falconers
   sew, or **seel**, up the eyes of a
   hawk)
44 **Scarf up** blindfold

Cancel and tear to pieces that great bond
Which keeps me pale! Light thickens and the crow
Makes wing to th' rooky wood.
Good things of day begin to droop and drowse
Whiles night's black agents to their preys do rouse.   50
Thou marvel'st at my words. But hold thee still:
Things bad begun make strong themselves by ill.
So prithee, go with me.   *Exeunt.*

46 **bond** bond (in the natural order) of life/moral law
47 **pale** pale with fear
   thickens grows dense, darkens
48 **rooky** i.e., black and filled with rooks
50 **to their . . . rouse** wake and rise up to start hunting
51 **hold thee still** keep constant, maintain your resolve

☩

Rehearsing the Scene

Lady Macbeth's opening soliloquy reveals her inner restlessness, but as her husband enters she turns at once to tell him not to dwell on his secret thoughts. In answer he expresses the torture they both feel, reestablishing the "we" which his wife had used before he entered. Without having heard her words, he echoes her envy of Duncan, elaborating it, but remembers the possibility of "peace" rather than "content" (ll. 2 and 17). The incomplete verse-line 23 indicates a pause or silence before Lady Macbeth draws him towards practical business and his next task, offering neither comfort nor reproof for what he has just said. Now he can agree very simply and, by calling her "love," he seems to recognize her power to help him escape from their mutual fears.

For a moment Macbeth talks like she does, with pretended good humor and good heart, but a bitter and dark irony enters his speech which she at once detects: "You must leave this" (l. 32). He has not directly contradicted her, but she has no need to name the self-torture she rebukes and seeks to avoid; they understand each other completely. They could hold each other in their arms here. Macbeth now calls her "dear wife" (l. 33) and, pretending to good spirits, speaks directly of the pain in his heart.

Now the scene develops in a new direction. Indirectly he begins to talk of the next murder he has already set in motion. His wife seems to understand his intention or else suggests he should do what he has already done. Macbeth's spirits rise and he encourages her to be "jocund"—a word, in Shakespeare's plays, more carefree than her "bright and jovial" (l. 25). For example:

> As gentle and as jocund as to jest
> Go I to fight.   (*Richard II*, I.iii.95-96)

> The jocund day
> Stands tiptoe on the misty mountain tops . . .
>   (*Romeo and Juliet*, III.v.9-10)

But Macbeth's thoughts for himself are different. He becomes immersed in quite different visions; and he is strengthened by them too. Marvelously detailed and sensitive, his evocation of the planned assassination of Banquo and Fleance is dark, quiet and mysterious, like the coming of night in the natural world. Lady Macbeth asks only the simplest question now (l. 41), and this prompts him to protect her and to use his most intimate and contented way of addressing her—"dearest chuck." But then he turns away, summoning the night as if he were more powerful than Hecate, becoming at one with predatory and annihilating forces.

Perhaps some wordless response to the horror should come from Lady Macbeth which calls for his "Thou marvel'st at my words" (l. 51). But he may associate instinctively with her fears, without prompting, because he needs her to "hold" with him constantly. Perhaps his acceptance of "Things bad begun make strong themselves by ill" is linked by rhyme to his admonition of his wife to show that it is accompanied by a movement towards her, so that he seems to be made "strong" by her, as well as by his own committal to darkness and blood. Or does "So prithee, go with me" indicate that he knows that unless she is called to follow she will not do so? Does he fear that he has moved so far into "ill" that he will now have to act alone?

Macbeth is notoriously full of action and spectacle, but the action of this scene is what happens when the two protagonists meet. Macbeth enters because his wife has asked for him. He leaves the stage after he has asked her to go with him. The strongest and most significant action is within the two characters, their individual grappling with uncertainty, isolation, guilt, a need for peace and, perhaps in Macbeth only, a need for pride. Although it is possible to play the scene without them touching each other, they influence each other constantly, their relationship changing with the interplay. This is why the writing is so dense, needing many annotations and patient study to follow its double meanings, fine distinctions and multiple associations. The action is within these two characters, underneath what they say and fired partly by their sense of each other's presence.

Actors will find the words difficult to master until their characters' basic and inner actions begin to become clear to them. Yet the characters are implicit in those very words. The study process must develop in two ways: searching the words for clues to character; and using the action of being together to explore and establish each character's reality.

It may be helpful to ask which is the most important, most crucial and necessary, action for each character. 1) He protects his wife from knowledge of his new crime. He identifies himself with darkness, the witches, blood and evil. He denies the truth of "what's done is done." He sees life as a "fever," full of madness and violence. He realizes he would rather be dead than be uncertain and alive. 2) She tells her husband to pay no attention to what has been done and reminds him of what can be done. She senses that Macbeth cannot throw off his fears and so she suggests that these feelings may die if his rivals die. (She does not remind him of the witches' prophesy, but she dares to look to the future and so may arouse his thoughts of them so that they surface in the mention of Hecate.) She makes equal cause with him, speaking more directly and simply about what must be done. That is her last word, but not her last response: she may, indeed, "marvel" at his words (l. 52), regaining his attention although remaining silent. She may respond to "Hold thee still" and certainly she must respond to his request that she should go with him. She is necessary to him, in some way; and Shakespeare's handling of the scene insists that she responds to this.

For Macbeth, the culmination of this scene is sustained with words, but for Lady Macbeth, when attention is brought to bear finally on her, there is not a single word to say. Her silent movement across the stage, choosing either to go *with* him, as he goes, or to move in her own time and with her own purpose, marks the conclusion of the scene. She has to be *what she is*: is this her most important action? For the silent movement to be fully expressive, she must have responded in her mind and body to every word Macbeth has spoken. Is it an act of courage, of love, of committal to violence, of despair, of defeat? Whatever the actress finds herself able to make this exit express, it will gain closest possible attention by contrast to the many words given to Macbeth at the close of the scene.

13

Antony and Cleopatra

Act I, Scene iii

ANTONY and CLEOPATRA

✠

Mark Antony, one of the three rulers of the world after the death of Julius Caesar, has quartered his army in Egypt where he spends his time with Cleopatra, the Queen of Egypt. To his soldiers it looks as though:

> his captain's heart
> Which in the scuffles of great fights hath burst
> The buckles on his breast, reneges (renounces) all temper
> And is become the bellows and the fan
> To cool a gypsy's lust.   (I.i.6-10)

Messengers from Rome counsel his return with their news of civil and foreign wars which demand his attention. Antony resolves that:

> These strong Egyptian fetters I must break
> Or lose myself in dotage.   (I.ii.117-18)

Further news of his wife's death strengthens anew his resolve to depart. He orders his officers to get ready to leave.

Cleopatra has heard a report of Antony's decision from one of her spies. But when his entry is announced, she determines to be "sick and sullen" (I.iii.13). He enters alone.

✠

ANTONY
   I am sorry to give breathing to my purpose—
CLEOPATRA
   Help me away dear Charmian! I shall fall.
   It cannot be thus long, the sides of nature
   Will not sustain it.

---

1 **breathing** utterance   3 **sides of nature** human frame

ANTONY   Now my dearest queen—
CLEOPATRA
Pray you stand farther from me.
ANTONY   What's the matter?   5
CLEOPATRA
I know by that same eye there's some good news.
What, says the married woman you may go?
Would she had never given you leave to come!
Let her not say 'tis I that keep you here,
I have no power upon you; hers you are.   10
ANTONY
The gods best know—
CLEOPATRA   O never was there queen
So mightily betrayed! Yet at the first
I saw the treasons planted.
ANTONY   Cleopatra—
CLEOPATRA
Why should I think you can be mine and true
(Though you in swearing shake the thronèd gods)   15
Who have been false to Fulvia? Riotous madness
To be entangled with those mouth-made vows
Which break themselves in swearing.
ANTONY   Most sweet queen—
CLEOPATRA
Nay, pray you seek no color for your going
But bid farewell and go. When you sued staying,   20
Then was the time for words, no going then;
Eternity was in our lips and eyes,
Bliss in our brows' bent, none our parts so poor
But was a race of heaven; they are so still
Or thou, the greatest soldier of the world,   25
Art turned the greatest liar.

13 **planted** set (ready to grow/operate)
17 **mouth-made** i.e., words only
18 **in swearing** as they are spoken
19 **color** excuse, pretext
20 **sued staying** begged to stay

23 **our brow's bent** the curve of my eyebrows
parts parts of body/abilities
24 **race of heaven** taste of heaven heavenly disposition, inheritance

ANTONY   How now, lady?

CLEOPATRA

   I would I had thy inches; thou shouldst know
   There were a heart in Egypt.

ANTONY   Hear me queen.

   The strong necessity of time commands
   Our services awhile but my full heart   30
   Remains in use with you. Our Italy
   Shines o'er with civil swords; Sextus Pompeius
   Makes his approaches to the port of Rome;
   Equality of two domestic powers
   Breed scrupulous faction; the hated, grown to
      strength,   35
   Are newly grown to love; the condemned Pompey,
   Rich in his father's honor, creeps apace
   Into the hearts of such as have not thrived
   Upon the present state, whose numbers threaten;
   And quietness, grown sick of rest, would purge   40
   By any desperate change. My more particular,
   And that which most with you should safe my going,
   Is Fulvia's death.

CLEOPATRA

   Though age from folly could not give me freedom,
   It does from childishness. Can Fulvia die?   45

ANTONY

   She's dead, my queen.
   Look here and at thy sovereign leisure read
   The garboils she awaked. At the last, best:
   See when and where she died.

---

28 **Egypt** Cleopatra/the country
31 **in use with you** for your advantage, profit/in trust with you
32 **Shines o'er** is bright, glitters
   civil drawn in civil war
34-35 **Equality . . . faction** two evenly matched rulers at home encourage quarrels over small issues
35-36 **the hated . . . to love** those who were hated are loved when they gain power
36 **condemned Pompey** (he was banished by the Senate for being a threat to peace)
40 **purge** let blood (to cleanse the body of impurities)
41 **desperate** reckless
   particular personal concern
42 **safe** make safe
48 **garboils** commotion, rows

CLEOPATRA   O most false love!
Where be the sacred vials thou shouldst fill   50
With sorrowful water? Now I see, I see,
In Fulvia's death how mine received shall be.

ANTONY
Quarrel no more but be prepared to know
The purposes I bear which are, or cease,
As you shall give th' advice. By the fire   55
That quickens Nilus' slime, I go from hence
Thy soldier-servant, making peace or war
As thou affects.

CLEOPATRA   Cut my lace Charmian, come—
But let it be: I am quickly ill and well,
So Antony loves.

ANTONY   My precious queen forbear,   60
And give true evidence to his love which stands
An honorable trial.

CLEOPATRA   So Fulvia told me.
I prithee turn aside and weep for her
Then bid adieu to me, and say the tears
Belong to Egypt. Good now, play one scene   65
Of excellent dissembling and let it look
Like perfect honor.

ANTONY   You'll heat my blood. No more.

CLEOPATRA
You can do better yet; but this is meetly.

ANTONY
Now by my sword—

CLEOPATRA   And target. Still he mends
But this is not the best. Look prithee, Charmian,   70

---

50 sacred vials (Romans were said
    to collect tears in vials to place
    in the tombs of loved ones)
55-56 fire . . . slime sun that generates
    life in the mud of the Nile valley
58 affects at inclined;
    Cut my lace cut the laces of my

bodice (speaking as if gasping for
breath)
60 So if/as
61 give true evidence bear true wit-
    ness; stands can stand up to
68 meetly quite good, not bad
69 target small shield

How this Herculean Roman does become
The carriage of his chafe.

ANTONY   I'll leave you, lady.

CLEOPATRA
Courteous lord, one word.
Sir, you and I must part, but that's not it.
Sir, you and I have loved, but there's not it,   75
That you know well. Something it is I would—
O my oblivion is a very Antony
And I am all forgotten.

ANTONY   But that your royalty
Holds idleness your subject, I should take you
For idleness itself.

CLEOPATRA   'Tis sweating labor   80
To bear such idleness so near the heart
As Cleopatra this. But sir forgive me,
Since my becomings kill me when they do not
Eye well to you. Your honor calls you hence
Therefore be deaf to my unpitied folly   85
And all the gods go with you. Upon your sword
Sit laurel victory and smooth success
Be strewed before your feet!

ANTONY   Let us go. Come.
Our separation so abides and flies
That thou residing here goes yet with me   90
And I hence fleeting here remain with thee.
Away!   *Exeunt.*

71-72 **become . . . chafe** looks good
       when acting his anger
77-78 **my oblivion. . . . forgotten** (1) I
       am as forgetful as Antony and I
       have forgotten what to say (2) my
       mind forgets everything but Anto-
       ny and I forget myself entirely

78-80 **But . . . idleness itself** if you
       were not in control of all these
       follies, I would think you were
       quite foolish
   81 **bear** (pun on the **labor** of child-
       birth)
   83 **becomings** attractions, efforts
   84 **Eye** look

✠

Rehearsing the Scene

Cleopatra is in her own private apartment and as Antony enters she pretends (as she has just said she would) to be "sick and sullen." Probably she lies down on a couch, as if about to collapse and needing air and space. Antony, the visitor who feels at first very much at home, cannot complete what he wants to say, but has to put his own business aside to ask, brusquely or urgently, "What's the matter?" At this point, as he yields, Cleopatra changes; but only to mock and reprove him.

In the play, Cleopatra is attended in this scene by Charmian and Iras. At a late stage of rehearsal for this scene, it would be helpful to add two silent attendants, or perhaps several more, all women, to whose sympathetic ears Cleopatra can address a number of observations: for example, lines 2, 6, 11-13, part of 44-45, 51-52, 57-59, the second half of 68, and 69-72. Without supporting players, Cleopatra can still speak these lines away from Antony, addressing the walls, if nothing else. The immediate effect of so playing against Antony's expectations might be even stronger if she is alone, but the results of doing so will not be sustained as well without the solicitous reponses of attendants.

Much of the strength of this scene derives from the changing interplay between the two lovers, contrasting his more static strength and her variable vitality. Cleopatra seems to have so much life because she is presented in many guises: in playacting, pretending to sickness, misunderstanding or naiveté, in mockery and teasing, in self-deprecation, passing rapidly into confidence and easy assertion of command. She is able to say much in few words—"hers you are," "Can Fulvia die?", "so Antony loves"— and, later in the scene, she rises to sustained eloquence. Cleopatra uses words boldly and freshly in clashing conjunctions. She also uses repetitions so that simple words grow in power as if they were refrains (see ll. 19-26, 73-78, 86-88). At times her speech has strong and simple rhythms—almost like an incantation—and then precise words represent the simple facts of physical contact and glorious words the effect of sexual awareness and her power over Antony. The actress should concentrate on fulfilling each moment as it comes. Imaginatively and physically, she must be as alive as possible, taking careful thought, and plenty of time in rehearsal and study, in order to make the text at one with her response to it, moment by moment. So the audience may share the sensual reality and deep self-awareness of

> 'Tis sweating labor
> To bear such idleness so near the heart
> As Cleopatra this. (ll. 80-82)

Such lines should be taken very slowly and strongly, at least until the actress can make this great journey through the mind and body with full imaginative committal. Having rehearsed patiently and truthfully, the sheer variety of performance will dazzle and carry conviction.

The actor of Antony works by contrasting means. For the first twenty-eight lines he says little, but he has to hear a great deal and maintain his initiative, turning aside from much of what has been said until he insists "Hear me queen." At this point, either Cleopatra gives him total attention, almost provoking him to have his say, or he presses on regardless of whether he has an appropriate audience or not. Until now his inability to speak may have been laughable, but if Antony remains motionless and takes his own time throughout this passage and resists succumbing to the emotional climate Cleopatra establishes, he can draw attention strongly enough to quench the incipient comedy. Now Antony commands attention clearly stating why he needs to leave: he gives a global picture of the political situation, expressed economically but finely, and viewed from several different aspects—immediate and long-range, reflective and informative. By the close of his speech, he has complete attention; and when he gives news of Fulvia's death, without comment, it is some time before Cleopatra is ready to reply (as indicated by the incomplete verse line, 43).

If the actor manages Antony's single long speech with the ease and variety of attack its complexity requires, his following interplay with Cleopatra when he has to struggle again for a serious hearing can turn the laughter against the Queen. Both characters at moments could seem to be almost comic: and both should hold back laughter by maintaining a deeper engagement under the verbal interchanges, a consciousness of each other which is not expressed adequately in words or action until the end of the scene.

It is Antony who forces attention on the underlying passion: "You'll heat my blood. No more. . . . Now by my sword. . . . I'll leave you lady" (ll. 67-72). Again a half-line registers that Cleopatra has to change her response, and this time the difference in tone is huge: "Courteous lord, one word." If he has provided an unhurried and full counterplay to her throughout the scene, physically assured and fully imagined, the silence and then these four words will provide a moment of strength and inward understanding.

Throughout the scene the balance between comedy and drama (or, even, incipient tragedy) is often in doubt, and performances could tip irrevocably one way or the other at several moments. It is good—exciting for the actors and audience—to keep this issue open until the very close, when he speaks with the resonance and simplicity she had used earlier.

14

Cymbeline

Act III, Scene ii

PISANIO and IMOGEN

✠

The scene is Ancient Britain at the court of King Cymbeline. It is a strange court—"You do not meet a man but frowns" (I.i.1)—where Imogen, the king's only daughter, is kept under house arrest, her husband having been banished from the land as soon as it was known she had married against her father's wish. The husband, Leonatus Posthumus, had been brought up at court as an honor to his family after the death of both parents: he is "a poor but worthy gentleman" (I.i.7).

As an exile in Italy, Posthumus had boasted about Imogen's faithfulness, but after being confronted with what looks like evidence that Imogen has been unfaithful he orders Pisanio his servant to kill Imogen. Pisanio has just received his master's letter and another for his mistress.

✠

PISANIO

How? of adultery? Wherefore write you not
What monsters her accuse? Leonatus!
O master, what a strange infection
Is fall'n into thy ear! What false Italian,
As poisonous-tongued as handed, hath prevailed   5
On thy too ready hearing? Disloyal? No.
She's punished for her truth and undergoes,
More goddesslike than wifelike, such assaults
As would take in some virtue. O my master,
Thy mind to her is now as low as were   10
Thy fortunes. How? That I should murder her,

3 **strange** foreign	9 **take in** defeat
7 **truth** loyalty, honesty	**virtue** strength, power/moral
undergoes endures	good
	10 **to** compared with

Upon the love and truth and vows which I
Have made to thy command? I her? Her blood?
If it be so to do good service, never
Let me be counted serviceable. How look I   15
That I should seem to lack humanity
So much as this fact comes to? (*Reading.*) "Do't! The
    letter
That I have sent her, by her own command
Shall give thee opportunity." O damned paper,
Black as the ink that's on thee! Senseless bauble,   20
Art thou a fedary for this act and look'st
So virginlike without? Lo, here she comes.

Enter IMOGEN.

I am ignorant in what I am commanded.
IMOGEN
How now, Pisanio?
PISANIO
Madam, here is a letter from my lord.   25
IMOGEN
Who, thy lord? That is my lord Leonatus!
O learn'd indeed were that astronomer
That knew the stars as I his characters;
He 'ld lay the future open. You good gods,
Let what is here contained relish of love,   30
Of my lord's health, of his content—yet not
That we two are asunder, let that grieve him:
Some griefs are med'cinable, that is one of them
For it doth physic love—of his content
All but in that. Good wax, thy leave. Blest be   35

15 **serviceable** willing to serve
17 **fact** deed, crime
20 **senseless** incapable of feeling/
    foolish
21 **fedary for** accomplice in
23 **am ignorant in** i.e., will pretend
    to be ignorant of

27 **astronomer** astrologer
28 **characters** handwriting
30 **relish** have a taste
31 **not** i.e., not content
33 **med'cinable** able to heal
34 **physic** keep in health

You bees that make these locks of counsel. Lovers
And men in dangerous bonds pray not alike;
Though forfeiters you cast in prison yet
You clasp young Cupid's tables. Good news, gods!

(*Reading.*) "Justice and your father's wrath, should he   40
take me in his dominion, could not be so cruel to me
as you, O the dearest of creatures, would even renew
me with your eyes. Take notice that I am in Cambria at
Milford Haven. What your own love will out of this
advise you, follow. So he wishes you all happiness,   45
that remains loyal to his vow, and your increasing in
love.   *Leonatus Posthumus*."

O for a horse with wings! Hear'st thou, Pisanio?
He is at Milford Haven. Read and tell me
How far 'tis thither. If one of mean affairs   50
May plod it in a week, why may not I
Glide thither in a day? Then, true Pisanio,
Who long'st like me to see thy lord, who long'st—
O let me bate—but not like me, yet long'st,
But in a fainter kind—O not like me   55
For mine's beyond beyond!—say, and speak thick—
Love's counselor should fill the bores of hearing
To th' smothering of the sense—how far it is
To this same blessed Milford. And by th' way
Tell me how Wales was made so happy as   60
T' inherit such a haven. But first of all,
How we may steal from hence; and for the gap

36 **locks of counsel** i.e., waxen seals
37 **in . . . bonds** in danger of forfeit-
     ing legal bonds
38 **you** i.e., waxen seals
39 **clasp . . . tables** keep secret the
     contents of love-letters or other
     writings in notebooks (**tables**)
41-43 **could not . . . renew me** i.e.,
       the force of Cymbeline's cruelty
       could not be so great as the force

of Imogen's restorative power
43 **Cambria** Wales
50 **mean affairs** ordinary business
54 **bate** modify (the last statement)
56 **thick** many words at a time
57 **bores of hearing** ears
59 **by** along

That we shall make in time from our hence-going
And our return, to excuse. But first, how get hence?
Why should excuse be born or ere begot?   65
We'll talk of that hereafter. Prithee speak,
How many score of miles may we well rid
'Twixt hour and hour?

PISANIO   One score 'twixt sun and sun,
Madam, 's enough for you, and too much too.

IMOGEN
Why, one that rode to's execution, man,   70
Could never go so slow. I have heard of riding wagers
Where horses have been nimbler than the sands
That run i' th' clock's behalf. But this is fool'ry.
Go bid my woman feign a sickness, say
She'll home to her father; and provide me presently   75
A riding suit, no costlier than would fit
A franklin's housewife.

PISANIO   Madam, you're best consider.

IMOGEN
I see before me, man. Nor here, nor here,
Nor what ensues, but have a fog in them
That I cannot look through. Away, I prithee,   80
Do as I bid thee. There's no more to say.
Accessible is none but Milford way.   *Exeunt.*

---

64 **to excuse** i.e., tell me how to excuse (the syntax is very loose)
65 **or ere begot** or exist before
there is need (their departure
not yet having taken place)
67 **rid** cover, dismiss
72-73 **sands . . . behalf** sands of an
hour-glass (substituting for a
clock)

75 **presently** at once
77 **franklin** independent landowner
of modest means
78 **see before me** look (only) ahead;
Nor here, nor here i.e., to neither side
79 **what ensues** the consequences

✠

Rehearsing the Scene

The oddness, even weirdness, of the situation and the long unbroken speeches are offset by touches of startling reality: short, compulsive phrases, Imogen's broken, ungrammatical and almost nonsensical sentences, and Pisanio's long and baffled silence. Both actors need to react sharply and precisely, and with absolute belief in what they believe has happened and is happening. As Imogen says, they both see just what is "before" them, and act upon that (see line 78). Consequently a certain lightness is required in performance; in that way the deep feelings of both characters—grief and fear on one side, joy on the other—can be expressed without being muddied by the puzzlement which must also be present.

No stage properties are called for by the text beyond the two letters, and actors should probably do without any: their thoughts are too agile for either of them to sit down or engage in other business. No door or wall, or window, is called for, so the meeting seems to take place in the open. However, Imogen is a prisoner in a castle-palace, so she could behave as if under surveillance, not daring at first to open the letter and keeping excitement, for the most part, unnaturally low in expression.

Pisanio sets up the main action of the scene and then, unable to reveal what he knows, both watches and participates. His attempts to play down the drama and restrain Imogen's reaction can only be counterproductive. Seeing this, his prolonged silence from lines 48 to 68 may be chosen as a way to calm Imogen; he will need effort to do this because Imogen turns repeatedly towards him requiring a response, and each time he refuses. His hope of interposing, which keeps him with Imogen, finally dies; perhaps this is immediately after his last half-line (77), so that Imogen, at line 81, silences an already defeated and resigned man.

But it might also be possible to play Pisanio so that, in his perplexity and pain, he learns to keep actively involved, secure only in obeying the needs of each moment; so his final silence would be an active choice. Then, perhaps, Imogen is silencing herself at line 81, not her servant. In contrast to Imogen's volatility, this Pisanio could become the stronger presence on stage.

Imogen has only one moment at the start of the scene when she may respond to Pisanio's troubled spirit. Then, very quickly, she translates what he has said into her own terms, and soon her joy and haste are touched only lightly with instinctive fear. The letter she reads is curiously constructed, beginning with a negative statement and then an avoidance of precise instruction. Moreover it contains no explanation why Posthumus is risking his life by returning to Britain. The contrast between Pisanio, questioning as he reads his letter, and Imogen, reading without pause or comment, is surely intentional and suggests that she does not hesitate or falter as she reads. Certainly she does not hesitate to react having finished it. Her mind is now hyperactive, conscious of future happiness and present difficulty, drawing Pisanio into her thoughts and yet distancing herself from him. Some images persist in her speech—flying, gliding, speed; strength, crowding, filling; longing, birth, death, risk, time, sickness—but they are all only touched on briefly. None holds the speaker's attention and none is developed with progressive power and richness of association, as in so much of Shakespeare's writing. She is eager, volatile, always moving forward in her thoughts.

Lines 64, 71 and 75 have several syllables over the usual count of ten or eleven, and each should, possibly, be printed as two half-lines, so indicating a pause for breath before the new sentence begins. But with some difficulty all three could be crushed, with major elisions, into a normal measure and so represent Imogen's mind struggling to keep up with her quick imagination. Both ways of speaking them could be explored.

The clearest metrical key to Imogen's state of mind lies in lines 78-82, where each sentence is strong, clear and short-phrased, and most of the words are simple monosyllables. After impulsive questioning and decisive instructions, these lines need to be spoken slowly to be comprehensible. Imogen may talk like someone in a dream, quietly, one phrase at a time, and with a sense of wonder; like someone waking slowly, focusing on only one reality and that distant from her. The last line of the scene, in contrast, flows smoothly and rapidly, with a rising rhythm despite its negative construction. The active finish of the scene suggests Imogen may well run offstage, before Pisanio.

15

The Winter's Tale

Act IV, Scene iv

FLORIZEL and PERDITA

✠

Two young persons enter; one appears to be a goddess, the other a shepherd. Perdita is dressed as queen of the shepherd's feast and Florizel, who is a prince, sole heir to his father's kingdom of Bohemia, is on holiday. Nor is Perdita an ordinary shepherdess; she was abandoned as a baby on the sea coast and, although no one here knows it, she is the daughter of Leontes, King of Sicily.

The setting for this scene is the countryside; the time, early summer, when the sheep have just been sheared.

✠

FLORIZEL

These your unusual weeds to each part of you
Do give a life: no shepherdess, but Flora
Peering in April's front. This your sheep-shearing
Is as a meeting of the petty gods
And you the queen on't.

PERDITA   Sir, my gracious lord,   5
To chide at your extremes it not becomes me—
O pardon that I name them! Your high self,
The gracious mark o' th' land, you have obscured
With a swain's wearing and me, poor lowly maid,
Most goddesslike pranked up. But that our feasts   10
In every mess have folly and the feeders

---

1 **weeds** clothes
2 **Flora** Roman goddess of flowers and springtime
3 **Peering** just coming into sight
  front forehead, beginning
  sheep-shearing rural feast at the beginning of summer
6 **extremes** extravagances, exaggerations

8 **mark** example, person of note
9 **swain's wearing** clothes of a young peasant (or lover: *poetic*)
10 **pranked up** tricked out (in Shakespeare's source she was attired in flowers and garlands)
11 **mess** dish/social rank at a banquet

Digest it with a custom, I should blush
To see you so attired; swoon, I think,
To show myself a glass.

FLORIZEL   I bless the time
When my good falcon made her flight across   15
Thy father's ground.

PERDITA   Now Jove afford you cause!
To me the difference forges dread; your greatness
Hath not been used to fear. Even now I tremble
To think your father by some accident
Should pass this way, as you did. O the fates!   20
How would he look to see his work, so noble,
Vilely bound up? What would he say? Or how
Should I, in these my borrowed flaunts, behold
The sternness of his presence?

FLORIZEL   Apprehend
Nothing but jollity. The gods themselves,   25
Humbling their deities to love, have taken
The shapes of beasts upon them. Jupiter
Became a bull and bellowed; the green Neptune
A ram and bleated; and the fire-robed god,
Golden Apollo, a poor humble swain   30
As I seem now. Their transformations
Were never for a piece of beauty rarer
Nor in a way so chaste, since my desires
Run not before mine honor nor my lusts
Burn hotter than my faith.

PERDITA   O but sir,   35
Your resolution cannot hold when 'tis
Opposed, as it must be, by th' power of the king.
One of these two must be necessities

---

12 **Digest . . . custom** tolerate it because is a tradition
17 **difference** (in our social ranks)
22 **bound up** (referring to Florizel's
clothes: like a great book shoddi-
ly bound)
23 **flaunts** finery

27-30 **Jupiter . . . Neptune . . . Apollo**
(so Jupiter and Neptune won Eu-
ropa and Theophane;
Apollo served as a shepherd to
help Admetus win Alcestis—so
Ovid told the stories)
32 **piece of** person created by
33 **in a way** i.e., loved in a manner

Which then will speak, that you must change this
   purpose
Or I my life.

FLORIZEL   Thou dearest Perdita,   40
With these forced thoughts, I prithee darken not
The mirth o' th' feast: or I'll be thine, my fair,
Or not my father's. For I cannot be
Mine own nor anything to any, if
I be not thine. To this I am most constant   45
Though Destiny say no. Be merry, gentle;
Strangle such thoughts as these with anything
That you behold the while. Your guests are coming;
Lift up your countenance as it were the day
Of celebration of that nuptial which   50
We two have sworn shall come.

PERDITA   O Lady Fortune,
Stand you auspicious!

FLORIZEL   See, your guests approach.
Address yourself to entertain them sprightly
And let's be red with mirth.

40 **I my life** i.e., I must lose my life   42 **or** either
41 **forced**   far-fetched,   unnatural

✠

Rehearsing the Scene

The main challenge to actors is to make the scene credible
without underplaying any of its various elements. These characters must have ease, clarity and grace, and be keenly aware of
each other's sexual attractiveness. In fact, the scene is much less
simple than appears at first, however clear in meaning.

Perdita has to appear as gentle, generous and brave as the
very first flowers of the spring: these are the attributes of the
goddess Flora whose image comes to Florizel's mind as he gazes
in admiration at her. The holiday clothes are right for her natural
beauty but, like the year's earliest days of sunshine, she will

sometimes appear timid and unsure.

Florizel has never worked as a shepherd, so his clothes show no sign of wear and tear. He seems tireless; it is holiday time, and he is as fit and vigorous as if he had just been created, fully grown.

Perdita's entry is difficult in that it is silent and she has no positive action to play; yet she draws Florizel's attention constantly. It may be helpful to choose some music to play at this moment and to improvise a dancing, laughing or playful entry for the two lovers. Perdita's references to "extremes" and "follies" (ll. 6 and 11) and the possibility that she might "blush" or "swoon" (ll. 12 and 13), together with Florizel's talk of the "petty gods," all indicate the appropriate mood for this opening. It might also be useful to look at some Renaissance paintings of gods and mortals in springtime—for example, by Giorgione, Titian, Botticelli—and photographs and videos of present-day celebrations in the country at springtime.

Florizel starts to speak on a high note, although "Peering in April's front" (l. 3) adds the tentativeness of early spring to the later celebration. This note is taken up by Perdita immediately after he has spoken of a "queen" (l. 5); she is apprehensive and embarrassed as soon as she is reminded that her lover is truly a prince. Florizel is reassuring and bold in reply: his short response has a sustained phrasing which cuts across the line endings; it has a strong and rising rhythm until the close, and it evokes an image of a lonely hunter—this last feature not so comforting. Perdita is not deflected by his reply but, rather, becomes more precise and careful in expressing her concerns.

There is humor in all this, as well as drama. In days of royal rule, it was unthinkably dangerous for a prince to marry a commoner: politically it would be suicide and, beyond that, a dereliction of duty. But Florizel professes not to hear any of this in what Perdita says. He takes the unruly gods for his precedent and the rhythms of his verse are strong as each deity is introduced at the line endings. Talk of bellowing and bleating (see ll. 28 and 29) invites imitation and pleasure in speaking of the gods. He is probably teasing Perdita, trying to help her to forget fear; he professes to take account only of the sexuality of their encounter, and promises self-control (ll. 33-37). Perhaps there is some ambiguity here, for "honor" and "faith" can also allude to the responsibilities of being a prince.

When Perdita presses her argument and shows good cause to fear for the happiness of them both and for her own life, Florizel answers with more consideration, more at the level of her proper concerns.

As Florizel renews his promises, the "mirth o' th' feast" can be re-established. The two make their own stand even in the face of "Destiny" (l. 46): they are brave enough to love each other against absolute odds. Perhaps the guests who now approach should be represented by strong and lively music, a sound in contrast to the music at the beginning of the scene. In answering its call, the two actors can draw this encounter to whatever close seems appropriate. (As so often, Shakespeare has created a concluding moment for which performers must find their own truth to play.) Here there is scope for alternative interpretations: is Perdita "red with mirth" (l. 54) or not, and is Florizel prepared to trust "Lady Fortune"? Are their differences quite forgotten or resolved?

Perhaps a word may be said about the task of playing a prince and a princess. There is no need to borrow "royal" or "privileged" gestures and behavior—certainly they would be wrong for Perdita, who has never lived in luxury. Florizel can have some rebellious fun with them, but this should not take too much attention. These two are young persons born to enjoy life and to grow into responsibility for the lives of others: these are the most important facts about them, and ones which can be imaginatively shared by any actors. They are frightened by the world in which they live, but committed to the pleasures of their springtime.

SCENES
FOR
TWO
ACTRESSES

16

The Comedy of Errors
Act II, Scene i and Act IV, Scene ii
ADRIANA and LUCIANA

✠

The action is set outside a Merchant's house in Ephesus where, in the first of these two short scenes, two sisters, Adriana and Luciana, await the return of Adriana's husband for the midday meal.

Between the first and second scene, Adriana has found her husband and reproached him, but he behaved strangely, as if he did not know her: the man she is accosting is *not* her husband, but his long forgotten twin brother from Syracuse. (This is Shakespeare's earliest use of the device of mistaken identity.) The twin conceals his origins because there is a death penalty on anyone from Syracuse who is found in Ephesus.

To further complicate matters, the visting twin has declared love for Luciana in the most extravagant terms:

> Are you a god? Would you create me new?
> Transform me then, and to your power I'll yield.
>
> (III.ii.39-40)

Luciana, who now believes that her sister's husband has proposed to her, withdraws in confusion to find Adriana; the second scene then follows.

✠

ADRIANA
Neither my husband nor the slave returned
That in such haste I sent to seek his master.
Sure, Luciana, it is two o'clock.
LUCIANA
Perhaps some merchant hath invited him

---

1 **slave** Dromio, the servant

And from the mart he's somewhere gone to dinner.   5
Good sister let us dine and never fret;
A man is master of his liberty.
Time is their master and when they see time,
They'll go or come; if so, be patient sister.

ADRIANA
Why should their liberty than ours be more?   10

LUCIANA
Because their business still lies out o' door.

ADRIANA
Look when I serve him so, he takes it ill.

LUCIANA
O, know he is the bridle of your will.

ADRIANA
There's none but asses will be bridled so.

LUCIANA
Why headstrong liberty is lashed with woe.   15
There's nothing situate under heaven's eye
But hath his bound, in earth, in sea, in sky.
The beasts, the fishes and the winged fowls
Are their males' subjects and at their controls;
Man, more divine, the master of all these,   20
Lord of the wide world and wild wat'ry seas,
Indued with intellectual sense and souls,
Of more preeminence than fish and fowls,
Are masters to their females and their lords;
Then let your will attend on their accords.   25

ADRIANA
This servitude makes you to keep unwed.

LUCIANA
Not this, but troubles of the marriage bed.

ADRIANA
But were you wedded, you would bear some sway.

5 **mart** time for buying and selling
9 **go or come** (reversing the usual order of the verbs)
11 **still** always
12 **Look when** whenever
15 **lashed** punished
19 **controls** command
22 **intellectual sense** reason
25 **accords** consent
28 **sway** rule, authority

LUCIANA

Ere I learn love, I'll practice to obey.

ADRIANA

How if your husband start some other where?   30

LUCIANA

Till he come home again, I would forbear.

ADRIANA

Patience unmoved! No marvel though she pause;
They can be meek that have no other cause.
A wretched soul, bruised with adversity,
We bid be quiet when we hear it cry   35
But were we burd'ned with like weight of pain,
As much or more we should ourselves complain.
So thou, that hast no unkind mate to greive thee,
With urging helpless patience would relieve me;
But if thou live to see like right bereft,   40
This fool-begged patience in thee will be left.

LUCIANA

Well I will marry one day, but to try.

☩

ADRIANA

Ah Luciana, did he tempt thee so?
Mightst thou perceive austerly in his eye
That he did plead in earnest? Yea or no?
Looked he or red or pale, or sad or merrily?
What observation mad'st thou in this case   5
Of his heart's meteors tilting in his face?

30 **start . . . where** fly off to some other woman
32 **pause** hesitate, take time to think (i.e., before getting married)
33 **cause** matter in dispute
39 **helpless** useless (opposite of helpful)
40 **like right bereft** yourself suffer the same loss of rights/justice
41 **fool-begged** idiotic, gained (like a fool) by asking for it

2 **austerely** paying strict attention
6 **meteors tilting** signs of fiery passions in conflict

LUCIANA

First he denied you had in him no right.

ADRIANA

He meant he did me none; the more my spite.

LUCIANA

Then swore he that he was a stranger here.

ADRIANA

And true he swore though yet forsworn he were.   10

LUCIANA

Then pleaded I for you.

ADRIANA   And what said he?

LUCIANA

That love I begged for you he begged of me.

ADRIANA

With what persuasion did he tempt thy love?

LUCIANA

With words that in an honest suit might move.

First he did praise my beauty then my speech.   15

ADRIANA

Didst speak him fair?

LUCIANA   Have patience, I beseech.

ADRIANA

I cannot, nor I will not, hold me still.

My tongue, though not my heart, shall have his will.

He is deformed, crooked, old and sere,

Ill-faced, worse bodied, shapeless everywhere,   20

Vicious, ungentle, foolish, blunt, unkind,

Stigmatical in making, worse in mind.

LUCIANA

Who would be jealous then of such a one?

No evil lost is wailed when it is gone.

---

7 **denied . . . right** (a double negative, either intensifying or deny-
ing the statement)
8 **spite** injury, vexation
14 **honest** honorable

16 **him fair** kindly, favorably to him
18 **his** its
20 **shapeless** ugly, unshapely
22 **Stigmatical in making** congen-
tally deformed

ADRIANA

Ah but I think him better than I say;   25
And yet would herein others' eyes were worse.
Far from her nest the lapwing cries away;
My heart prays for him though my tongue do curse.

26 **worse** (so they would not see his deformity)

27 **lapwing** peewit (the bird draws intruders away from its nest by crying out at a distance from it)

✠

Rehearsing the Scene

These short exchanges offer sharp contrasts in the respective feelings, actions and situations of the two characters. Their different attitudes about matrimony, men and life give rise to constant comic disharmony. The two scenes can be played with no more break between them than the time required to leave the acting area and return with fresh impetus.

The meter in these scenes is mostly strong and regular, and changes in rhythm can be clues to changes in action. At the start of the first passage, a change of rhythm between lines 1-2 and line 3 can be an opportunity to bring out Adriana's impatience so that it starts ticking away like a time bomb that explodes at the close of the scene. After a sentence that flows fluently through two lines, the next sentence breaks into three sections within a single verse line, its last phrase a challenge which is intended to be unanswerable. Luciana's reply is so smooth, so vague about Adriana's concerns, so easily comprehensive about men in general, that Adriana is determined to puncture her innocent sister's confident opinions about men in love, with one-line arguments. Luciana's ardor is undimmed as she rhapsodizes about the mastery of men (ll. 15-25). Is Luciana expressing her own desire to find a strong, capable and near-divine master who will give her entry to the "wide world and wild wat'ry seas"? Or is she merely repeating what she has been taught? Or does she speak teasingly, as if she knows what will anger her sister most? Line 27 could support any one of these interpretations, "troubles" suggesting several different ironies. Adriana, in her put-down of the inexperienced Luciana, offers her own justification in terms of a motherly concern for suffering (ll.34-35).

To conclude the episode, Luciana manages to have the last word. Here and throughout the scene, the actress playing Luciana must explore whether she is genuinely gullible and quick-thinking, or as sure of herself as she behaves.

The tone changes with the second episode's first line. Adriana is envious as well as reproving, and ignorant of the details of what has happened. In the earlier scene, the two sisters debate the general virtues and nature of men. The second scene becomes an investigation of the behavior of one man, Adriana's husband. The meter of the scene reflects this shift. Here lines will be shared between the two speakers, Adriana jumping in with her question at line 11 and incapable of saying more than a few indignant words at line 16. Although she is at first dependent on Luciana's answers, she takes over at the end of the scene in angry castigation of her absent husband. When Luciana asks the question that supplies an irrefutable proof that Adriana has not told the full truth, the married woman confesses to her heart's concerns (see also l. 18, which prepares for this). The scene concludes with Adriana's analogy of the fluttering, frightened and helpless bird protecting its young. The actress might take this conceit as a guide to physical performance at this point. But is she speaking only for herself, or against the injustice of marriage in general, or simply to silence her sister?

What effects of her bizarre romantic encounter register in Luciana's behavior? One should recall that Luciana had listened to this suit without saying very much to stop it. Line 14 hints that she has been "moved," in some measure. Her refusal at first to answer Adriana's questions suggests anxiety and perplexity. The brevity of what she does say may imply that her mind remains preoccupied by the strange encounter. Every word she speaks may betray excitement and some pleasure.

An open mind and full physical involvement will reveal many opportunities for both passion and comedy. In the first episode, Adriana should be on the lookout for her husband, and so restless; Luciana focuses on her ideal man, and apparently is "unmoved"—perhaps unmoving. In the second, it is Luciana who is focused on the "husband", and Adriana must struggle to win her attention.

17

The Two Gentlemen of Verona
Act I, Scene ii
JULIA and LUCETTA

✠

Proteus is in love with Julia:

> Thou, Julia, thou hast metamorphosed me,
> Made me neglect my studies, lose my time,
> War with good counsel, set the world at naught;
> Made wit with musing weak, heart sick with thought.

(I.i.66-99)

Julia and her maid Lucetta confer about Julia's suitors.

✠

JULIA
> But say Lucetta, now we are alone,
> Wouldst thou then counsel me to fall in love?

LUCETTA
> Ay madam, so you stumble not unheedfully.

JULIA
> Of all the fair resort of gentlemen
> That every day with parle encounter me,   5
> In thy opinion which is worthiest love?

LUCETTA
> Please you repeat their names, I'll show my mind
> According to my shallow simple skill.

JULIA
> What think'st thou of the fair Sir Eglamour?

LUCETTA
> As of a knight well-spoken, neat and fine;   10

---

4 **resort** company
5 **parle** talk

10 **neat** elegant
fine highly accomplished, refined

But were I you, he never should be mine.

JULIA
What think'st thou of the rich Mercatio?

LUCETTA
Well of his wealth but of himself so so.

JULIA
What think'st thou of the gentle Proteus?

LUCETTA
Lord, Lord! To see what folly reigns in us!   15

JULIA
How now! What means this passion at his name?

LUCETTA
Pardon dear madam, 'tis a passing shame
That I, unworthy body as I am,
Should censure thus on lovely gentlemen.

JULIA
Why not on Proteus as of all the rest?   20

LUCETTA
Then thus: of many good I think him best.

JULIA
Your reason?

LUCETTA
I have no other but a woman's reason,
I think him so because I think him so.

JULIA
And wouldst thou have me cast my love on him?   25

LUCETTA
Ay if you thought your love not cast away.

JULIA
Why, he of all the rest hath never moved me.

LUCETTA
Yet he of all the rest, I think, best loves ye.

JULIA
His little speaking shows his love but small.

13 **so so** good/not very good
16 **passion** passionate speech, out-
    burst
17 **passing** extreme

19 **censure** pass judgement
27 **moved** proposed to

LUCETTA

Fire that's closest kept burns most of all. 30

JULIA

They do not love that do not show their love.

LUCETTA

O they love least that let men know their love.

JULIA

I would I knew his mind.

LUCETTA

Peruse this paper madam.

JULIA

"To Julia." —Say from whom. 35

LUCETTA

That the contents will show.

JULIA

Say, say who gave it thee.

LUCETTA

Sir Valentine's page; and sent, I think, from Proteus.
He would have given it you but I, being in the way,
Did in your name receive it. Pardon the fault I pray. 40

JULIA

Now by my modesty, a goodly broker!
Dare you presume to harbor wanton lines?
To whisper and conspire against my youth?
Now trust me, 'tis an office of great worth,
And you an officer fit for the place. 45
There take the paper; see it be returned
Or else return no more into my sight.

LUCETTA

To plead for love deserves more fee than hate.

JULIA

Will ye be gone?

LUCETTA   That you may ruminate.   *Exit.*

JULIA

And yet I would I had o'erlooked the letter. 50

---

41 **broker** go-between   50 **o'erlooked** perused

It were a shame to call her back again
And pray her to a fault for which I chid her.
What fool is she that knows I am a maid
And would not force the letter to my view
Since maids in modesty say "no" to that   55
Which they would have the profferer construe "ay."
Fie, fie, how wayward is this foolish love
That, like a testy babe, will scratch the nurse
And presently, all humbled, kiss the rod!
How churlishly I chid Lucetta hence   60
When willingly I would have had her here!
How angerly I taught my brow to frown
When inward joy enforced my heart to smile!
My penance is to call Lucetta back
And ask remission for my folly past.   65
What ho! Lucetta!

Enter LUCETTA, *and lets the letter fall to the ground.*

LUCETTA   What would your ladyship?
JULIA
Is't near dinnertime?
LUCETTA   I would it were
That you might kill your stomach on your meat
And not upon your maid.   *She picks up the letter.*
JULIA
What is't that you took up so gingerly?   70
LUCETTA
Nothing.
JULIA
Why didst thou stoop then?
LUCETTA
To take a paper up that I let fall.

52 **to a fault** to commit a fault
58 **testy** fretful
59 **presently** immediately

68 **kill** satisfy/subdue
    stomach (1) appetite (2) anger
69 **maid** (wordplay on **maid**, pro-
    nounced *mate*)

JULIA

And is that paper nothing?

LUCETTA

Nothing concerning me.   75

JULIA

Then let it lie for those that it concerns.

LUCETTA

Madam, it will not lie where it concerns
Unless it have a false interpreter.

JULIA

Some love of yours hath writ to you in rhyme.

LUCETTA

That I might sing it madam, to a tune.   80
Give me a note: your ladyship can set.

JULIA

As little by such toys as may be possible.
Best sing it to the tune of "Light o' love."

LUCETTA

It is too heavy for so light a tune.

JULIA

Heavy! Belike it hath some burden then?   85

LUCETTA

Ay and melodious were it, would you sing it.

JULIA

And why not you?   **LUCETTA**   I cannot reach so high.

JULIA

Let's see your song. (*Takes the letter.*) How now,
   minion!

LUCETTA

Keep tune there still, so you will sing it out;

---

77 **lie** deceive (pun on **lie** = remain, l. 76)
81 **note** musical note/letter **set** set to music/write (a letter)
82 **As little by** as little store by (wordplay on **set** store; see l. 81) **toys** trifles
83 **Light o' love** (a popular tune of the time)

85 **burden** (1) load (2) musical refrain (3) 'a woman's burden' (bawdy)
87 **high** (1) too high a note to sing (2) too high in social scale
89 **tune** (1) correct musical pitch (2) mood, humor

And yet methinks I do not like this tune.   90

JULIA

You do not?

LUCETTA   No madam, 'tis too sharp.

JULIA

You minion, are too saucy.

LUCETTA

Nay, now you are too flat
And mar the concord with too harsh a descant.
There wanteth but a mean to fill your song.   95

JULIA

The mean is drowned with your unruly bass.

LUCETTA

Indeed I bid the base for Proteus.

JULIA

This babble shall not henceforth trouble me.
Here is a coil with protestation.   *Tears the letter.*
Go get you gone and let the papers lie;   100
You would be fing'ring them to anger me.

LUCETTA

She makes it strange. But she would be best pleased
To be so ang'red with another letter.   *Exit.*

JULIA

Nay, would I were so ang'red with the same!
O hateful hands, to tear such loving words!   105
Injurious wasps, to feed on such sweet honey
And kill the bees that yield it with your stings!
I'll kiss each several paper for amends.

91 **sharp** (1) out of musical tune (2) spoken too sharply, or struck too hard
93 **flat** (1) out of musical tune (2) downright in attitude
94 **descant** variation of tune or mood
95 **wanteth** lacks
   mean tenor part (i.e., Proteus)
96 **mean** (1) tenor part (2) well ordered   mood
   bass (1) bass part (2) base, low conduct
97 **bid the base** (from a game of challenge and chase; with pun on bass)
99 **coil with protestation** fuss over a declaration of love
101 **fing'ring** (1) stealing (2) playing with (as on a musical instrument)
102 **makes it strange** pretends to indifference
106 **wasps** (her fingers)
108 **several** separate

Look, here is writ "kind Julia." Unkind Julia,
As in revenge of thy ingratitude,   110
I throw thy name against the bruising stones,
Trampling contemptuously on thy disdain.
And here is writ "love-wounded Proteus."
Poor wounded name! My bosom, as a bed,
Shall lodge thee till thy wound be throughly healed;   115
And thus I search it with a sovereign kiss.
But twice or thrice was "Proteus" written down.
Be calm, good wind, blow not a word away
Till I have found each letter in the letter,
Except mine own name: that some whirlwind bear   120
Unto a ragged, fearful, hanging rock
And throw it thence into the raging sea.
Lo here in one line is his name twice writ,
"Poor forlorn Proteus, passionate Proteus,
To the sweet Julia." That I'll tear away —   125
And yet I will not, sith so prettily
He couples it to his complaining names.
Thus will I fold them one upon another:
Now kiss, embrace, contend, do what you will.

Enter LUCETTA.

LUCETTA
Madam,   130
Dinner is ready and your father stays.
JULIA
Well let us go.
LUCETTA
What, shall these papers lie like telltales here?
JULIA
If you respect them, best to take them up.

110 **As** thus	126 **sith** since
115 **throughly** thoroughly	131 **stays** is waiting
116 **search** probe (to cleanse and so cure a wound)	134 **respect** care about, value
	best it were best
121 **ragged** rugged	

LUCETTA

Nay, I was taken up for laying them down.   135
Yet here they shall not lie for catching cold.

JULIA

I see you have a month's mind to them.

LUCETTA

Ay madam, you may say what sights you see;
I see things too although you judge I wink.

JULIA

Come, come; will't please you go?   *Exeunt.*   140

---

135 **taken up** reprimanded
136 **for** for fear of

137 **month's mind** great longing
      (used of desire for various foods
      during pregnancy)
139 **wink** close my eyes, see nothing

✠

Rehearsing the Scene

The dramatic interest in this scene does not center on whether Julia loves Proteus, or on what sort of man he is. Both characters show what they think about all this very early on. Rather this scene between two very differently circumstanced women is about trust.

Can Julia trust her own feelings, and can she trust Lucetta, her maid? She feels the need to speak about her love, and yet she fears to do so openly; as she prevaricates and changes her mind, an actress can show how Julia learns about tenderness and the violence of her own feelings.

Lucetta can be played quite coolly, as if she enjoys the opportunity of manipulating the reactions of her mistress; so she may be much the older and wiser of the two, and protective towards her mistress as she leads her towards a fuller self-knowledge. Or Lucetta's humor can be cynical and her motivation rebellion against the authority of her mistress. A third choice, would be for the actress to show Lucetta sharing the excitement of her mistress, and only pretending to greater wisdom; so she would become "too saucy" (l. 82) because that expresses her pleasure in discovering Julia's strength of feeling. However she is played, the actress will find that Shakespeare has given her lines that control effortlessly the way in which the action of the scene develops; consciously or unconsciously, the maid is in control of the mistress.

All these issues will arise as soon as rehearsals start. Why does Julia need to talk to Lucetta? Why does Lucetta talk at once about stumbling? Is Julia impetuous and insecure by nature, or does Lucetta take every opportunity to fight her with words, picking up "counsel" and "fall" from Julia's very first speech? Why does Lucetta laugh or protest as soon as Julia mentions Proteus (ll. 14-15)? Julia calls this reaction a "passion"; so whichever way it is played, it must be strong enough to call for the apology of lines 17-19. In all this tone is a crucial factor: the whole exchange could be light enough for Julia to be laughing with happiness, right up to lines 61-65 and beyond.

Most of the questions which will arise between the two actresses are about the relative power and security of the two characters. The change to a short verse-measure (three feet only to each line) at line 33, marks a decisive moment when Julia speaks very simply and Lucetta reveals that she has been withholding a very significant fact—her possession of Proteus's letter—all the way through their opening talk. Lucetta would have to be played very stupidly if she had been merely forgetful that the letter had arrived: her pleasurable manipulation of her mistress becomes obvious here.

At line 41, Julia starts defending herself by attacking Lucetta, and so loses what she most desires at that moment—possession of the letter. As soon as she is alone, she taunts her servant for being a fool, only to be led to see her own folly and her own childishness. When she tries to reverse her hasty decision, she is confronted with Lucetta ready to taunt her further by dropping the letter on to the floor. Again the verse changes to the shorter measure, which Lucetta introduces by tightening the tension with an isolated "nothing" (l. 71).

Now the two start a more deliberate wordplay, in a series of puns on musical terms. Lucetta wins easily because, as the talk becomes more sexual, Julia tears up the letter which she longs to possess. Before Lucetta leaves the stage a second time she has a speech (ll. 102-3) which seems to be addressed to the audience so that she can establish her superior understanding. But no aside is marked in the text because Lucetta could say this to herself in such a way that her mistress has to hear and so come to a fuller understanding herself. (Julia's following words show that she did hear—which is against stage conventions governing asides.)

Left alone, Julia can play her second soliloquy in several ways: (1) Totally distraught, and becoming funnier all the time; for this, it will be convenient if Lucetta has torn the letter into very small pieces. (2) Carefully and deliberately, working soberly to piece the letter together, and becoming funnier and more effectively pathetic as she proceeds; for this, the pieces should be fairly large and not too numerous.

The ending is finely balanced. It will become a competition between the two actresses to see who manages with greater dignity, or with greater pleasure. Perhaps she who plays Julia will have more difficulty in concluding on top, for her last line seems to leave the last decisive choice to Lucetta—how does she acquiesce?

Some chairs, or a long bench or couch, with other furniture, could be useful to give the sense of a private apartment and to encourage activity which would accentuate the mistress-servant relationship and provide places of refuge or resource in the cat-and-mouse game between the two. Alternatively, the scene might be played as if the two women had just escaped from some family room and they are "alone" on a terrace outside, or in some great hall or garden where movement and speech is unrestricted.

18

Romeo and Juliet

Act II, Scene v

JULIET and the NURSE

✠

Juliet met Romeo for the first time last night when he arrived un-
expectedly at the annual party given by her parents. She is fourteen
years old and an only child. After dancing together, the stranger and
she had talked and kissed before parting. Later in the garden under
her bedroom window, Romeo declared his love and Juliet told him to
send word saying where and when they could be married. As they are
the sole heirs of two powerful families locked in a bitter, dangerous
feud, their passion and devotion require great secrecy.

Juliet has sent her Nurse to receive Romeo's message and is waiting her return. Probably she is in the garden, on the lookout, and
dressed ready to go to any rendezvous Romeo names.

The Nurse lives for Juliet, both her own child and her husband
having died many years previously. As a servant in the Capulet house
she has looked after Juliet since birth and enjoys great familiarity with
the whole household. She is proud of her long service.

There is no need for the Nurse's attendant, Peter, to be present;
he can be dealt with as an offstage character.

✠

JULIET
　The clock struck nine when I did send the nurse.
　In half an hour she promised to return.
　Perchance she cannot meet him. That's not so.
　O she is lame! Love's heralds should be thoughts
　Which ten times faster glide than the sun's beams   5
　Driving back shadows over low'ring hills,

3 **Perchance** perhaps

Therefore do nimble-pinioned doves draw Love
And therefore hath the wind-swift Cupid wings.
Now is the sun upon the highmost hill
Of this day's journey and from nine till twelve   10
Is three long hours; yet she is not come.
Had she affections and warm youthful blood,
She would be as swift in motion as a ball;
My words would bandy her to my sweet love
And his to me.   15
But old folks, many feign as they were dead:
Unwieldy, slow, heavy, and pale as lead.

Enter NURSE *and* PETER.

O God, she comes! O honey Nurse, what news?
Hast thou met with him? Send thy man away.

NURSE

Peter, stay at the gate.   *Exit* PETER.   20

JULIET

Now good sweet Nurse!—O Lord, why lookest thou
    sad?
Though news be sad, yet tell them merrily;
If good, thou shamest the music of sweet news
By playing it to me with so sour a face.

NURSE

I am aweary, give me leave awhile.   25
Fie, how my bones ache! What a jaunce have I!

JULIET

I would thou hadst my bones and I thy news.
Nay come, I pray thee speak. Good, good Nurse,
    speak.

NURSE

Jesu, what haste! Can you not stay awhile?
Do you not see that I am out of breath?   30

7   **nimble-pinioned** swift-winged
    doves (sacred to Venus, they
    draw her chariot)
8   **Cupid** (the blindfolded son of
    Venus)
9   **is . . . hill** it is midday

12 **affections** feelings
16 **feign** act, appear
20 **stay . . . gate** wait at the entrance
25 **give me leave** let me alone
26 **jaunce** jaunt, weary journey
29 **stay** wait

JULIET

How art thou out of breath when thou hast breath
To say to me that thou art out of breath?
The excuse that thou dost make in this delay
Is longer than the tale thou dost excuse.
Is thy news good or bad? Answer to that.   35
Say either and I'll stay the circumstance.
Let me be satisfied, is't good or bad?

NURSE   Well you have made a simple choice; you know
not how to choose a man. Romeo? No, not he.
Though his face be better than any man's, yet   40
his leg excels all men's, and for a hand and a foot,
and a body, though they be not to be talked on,
yet they are past compare. He is not the flower of
courtesy, but I'll warrant him as gentle as a lamb. Go
thy ways, wench; serve God. What, have you dined   45
at home?

JULIET

No, no. But all this did I know before.
What says he of our marriage? What of that?

NURSE

Lord, how my head aches! What a head have I!
It beats as it would fall in twenty pieces.   50
My back—a t' other side—ah my back, my back!
Beshrew your heart for sending me about
To catch my death with jauncing up and down!

JULIET

I' faith I am sorry that thou art not well.
Sweet, sweet, sweet Nurse, tell me, what says my
  love?   55

NURSE   Your love says, like an honest gentleman, and
a courteous, and a kind, and a handsome, and I
warrant a virtuous—where is your mother?

---

36 **stay the circumstance** wait for
  details
38 **simple** foolish
42 **not . . . talked on** not worth
  mentioning

51 **a** on
52 **Beshrew** a curse on
53 **jauncing** traipsing
56 **honest** honorable

JULIET

Where is my mother? Why she is within.
Where should she be? How oddly thou repliest!   60
"Your love says, like an honest gentleman,
'Where is your mother?'"

NURSE   O God's Lady dear!

Are you so hot? Marry come up, I trow.
Is this the poultice for my aching bones?
Henceforward do your messages yourself.   65

JULIET

Here's such a coil! Come, what says Romeo?

NURSE

Have you got leave to go to shrift today?

JULIET

I have.

NURSE

Then hie you hence to Friar Lawrence' cell;
There stays a husband to make you a wife.   70
Now comes the wanton blood up in your cheeks;
They'll be in scarlet straight at any news.
Hie you to church. I must another way,
To fetch a ladder by the which your love
Must climb a bird's nest soon when it is dark.   75
I am the drudge and toil in your delight,
But you shall bear the burden soon at night.
Go. I'll to dinner. Hie you to the cell.

JULIET

Hie to high fortune! Honest Nurse, farewell. *Exeunt.*

63 **hot** in a passion, angry
   Marry . . . trow By the Virgin,
   come off it, I should think
66 **coil** fuss
67 **shrift** confession
69 **hie** haste

72 **straight** straightway
75 **bird's nest** i.e. Juliet's room
   (**bird** = maiden)
76 **in** for
77 **bear the burden** do the work/
   bear the weight of your lover

✠

Rehearsing the Scene

Juliet and her nurse could hardly be closer to each other, knowing each other intimately. While Juliet is 'hot' to get on with her life and her new love, the Nurse will suffer a real loss in Juliet's departure. Juliet is only fourteen years old, and the nurse continues to treat the future bride like a child.

Much depends on how confident Juliet is at the beginning of the scene, how secure in comparing her love-thoughts to the "sun's beams" (l. 5). How aware is she of the uncertainties of "nimble-pinioned" birds, and of blind Cupid?

The Nurse may delay her news deliberately, either for her own pleasure or to test Juliet's seriousness. Or she can be, quite literally, "out of breath" (l. 30).

Does Juliet actually rub her Nurse's aching back (see l. 51), or is she too caught up in her own thoughts and feelings to be able to respond? At what point does she shift from demanding the news to cajoling it out of her faithful Nurse? Perhaps the Nurse gets full attention by her account of Romeo's physical attractions. "Go thy ways, wench" (ll. 44-45) may follow a pause in which both have become silent, still and happy in the contemplation of Romeo's virtues as a lover; or the Nurse can push ahead without further ado, confident that she is totally in charge and Juliet ready to do anything she says.

"Here's such a coil," some dozen lines from the end of the scene, suggests a climax in their talk, whether it occurs instinctively or because it has been engineered. Thereafter Juliet has little to say, but much to realize and enjoy—and, perhaps, to fear. The Nurse alludes now to sexual arousal and adventure with greater openness. Juliet's wordplay on "hie" and "high" can express her quick excitement.

Nurse and Juliet leave in opposite directions, the one in slower tempo into the house, the other, more quickly, in the direction from which the Nurse had entered. Juliet does not stop to thank the Nurse, but she may kiss or hug her before running off.

19

Romeo and Juliet

Act III, Scene v

LADY CAPULET and JULIET

✠

Sent by her husband, Lady Capulet enters Juliet's bedroom in the
first light of morning. Her task is to persuade her daughter to a quickly arranged marriage with Paris, a young nobleman whom she hardly
knows at all. This is the first Juliet has heard of the plan.

In secret, Juliet has married Romeo, heir of the Montague family,
the implacable rivals to the Capulets. Soon thereafter Romeo was
drawn into a duel with Tybalt, son of Lady Capulet's brother and Juliet's cousin. Tybalt is killed and Romeo subsequently banished upon
pain of death. After one night together, the lovers parted, leaving Juliet alone. At that last separation, Juliet's "ill-divining soul" had feared
that they would never meet again. She is now very close to tears, if
not actually weeping.

✠

Enter LADY CAPULET, *to* JULIET.

LADY CAPULET
Ho daughter, are you up?

JULIET
Who is't that calls? It is my lady mother.
Is she not down so late or up so early?
What unaccustomed cause procures her hither?

LADY CAPULET
Why how now, Juliet?

JULIET   Madam, I am not well.   5

LADY CAPULET
Evermore weeping for your cousin's death?
What, wilt thou wash him from his grave with tears?

---

3 **not . . . late** so late getting to bed   **procures** brings
4 **unaccustomed** unusual, strange

And if thou couldst, thou couldst not make him live
Therefore have done. Some grief shows much of love
But much of grief shows still some want of wit.   10

JULIET

Yet let me weep for such a feeling loss.

LADY CAPULET

So shall you feel the loss, but not the friend
Which you weep for.

JULIET   Feeling so the loss,
I cannot choose but ever weep the friend.

LADY CAPULET

Well girl, thou weep'st not so much for his death   15
As that the villain lives which slaughtered him.

JULIET

What villain, madam?

LADY CAPULET   That same villain Romeo.

JULIET (*Aside.*)

Villain and he be many miles asunder—
God pardon him! I do with all my heart,
And yet no man like he doth grieve my heart.   20

LADY CAPULET

That is because the traitor murderer lives.

JULIET

Ay madam, from the reach of these my hands.
Would none but I might venge my cousin's death!

LADY CAPULET

We will have vengeance for it, fear thou not.
Then weep no more: I'll send to one in Mantua   25
Where that same banished runagate doth live,
Shall give him such an unaccustomed dram
That he shall soon keep Tybalt company,

10 **still** always
11 **feeling** deeply felt
12 **but not** but not be affected by
14 **friend** lover (*pun*)
20 **like he** as he does (by his absence)
22 **hands** (for lovemaking/for vengeance)

23 **Would . . . death!** (so Romeo would be spared/so vengeance might be fit)
26 **runagate** fugitive
27 **unaccustomed dram** unlooked for dose (of poison)

And then I hope thou wilt be satisfied.

JULIET

Indeed I never shall be satisfied   30
With Romeo till I behold him . . . Dead! . . .
Is my poor heart so for a kinsman vexed.
Madam, if you could find out but a man
To bear a poison, I would temper it
That Romeo should, upon receipt thereof,   35
Soon sleep in quiet. O how my heart abhors
To hear him named and cannot come to him
To wreak the love I bore my cousin
Upon his body that hath slaughtered him!

LADY CAPULET

Find thou the means and I'll find such a man.   40
But now I'll tell thee joyful tidings, girl.

JULIET

And joy comes well in such a needy time.
What are they, beseech your ladyship?

LADY CAPULET

Well, well, thou hast a careful father, child,
One who, to put thee from thy heaviness,   45
Hath sorted out a sudden day of joy
That thou expects not nor I looked not for.

JULIET

Madam, in happy time! What day is that?

LADY CAPULET

Marry, my child, early next Thursday morn
The gallant, young, and noble gentleman,   50
The County Paris, at Saint Peter's Church
Shall happily make thee there a joyful bride.

JULIET

Now by Saint Peter's Church and Peter too,

---

29 **satisfied** (in vengeance)
30 **satisfied** repaid/sexually fulfilled
34 **temper** mix/modify
36 **sleep in quiet** die/sleep peace-
fully
38 **wreak** avenge/express

39 **his body that** the body of him
who
44 **careful** caring
45 **heaviness** sorrow
46 **sorted out** arranged
48 **in . . . time** it's the right time

He shall not make me there a joyful bride!
I wonder at this haste, that I must wed   55
Ere he that should be husband comes to woo.
I pray you tell my lord and father, madam,
I will not marry yet; and when I do, I swear
It shall be Romeo, whom you know I hate,
Rather than Paris. These are news indeed!   60

LADY CAPULET
Here comes your father. Tell him so yourself
And see how he will take it at your hands.

✠

Rehearsing the Scene

Lady Capulet comes to convey her husband's wishes; either
she is a very strong and decisive woman, or one who acts only on
impulse. Seeing Tybalt lying dead in the public street, she, and
not her husband, had demanded that the prince should revenge
his death by killing Romeo. It was she who countered Benvolio's
account of what had happened with an invented and exaggerated
version of her own, and called again for vengeance and Romeo's
death. In this scene, Lady Capulet who is not aware of her daughter's affection for Romeo may be trying, rather desperately, to
comfort her daughter by inventing a story about a plot to poison
Romeo by "one in Mantua" (1. 25). But alternatively, she could be
very controlled and purposeful, and her talk of revenge an account of a genuine and ruthless plan. Many variations are possible between these two readings. But whichever is chosen for the
beginning of the scene must decide how it finishes; Lady Capulet
can be glad to relinquish her task to her "careful" husband; or
her praise of him at line 44 can be sarcastic and her concluding
words as he enters imply her own power over him.
Juliet is discovered in a state of inconsolable mourning, for
her cousin and for Romeo's very recent departure from their marriage bed. Her words express her divided mind and feelings in
many double meanings, one being appropriate to herself, the
other intended for her mother's ears. How conscious is Juliet of
this deception, how in control of both meanings? Is she in real
danger of disclosing her love for Romeo? Line 18 must be spok-

en aside but her following words can be so passionate that were her mother not lost in her own thoughts she must understand their secret meaning.

Some actresses have played Lady Capulet as a woman with the same strong passions as her daughter; having only one daughter herself and her husband being much older, she has been played as a woman with unusually strong feeling and possessiveness towards her brother's son.

After Lady Capulet changes the subject of their talk at line 41, both characters are revealed in new ways: the mother speaks with kindness, after her own fashion; Juliet with assurance and rapid, unambiguous, invention. Does either of these new "roles" come easily?

20

The Merchant of Venice

Act I, Scene ii

PORTIA and NERISSA

✠

Bassanio has told the audience all it needs to know about Portia
and her waiting-woman before they come on stage for the first time in
this scene:

> In Belmont is a lady richly left
> And she is fair and, fairer than that word,
> Of wondrous virtues. Sometimes from her eyes
> I did receive fair speechless messages.
> Her name is Portia, nothing undervalued
> To Cato's daughter, Brutus' Portia;
> Nor is the wide world ignorant of her worth,
> For the four winds blow in from every coast
> Renowned suitors . . .   (I.i.161. ff.)

Portia and Nerissa enjoy a respite during the continual parade of suitors who seek her hand and her fortune.

✠

PORTIA By my troth Nerissa, my little body is aweary
    of this great world.
NERISSA You would be, sweet madam, if your miseries
    were in the same abundance as your good
    fortunes are. And yet for aught I see, they are as sick   5
    that surfeit with too much as they that starve with
    nothing. It is no mean happiness therefore, to be
    seated in the mean; superfluity comes sooner by white
    hairs, but competency lives longer.
PORTIA Good sentences and well pronounced.   10

1 **troth** faith
6 **surfeit** are overfed, glutted
7 **mean** slight (pun on golden
   mean)
8-9 **superfluity . . . hairs** excess is
   more ageing

9 **competency** moderate means
10 **sentences** sayings, aphorisms
   (pun on legal sense)
   pronounced spoken (pun on
   delivering legal judgements, or
   sentences)

NERISSA They would be better if well followed.

PORTIA If to do were as easy as to know what were good
to do, chapels had been churches and poor men's
cottages princes' palaces. It is a good divine that
follows his own instructions; I can easier teach twenty   15
what were good to be done than to be one of the
twenty to follow mine own teaching. The brain may
devise laws for the blood but a hot temper leaps o'er
a cold decree; such a hare is madness the youth to skip
o'er the meshes of good counsel the cripple. But this   20
reasoning is not in the fashion to choose me a husband.
O me, the word "choose"! I may neither choose who
I would nor refuse who I dislike, so is the will of a
living daughter curbed by the will of a dead father. Is it
not hard, Nerissa, that I cannot choose one nor   25
refuse none?

NERISSA Your father was ever virtuous and holy men
at their death have good inspirations. Therefore the
lott'ry that he hath devised in these three chests of
gold, silver and lead, whereof who chooses his mean-   30
ing chooses you, will no doubt never be chosen by any
rightly but one who you shall rightly love. But what
warmth is there in your affection towards any of these
princely suitors that are already come?

PORTIA I pray thee overname them and as thou namest   35
them I will describe them and according to my
description level at my affection.

NERISSA First there is the Neapolitan prince.

PORTIA Ay that's a colt indeed, for he doth nothing
but talk of his horse and he makes it a great appropri-   40

---

13 **had been** would have been
18 **blood** passion, sexual appetite
    hot temper high spirits, passion-
    ate temperament
19 **cold decree** sober judgement
20 **meshes** nets, traps
21 **in the fashion** of the sort

23-24 **will . . . will** wish, sexual desire
    . . . will, last testament
35 **overname** i.e., go through the
    whole list
37 **level** aim, guess
39 **colt** young fool/young horse

ation of his own good parts that he can shoe him
himself. I am much afeard my lady his mother played
false with a smith.

NERISSA Then is there the County Palatine.

PORTIA He doth nothing but frown—as who should   45
say, "And you will not have me, choose!" He hears
merry tales and smiles not; I fear he will prove the
weeping philosopher when he grows old, being so
full of unmannerly sadness in his youth. I had rather
be married to a death's-head with a bone in his mouth   50
than to either of these. God defend me from these two!

NERISSA How say you by the French lord, Monsieur
Le Bon?

PORTIA God made him and therefore let him pass for
a man. In truth I know it is a sin to be a mocker,   55
but he! Why he hath a horse better than the Neapolitan's, a better bad habit of frowning than the
Count Palatine; he is every man in no man. If a
throstle sing, he falls straight a-cap'ring; he will fence
with his own shadow. If I should marry him, I   60
should marry twenty husbands. If he would despise
me, I would forgive him for if he love me to madness,
I shall never requite him.

NERISSA What say you then to Falconbridge, the young
baron of England?   65

PORTIA You know I say nothing to him for he
understands not me nor I him. He hath neither Latin,
French nor Italian and you will come into the court
and swear that I have a poor pennyworth in the

41 **parts** talents
44 **County** Count
45-46 **as . . . say** as much as to say
46 **And** if
   choose have it your own way
48 **weeping philosopher** another
   Heraclitus (who wept at the foolishness of people)
49 **unmannerly sadness** unseemly
   seriousness (pun on **man**, i.e.
   adult)
50 **death's-head** skull (**bones** were
   crossed underneath a skull on
   tombstones, not in its **mouth**)
59 **throstle** thrush
60-61 **should . . . should** were to . . .
   would have to
68-69 **come . . . swear** bear me witness
69 **pennyworth** (1) small quantity
   (2) bargain

English. He is a proper man's picture but alas, who   70
can converse with a dumbshow? How oddly he is
suited! I think he bought his doublet in Italy, his
round hose in France, his bonnet in Germany and
his behavior everywhere.

NERISSA What think you of the Scottish lord, his   75
neighbor?

PORTIA That he hath a neighborly charity in him for
he borrowed a box of the ear of the Englishman and
swore he would pay him again when he was able.
I think the Frenchman became his surety and sealed   80
under for another.

NERISSA How like you the young German, the Duke
of Saxony's nephew?

PORTIA Very vilely in the morning when he is sober
and most vilely in the afternoon when he is drunk.   85
When he is best he is a little worse than a man and
when he is worst he is little better than a beast. And
the worst fall that ever fell, I hope I shall make shift
to go without him.

NERISSA If he should offer to choose and choose the   90
right casket, you should refuse to perform your
father's will if you should refuse to accept him.

PORTIA Therefore for fear of the worst I pray thee set
a deep glass of Rhenish wine on the contrary casket,
for if the devil be within and that temptation   95
without, I know he will choose it. I will do anything,
Nerissa, ere I will be married to a sponge.

NERISSA You need not fear, lady, the having any of these
lords. They have acquainted me with their deter-

---

70 **is a proper . . . picture** i.e.,
   looks fine
72 **suited** (1) dressed (2) matched
   doublet upper garment
73 **round hose** lower garment,
   breeches or puffed-out hose

80 **Frenchman** (reference to the old
   alliance between France and
   Scotland, especially when the latter was at war with England)
86-87 **best . . . beast** (pun)
88 **make shift** find a way
94 **contrary** wrong

minations which is indeed to return to their home and   100
to trouble you with no more suit unless you may be
won by some other sort than your father's imposition
depending on the caskets.

PORTIA If I live to be as old as Sibylla, I will die as chaste
as Diana unless I be obtained by the manner of my   105
father's will. I am glad this parcel of wooers are so
reasonable for there is not one among them but I dote
on his very absence and I pray God grant them a fair
departure.

NERISSA Do you not remember, lady, in your father's   110
time, a Venetian, a scholar and a soldier that came
hither in company of the Marquis of Montferrat?

PORTIA Yes, yes, it was Bassanio!—as I think, so was he
called.

NERISSA True, madam. He, of all the men that ever my   115
foolish eyes looked upon, was the best deserving
a fair lady.

PORTIA I remember him well and I remember him
worthy of thy praise.

102 **sort** manner
      imposition command, charge
104 **Sibylla** Sibyl (Greek prophetess,
      who asked Apollo for the gift of
      long life)

105 **Diana** (virgin goddess of the
      hunt)
106 **parcel** company, set

✠

Rehearsing the Scene

Portia is constrained from choosing her own husband by her
father's will. This dictated that she must marry the man who is
able to solve the riddle of the caskets: which one, gold, silver or
lead, contains a picture of Portia. It was his plan that only a man
who truly loved Portia would choose the correct casket.

Portia has lapsed into reverie about the circumstances of her father's will. An actress might attempt to sound depths of personal suffering with Portia's first line, but the neat opposition of "little" and "great" makes any profundity unlikely. Nerissa's "sentences" are given in so sprightly a form that we are not surprised at Portia's pat response, or the quickness of Nerissa's rejoinder.

There are two ways to prevent this dialogue from becoming an exercise in verbal dexterity. The first is for Nerissa to remain in a quite different mind-set from Portia's. She addresses her mistress as "sweet madam," which suggests intimacy and respect; and her "sentences" imply that she has settled for a "competency" happily enough. But there is more to Nerissa than a homespun faith in happy endings. At the end of the scene it becomes clear that she has known all the while that the suitors Portia fears had already departed from the field. One cannot help but wonder whether Nerissa has allowed Portia to express her dislikes in order ultimately to build a case for her own favorite, Bassanio, whom she saves for last. Portia does try to hide how easily she remembers his name and to sound judicious in acquiescing to absolute praise of him; but Nerissa has achieved her aim and in her own way.

The waiting-woman is not bossily in charge of the mistress, but she presides over the scene, always ahead, never caught off balance. For example, see how smoothly she answers Portia's patronizing praise at lines 10-11, and how she speaks of the caskets in terms of "no doubt" (l. 31) when she knows already that the riddle has dispatched the current "parcel of wooers." When she says her own eyes are "foolish" (l. 116) could this imply that she has been laughing most of the time? Or does it mean that she is miserable at her own situation whenever she lets herself think of it, not unlike a professional fool?

Portia is seriously concerned with her responsibilities as the sole heiress of a very rich and famous man. Her field of concern takes in "poor men" as well as "princes," also teaching, law, and religion. She is aware of the dangers of "hot temper" and the "madness" of youth. The constraints imposed by her father's will invite a restless performance, perhaps propelling her from place to place, never still; or she may play compulsively with some object until she breaks it or gets bored with it. Or perhaps she holds herself very still, with difficulty, as if imprisoned.

What pleasure does Portia derive from her derision of the suitors? Does she enjoy mocking these men, impersonating each one in turn as the dialogue invites, finding in imitation of males an outlet for her own frustration and hot temper? The fact that all these men are duds makes the task easy; but instead of being bored, she makes the charade increasingly "beastly" (see l. 87).

The prose of the scene allows many changes of rhythm and tempo, and therefore more opportunity for idiosyncrasy than verse would do; but actors must respect and use its structure, as indicated by repetitions, antitheses, parallel phrases and word-play.

At the end of the scene, the two women have become closer and more open to each other. Perhaps they are laughing together now, or are both very quiet and still as they become increasingly aware of how much is truly at stake in the wooing match.

This scene can be delicate in performance, despite its elaborate sentences and a jocularity that seems forced at times. In a somewhat Chekhovian way, it can suggest an inner drama within these little bodies "aweary" of a great world. Sometimes mad thoughts are glimpsed briefly, as they leap over the meshes of crippling cleverness.

21

As You Like It

Act III, Scene ii

CELIA and ROSALIND

✠

After Duke Frederick's usurpation of the dukedom from Rosalind's father, Rosalind herself is banished from the court. Her cousin Celia runs away with her to the Forest of Arden. The two girls disguise themselves, with Rosalind posing as a man. Together with a loyal clown, Touchstone, they settle in the forest of Arden where Duke Senior is already in hiding with some faithful followers.

Also in the forest is Orlando, younger son of a gentleman loyal to the older duke. The girls have already met him, when he came to court to answer the challenge of Charles the Wrestler; in the first bout he had felled his adversary, but was subsequently banished from court because of the suspicions of Duke Frederick. However this was not before Rosalind had fallen in love with Orlando, and given him a chain as a favor.

This morning Rosalind and Celia find verses pinned on trees in the forest, all of them "deifying the name of Rosalind" (III. ii. 354), and they have been reading them aloud.

✠

CELIA Didst thou hear these verses?
ROSALIND O yes, I heard them all and more too; for
    some of them had in them more feet than the verses
    would bear.
CELIA That's no matter. The feet might bear the   5
    verses.
ROSALIND Ay, but the feet were lame and could not bear
    themselves without the verse and therefore stood

---

4 **bear** contain
5 **feet** pedestrians (pun on **feet** as metrical units)
7 **bear** endure
8 **stood** stopped/remained

lamely in the verse.

CELIA   But didst thou hear without wondering how   10
thy name should be hanged and carved upon these
trees?

ROSALIND   I was seven of the nine days out of the
wonder before you came, for look here what I found
on a palm tree. I was never so berhymed since   15
Pythagoras' time that I was an Irish rat, which I can
hardly remember.

CELIA   Trow you who hath done this?

ROSALIND   Is it a man?

CELIA   And a chain that you once wore, about his neck.   20
Change you color?

ROSALIND   I prithee who?

CELIA   O Lord, Lord, it is a hard matter for friends to
meet. But mountains may be removed with earth-
quakes and so encounter.   25

ROSALIND   Nay, but who is it?

CELIA   Is it possible?

ROSALIND   Nay, I prithee now with most petitionary
vehemence, tell me who it is?

CELIA   O wonderful, wonderful and most wonderful   30
wonderful, and yet again wonderful, and after that,
out of all whooping!

ROSALIND   Good my complexion! Dost thou think,
though I am caparisoned like a man, I have a doublet
and hose in my disposition? Once inch of delay more   35

13 **nine days** (a **nine days wonder** caused no great astonishment)
15 **palm tree** (an exotic tree for an English forest of Arden)
16 **Pythagoras** (Greek philosopher famous for believing in the trans-migration of souls after death); **that** when;
     Irish rat (Irish magicians were said to kill rats by rhymed spells)
18 **Trow** know
23-25 **hard matter . . . encounter** (allusion to proverb: "Friends may meet, but mountains never greet")
27 **Is it possible?** (i.e., not to know)
28 **prithee** beg you
32 **out . . . whooping** beyond all (bawdy) exclamations
33 **complexion** temperament, appearance (a mild oath)
34 **caparisoned** i.e., dressed (usually used of horses)
35-36 **One . . . discovery** one moment more of delay is like a long voyage of exploration to the South Seas

is a South Sea of discovery. I prithee tell me who is it
quickly, and speak apace. I would thou couldst
stammer that thou mightst pour this concealed man
out of thy mouth as wine comes out of a narrow-
mouthed bottle—either too much at once or none at   40
all. I prithee take the cork out of thy mouth, that I may
drink thy tidings.

CELIA So you may put a man in your belly.

ROSALIND Is he of God's making? What manner of man?
Is his head worth a hat or his chin worth a beard?   45

CELIA Nay, he hath but a little beard.

ROSALIND Why God will send more if the man will be
thankful. Let me stay the growth of his beard, if thou
delay me not the knowledge of his chin.   50

CELIA It is young Orlando that tripped up the wrestler's
heels and your heart both in an instant.

ROSALIND Nay but the devil take mocking! Speak sad
brow and true maid.

CELIA I' faith, coz, 'tis he.   55

ROSALIND Orlando?

CELIA Orlando.

ROSALIND Alas the day! What shall I do with my doublet
and hose? What did he when thou saw'st him? What
said he? How looked he? Wherein went he? What   60
makes he here? Did he ask for me? Where remains
he? How parted he with thee? And when shalt thou
see him again? Answer me in one word.

CELIA You must borrow me Gargantua's mouth first,
'tis a word too great for any mouth of this age's   65
size. To say "ay" and "no" to these particulars is more
than to answer in a catechism.

---

37 **apace** quickly
44 **of God's making** i.e., a normal
   human being
49 **stay** wait for
54-55 **sad . . . maid** seriously and
   truthfully
55 **coz** cousin

60 **Wherein went he** how was he
   dressed
60-61 **What makes he** what is he doing
64 **Gargantua** (Rabelais's giant; his
   writings were known in England
   at the time)

ROSALIND But doth he know that I am in this forest and in man's apparel? Looks he as freshly as he did the day he wrestled?

CELIA It is as easy to count atomies as to resolve the propositions of a lover, but take a taste of my finding him and relish it with good observance. I found him under a tree like a dropped acorn–

ROSALIND It may well be called Jove's tree when it drops such fruit. 75

CELIA Give me audience, good madam.

ROSALIND Proceed.

CELIA There lay he stretched along like a wounded knight– 80

ROSALIND Though it be pity to see such a sight, it well becomes the ground.

CELIA Cry "holla" to the tongue, I prithee; it curvets unseasonably. He was furnished like a hunter–

ROSALIND O ominous! He comes to kill my heart. 85

CELIA I would sing my song without a burden. Thou bring'st me out of tune.

ROSALIND Do you not know I am a woman? When I think, I must speak. Sweet, say on.

CELIA You bring me out. Soft. Comes he not here? 90

ROSALIND 'Tis he! Slink by and note him.

---

69 **freshly** in good health
71 **atomies** atoms, motes
   resolve answer
72 **propositions** questions, problems
73 **relish it** add a flavoring
   observance attention
75 **Jove's tree** (the oak was sacred to Jove, being thought the "king of trees")

77 **audience** attention, formal hearing
83 **holla** whoa (command to check a horse)
   curvets leaps, frisks
84 **furnished** equipped, dressed
85 **heart** (pun on *hart*)
86 **burden** refrain
90 **Soft** stay

✠

Rehearsing the Scene

In this scene, wordplay, metaphors and similes are the vocal expression of irrepressible excitement. Both Rosalind and Celia run towards bad puns as well as good ones; only by drawing several different worlds of experience together in their minds can they show the energy and wealth of their feelings. Puns also allow them to express their differences: they listen to each other intently, so that they may share the excitement and then outshine each other in delight. Perhaps they are also in competition, Celia not wishing to be left behind, not willing to allow Rosalind to hog all the limelight of love. Rosalind at times may pull back, so that her foolishness or weakness is not too obvious.

In acting this scene, it is important to find a physical performance which supports and occasionally contrasts with the verbal one. A good way to build the physical life of the scene might be for one actor to remain still while the other is constantly on the move. Movement on the part of one or both of the actors will be important to match the frenetic energy of thought.

It may help if several stepladders or piled-up objects are brought on to the acting area to stand in for the immobile trees of the forest. Both characters could be holding examples of Orlando's poems: Rosalind has to produce one at line 14, Celia might be reading another avidly at the top of the scene—and perhaps laughing at it.

When Celia asks, "Trow you who hath done this?" both girls are virtually certain who the writer is; but Rosalind cannot be absolutely sure until she has proof. Here is the trigger for the scene's action. When Rosalind pretends not to know the writer's identity, this tactic rebounds against her, awakening the full range of her emotions and unleashing the "vehemence" of her physical longing. Her wish to "drink thy tidings," line 42, prompts Celia's most sexually blatant response. Reassured that the writer is indeed Orlando, Rosalind's many questions come pouring out, unabashedly; and having now been given answers, she cannot stop speaking in reply, in a mixture of pleasure and fear.

When Celia reveals that she has actually seen Orlando, the game is all in her power. Then her continued playfulness can be sensed as a warm, caring affection for her cousin, the more engaging because Celia's imagery shows that she is aware of the helplessness, violence and physicality of love. An actress's first instinct will almost certainly be to play Celia sympathetically, both in her relationship to Rosalind and in her ideas about love, but it is possible to try a much colder, more antagonistic response. Celia might remain at a critical distance, believing that Rosalind has been mastered too completely by the idea of being in love. Or she might be enjoying Rosalind's predicament as the latest good joke, fully appreciating the irony of Rosalind declaring her love as a woman while dressed as a man.

22

Twelfth Night

Act I, Scene v

VIOLA and OLIVIA

✠

Viola, shipwrecked on the shores of Illyria, has disguised herself as a young man and become servant to Count Orsino, the ruler of this country. She falls in love with her master, but he is already in love with Olivia, a beautiful heiress who lives entirely alone after the death of her father and her brother, vowing to remain veiled for seven years.

Orsino has sent Cesario (as Viola is now called) to urge his suit to Olivia. By perseverance and quick wit he/she wins the prize of an interview with the reclusive Olivia.

✠

VIOLA The honorable lady of the house, which is she?

OLIVIA Speak to me; I shall answer for her. Your will?

VIOLA Most radiant, exquisite, and unmatchable beauty—   5

OLIVIA Whence came you, sir?

VIOLA I can say little more than I have studied, and that question's out of my part. Good gentle one, give me modest assurance if you be the lady of the house, that I may proceed in my speech.   10

OLIVIA Are you a comedian?

VIOLA No, my profound heart and yet by the very fangs of malice I swear I am not that I play. Are you the lady of the house?

OLIVIA If I do not usurp myself, I am.   15

9 **modest** reasonable
11 **comedian** actor (see **part**, l. 8)

12 **profound heart** perceptive and spirited lady
15 **usurp** supplant

VIOLA Most certain, if you are she, you do usurp yourself
for what is yours to bestow is not yours to reserve.
But this is from my commission. I will on with my
speech in your praise and then show you the heart
of my message. 20

OLIVIA Come to what is important in't. I forgive you
the praise.

VIOLA Alas, I took great pains to study it and 'tis
poetical.

OLIVIA It is the more like to be feigned; I pray you keep 25
it in. I heard you were saucy at my gates and allowed
your approach rather to wonder at you than to hear
you. Sure you have some hideous matter to deliver
when the courtesy of it is so fearful. Speak your office.

VIOLA I bring no overture of war, no taxation of 30
homage. I hold the olive in my hand. My words are
as full of peace as matter.

OLIVIA Yet you began rudely. What are you? What
would you?

VIOLA The rudeness that hath appeared in me have I 35
learned from my entertainment. What I am and
what I would are as secret as maidenhead: to your
ears, divinity; to any other's, profanation.

OLIVIA Well, sir, what is your text?

VIOLA Most sweet lady— 40

OLIVIA A comfortable doctrine and much may be
said of it. Where lies your text?

VIOLA In Orsino's bosom.

OLIVIA In his bosom? In what chapter of his bosom?

VIOLA To answer by the method, in the first of his 45

---

16 **usurp yourself** wrong yourself
17 **what** i.e., your hand in marriage
18 **from my commission** beyond
my instructions
21 **forgive you** release you from repeating
29 **when . . . fearful** since the for-
malities inspire such fear

office business
30 **taxation of** demand for
31 **olive** (symbol of peace)
36 **entertainment** reception
38 **divinity** i.e., a sacred message
41 **comfortable** comforting
45 **by the method** in the same style
(of theological discourse)

heart.

OLIVIA   O I have read it; it is heresy. Have you no more
to say?

VIOLA   Good madam, let me see your face.

OLIVIA   Have you any commission from your lord to   50
negotiate with my face? You are now out of your text.
But we will draw the curtain and show you the picture.
(*Unveils*.) Look you sir, such a one I was this
present. Is't not well done?

VIOLA   Excellently done, if God did all.   55

OLIVIA   'Tis in grain sir; 'twill endure wind and weather.

VIOLA
'Tis beauty truly blent whose red and white
Nature's own sweet and cunning hand laid on.
Lady, you are the cruel'st she alive   60
If you will lead these graces to the grave,
And leave the world no copy.

OLIVIA   O sir, I will not be so hard-hearted. I will give
out divers schedules of my beauty. I shall be
inventoried and every particle and utensil labeled to   65
my will: as, item, two lips, indifferent red; item, two
gray eyes, with lids to them; item, one neck, one
chin, and so forth. Were you sent hither to praise me?

VIOLA
I see you what you are—you are too proud.
But if you were the devil, you are fair.   70
My lord and master loves you. O such love
Could be but recompensed though you were crowned
The nonpareil of beauty.

OLIVIA   How does he love me?

51 **out . . . text** strayed from the
text (of your sermon)
52 **curtain** (paintings were protect-
ed by curtains)
53-54 **this present** at this time
56 **in grain** indelible
58 **blent** blended
59 **cunning** skillful
64 **schedules** statements

65 **utensil** article
65-66 **labeled . . . will** i.e., added as a
codicil
66 **indifferent** fairly
68 **praise** appraise/flatter
70 **if** as if
72 **but recompensed** no more than
repaid
73 **nonpareil of** unequalled in

VIOLA With adorations, with fertile tears,   75
With groans that thunder love, with sighs of fire.
OLIVIA
Your lord does know my mind; I cannot love him.
Yet I suppose him virtuous, know him noble,
Of great estate, of fresh and stainless youth,
In voices well divulged, free, learned and valiant,   80
And in dimension and the shape of nature
A gracious person; but yet I cannot love him.
He might have took his answer long ago.
VIOLA
If I did love you in my master's flame,
With such a suff'ring, such a deadly life,   85
In your denial I would find no sense;
I would not understand it.
OLIVIA   Why, what would you?
VIOLA
Make me a willow cabin at your gate
And call upon my soul within the house;
Write loyal cantons of contemned love   90
And sing them loud even in the dead of night;
Hallo your name to the reverberate hills
And make the babbling gossip of the air
Cry out "Olivia!" O you should not rest
Between the elements of air and earth   95
But you should pity me.
OLIVIA
You might do much. What is your parentage?
VIOLA
Above my fortunes, yet my state is well—
I am a gentleman.

75 **fertile** abundant
80 **In . . . divulged** of good reputation
81 **dimension** physique
85 **deadly life** living death
88 **willow** (emblem of a forlorn lover)
89 **my soul** i.e., Olivia
90 **cantons** songs
   contemned rejected
92 **reverberate** reverberating
93 **babbling . . . air** i.e., echo
98 **state** status, class

OLIVIA   Get you to your lord.
  I cannot love him. Let him send no more   100
  Unless, perchance, you come to me again
  To tell me how he takes it. Fare you well.
  I thank you for your pains. Spend this for me.

VIOLA
  I am no fee'd post, lady; keep your purse.
  My master, not myself, lacks recompense.   105
  Love make his heart of flint that you shall love
  And let your fervor like my master's be
  Placed in contempt. Farewell, fair cruelty.   *Exit.*

OLIVIA
  "What is your parentage"
  "Above my fortunes, yet my state is well—   110
  I am a gentleman." I'll be sworn thou art.
  Thy tongue, thy face, thy limbs, actions and spirit
  Do give thee fivefold blazon. Not too fast . . . soft, soft!
  Unless the master were the man. How now?
  Even so quickly may one catch the plague!   115
  Methinks I feel this youth's perfections
  With an invisible and subtle stealth
  To creep in at mine eyes. Well, let it be.

104 **fee'd post** paid messenger
113 **give . . . blazon** i.e., Cesario's
    voice, features, and so on, all

    proclaim him a gentleman
    soft take it slowly

✠

Rehearsing the Scene

   Viola/Cesario makes a confident entrance having penetrated
Olivia's security system. (Valentine, another of Orsino's servants,
had been turned back at the gate.) Her very first question is im-
pertinent, because Olivia would expect to be recognized as Lady
of the House, even with a veil over her face.

   Since Olivia has been told already where the messenger came
from, her question at line 6 must have some further significance.

After the two lines Olivia is able to discern on some level that Cesario's origins are more complicated than he/she states. Olivia interrupts Cesario's rehearsed speech and is clearly more fascinated by the messenger than his master. Some change in the tone of their exchange is indicated by the time Viola calls Olivia "Good gentle one".

Viola takes pleasure in pretending to be a blunt-speaking and disinterested male who uses flattery to get attention. She is also genuinely curious about Olivia, her rival for Orsino's love. Olivia uses mockery, reproof and the inbred superiority of a lady talking to a mere servant, to regain the upper hand, and to further explore the nature of this young man.

Both women discover in the other more than she bargained for. Surely the last reaction Viola would have expected from her portrayal of Cesario would be actually to arouse romantic interest from Olivia. Instead of advancing Orsino's cause she unwittingly begins to advance her own! The actors need only to play sincerely moment by moment and the comedy will take care of itself. Both characters show their personal feelings unmistakably in ways that can show deep concern and even pain. By her own admission Viola discovers there is something malicious in the sport she has with Olivia–"by the very fangs of malice" (ll. 12-13). Despite her ardent efforts, Viola's true character and nature assert themselves: "What I am and what I would are as secret as maidenhead" (ll. 36-37). Perhaps line 55 begins with frank admiration in "Excellently done," which Viola has to cover up by the brusque and cheeky qualification, "if God did all." Such lines need to be judged very carefully; they can be heavy-handed as wit, or clumsy as they reflect a shift of feeling. Olivia's inner feelings are mostly expressed through the brevity and number of her questions, when all that she is required to do is to listen to a message. An occasional sharpness or hesitation can reveal unspoken insecurity or sense of danger. Her speech concluding this scene (ll. 112-18) tells the actress what is affecting Olivia; it also offers Shakespeare's own directions to the actress playing Viola on how she should behave.

The change from prose to verse at line 58 invites Viola to change the tone decisively through the sustaining power of meter with its ability to lend force to particular words. Olivia at first resists the change, but when the nimble catalogue of her own attractions fails to raise a response, she follows it with first one brief question (l. 68) and then another (l. 74). Her next words are in verse, the first line being loaded with monosyllables; she can sound very sober or very beseeching. Then her verse becomes much lighter in rhythm, as if escaping from matters that threaten to be more serious.

At line 84, speaking of the flame and suffering of unrequited love, most Violas speak from the depths of their own feelings; she suffers like her master, but in longing for her master. Her images grow in scope and soon encompass the "dead of night," "reverberate hills" and the limitless elements of "air and earth." Some Violas hesitate before pronouncing "Olivia" (l. 94), as if about to name Orsino instead. The half-line 96 shows that a pause follows this amazing and glowing speech; and the whole scene can pivot on this silent moment. Olivia's next words reveal that she is affected deeply; perhaps they should be spoken very slowly and quietly, in strong contrast to Viola's fervor.

From line 97 onwards both women speak so that almost all the verse lines are broken into short phrases; both are controlling inner turmoil, and cannot speak with full assurance or truth. In a later scene, Viola notes that Olivia had

> . . . made good view of me, indeed so much
> That sure methought her eyes had lost her tongue,
> For she did speak in starts distractedly.
>
> (II.ii.16-18)

Olivia drops all pretense as soon as she is alone and remains silent for some time (109 is an incomplete verse line). All she can say at first is a repetition of Cesario's words; and a moment later she acknowledges that she has caught the "plague" of love and fallen for a servant. "Well, let it be" can be either solemn or dismissive, either pledging her love with absolute simplicity or accepting it all very lightly because that way is easier and more immediately pleasurable. Or possibly, she is very muddled: "blazon" and "plague," "perfections" and "stealth" suggest conflicting thoughts and feelings. Whichever way this soliloquy is spoken, Olivia is shown awakening to an obsessive love which wipes out all her vows of solitude and reserve.

23

Twelfth Night

Act III, Scene i

VIOLA and OLIVIA

✠

Viola, disguised as Cesario, has returned from her master Orsino and requested a second interview with Olivia. After their previous scene together (see scene 22), Viola had realized that Olivia had been "charmed" (II.ii.18) by the young man she is pretending to be. But back in Orsino's presence, she suffers so keenly from her hidden love for her master that she herself has suggested this second mission. Perhaps she hopes for some decisive rejection from Olivia which will free Orsino from his enslavement, or perhaps she wants only to know as soon as possible either the worst or the best:

> O Time, thou must untangle this, not I;
> It is too hard a knot for me t' untie. (II.ii.40-41)

Olivia comes out into the garden to greet Cesario herself, unable to wait even a moment longer for him to enter the house.

✠

VIOLA Most excellent accomplished lady, the heavens
  rain odors on you. (*A pause.*) My matter hath no
  voice, lady, but to your own most pregnant and
  vouchsafed ear.
OLIVIA Let the garden door be shut and leave me to   5
  my hearing. Give me your hand, sir.
VIOLA
  My duty, madam, and most humble service.
OLIVIA
  What is your name?

2-3 **hath no voice** cannot be spoken
  3 **pregnant** receptive (?)

4 **vouchsafed** condescending

VIOLA

Cesario is your servant's name, fair princess.

OLIVIA

My servant, sir? 'Twas never merry world
Since lowly feigning was called compliment.   10
Y' are servant to the Count Orsino, youth.

VIOLA

And he is yours, and his must needs be yours:
Your servant's servant is your servant, madam.

OLIVIA

For him, I think not on him: for his thoughts,
Would they were blanks rather than filled with me.   15

VIOLA

Madam, I come to whet your gentle thoughts
On his behalf.

OLIVIA   O by your leave, I pray you:
I bade you never speak again of him,
But would you undertake another suit,
I had rather hear you to solicit that   20
Than music from the spheres.

VIOLA   Dear lady —

OLIVIA

Give me leave, I beseech you. I did send,
After the last enchantment you did here,
A ring in chase of you. So did I abuse
Myself, my servant and, I fear me, you.   25
Under your hard construction must I sit,
To force that on you in a shameful cunning
Which you knew none of yours. What might you
    think?
Have you not set mine honor at the stake
And baited it with all th' unmuzzled thoughts   30

---

10 **lowly feigning** humble pretense
14 **For** as for
21 **music . . . spheres** (the celestial
   harmony, supposed to be caused
   by the movements of the planets
   and stars)
24 **abuse** wrong, disgrace

25 **my servant** (she had sent her
   steward, Malvolio, with the ring)
26 **construction** interpretation
29-30 **set . . . unmuzzled thoughts**
   i.e., the claims of honor are beset
   by those of love, like a bear bated
   by dogs at a stake

That tyrannous heart can think? To one of your
   receiving
Enough is shown: a cypress, not a bosom,
Hides my heart. So let me hear you speak.

VIOLA
I pity you.

OLIVIA   That's a degree to love.

VIOLA
No, not a grize, for 'tis a vulgar proof   35
That very oft we pity enemies.

OLIVIA
Why then methinks 'tis time to smile again.
O world, how apt the poor are to be proud:
If one should be a prey, how much the better
To fall before the lion than the wolf.   (*Clock strikes*.)   40
The clock upbraids me with the waste of time.
Be not afraid, good youth: I will not have you.
And yet, when wit and youth is come to harvest,
Your wife is like to reap a proper man.
There lies your way, due west.

VIOLA   Then westward ho!   45
Grace and good disposition attend your ladyship.
You'll nothing, madam, to my lord by me?

OLIVIA
Stay.
I prithee tell me what thou think'st of me.

VIOLA
That you do think you are not what you are.   50

OLIVIA
If I think so, I think the same of you.

31 **receiving** sensitivity
32 **cypress** veil of mourning
35 **grize** step
vulgar proof common experience
43 **come to harvest** i. e. when you are mature
44 **proper** fine
45 **due west** i. e., toward the setting sun

westward ho! (cry of London watermen ready to row up the Thames)
46 **good disposition** peace of mind
50 **you are not . . . are** You (by loving a servant) are not being the lady you are
51 **If . . . you** I, likewise, think you are the lord you are not

VIOLA

Then think you right: I am not what I am.

OLIVIA

I would you were as I would have you be.

VIOLA

Would it be better, madam, than I am?
I wish it might, for now I am your fool.   55

OLIVIA

O what a deal of scorn looks beautiful
In the contempt and anger of his lip!
A murd'rous guilt shows not itself more soon
Than love that would seem hid: love's night is noon.
Cesario, by the roses of the spring,   60
By maidhood, honor, truth and everything,
I love thee so that, maugre all thy pride,
Nor wit nor reason can my passion hide.
Do not extort thy reasons from this clause,
For that I woo, thou therefore hast no cause;   65
But rather reason thus with reason fetter,
Love sought is good, but given unsought is better.

VIOLA

By innocence I swear and by my youth,
I have one heart, one bosom and one truth,
And that no woman has, nor never none   70
Shall mistress be of it, save I alone.
And so adieu, good madam. Never more
Will I my master's tears to you deplore.

OLIVIA

Yet come again, for thou perhaps mayst move
That heart which now abhors to like his love. *Exeunt.*

---

55 **I am . . . fool** i. e., you are making a fool of me
59 **love's . . . noon** i. e., love is
plainly visible, even when hidden
61 **maidhood** virginity
62 **maugre** in spite of

64 **clause** premise
65 **For that** that because
   cause interest (in her love)
69 **heart** love
   bosom affection
   truth devotion

✠

Rehearsing the Scene

Olivia has more to say, but Viola receives more surprises and must extricate herself from a highly embarrassing situation.

With "Give me your hand" (l. 6), Olivia takes the initiative and steps very close to this servant who has so captured her affections. She breaks social decorum in doing this, and Viola is doubly respectful in reply: does she refuse to take Olivia's hand, or steel herself to do so? Olivia is not deterred, but rather presses on to ask the servant his name. After a pause, they continue to thrust and parry with words: both may be nervous until, in mid-line, Olivia breaks decorum yet again by interrupting to stop this exchange. Her mood then alters, and Viola must now hear a declaration of Olivia's idealized love, at first tactfully, but then apologetically and apprehensively expressed.

How should Viola respond when she says so little in reply? Viola may be surprised by the lengths to which Olivia will go, and perhaps startled by her passion. Is she constantly moving out of Olivia's reach throughout the scene? Or does she stand still resigned to her fate? Does she smile, or might she have to prevent a laugh? Is she "afraid" of what may come next, as Olivia believes (see l. 42)?

Perhaps line 31 should be printed as two half-lines indicating that Olivia waits for a reply to her question. But she may be so frightened of what she finds herself saying that she rushes on, until at line 33 (which has only nine syllables), at which point she does pause briefly. When Viola answers—probably with difficulty—"I pity you," Olivia is quick to respond, perhaps cutting her off in mid-sentence. By line 37, however, she has recovered some composure, and concludes the interview with a show of humor. Viola says farewell with some spirit (ll. 45-46), but then adds a question: is this because she remembers the need to make a sensible report of what has happened, or does she hope for some message that could shock Orsino from his love for Olivia?

Now the two young women have to face each other; there is no escape from Olivia's "Stay." For the next six lines both choose words very carefully; the talk is even more like a duel than their first exchanges. It is Viola who breaks the pattern this time, by showing what Olivia calls variously "scorn . . . contempt . . . anger." But Olivia must recognize a depth of feeling in Viola/Cesario's words because, after two lines spoken aside, she declares her love yet again, without any reserve. Perhaps she kneels before the servant, or takes the hand which had earlier been refused. Finally Olivia struggles to give Cesario reasons for accepting her love, as if aware of the madness of what she is proposing.

Viola's last speech is firm (and in rhyme, like Olivia's), and it will be tempting for the actress to leave on her own last words so that Olivia's concluding couplet has to be spoken as she is moving away or perhaps already offstage. But Viola's words are also considerate—she uses "*good* madam" for the first time in this scene—and she may be deeply moved by Olivia's fate, which is not altogether unlike her own. Possibly they both stand still for a last silent moment, either facing each other or turned away, both uncertain of the future. They would then leave in different directions, but at the same time and with something of the same sense of bewilderment and determination.

24

All's Well That Ends Well

Act I, Scene iii

HELENA and the COUNTESS

✠

Helena, "a poor physician's daughter", has been overheard talking aloud to herself of her hopeless love for the Countess's son Bertram, who has recently left for the King's court in Paris. This confirms the Countess's own suspicions. She calls Helena in to discuss the predicament.

When Helena's father had died, he had bequested his only daughter to the care of the Countess, who has come to "love [her] gentlewoman entirely" (I. iii. 100-1).

✠

HELENA
What is your pleasure madam?
COUNTESS   You know, Helen,
I am a mother to you.
HELENA
Mine honorable mistress.
COUNTESS   Nay a mother.
Why not a mother? When I said "a mother"
Methought you saw a serpent. What's in "mother"   5
That you start at it? I say I am your mother
And put you in the catalogue of those
That were enwombed mine. 'Tis often seen
Adoption strives with nature and choice breeds
A native slip to us from foreign seeds.   10
You ne'er oppressed me with a mother's groan
Yet I express to you a mother's care.

9-10 **choice...seeds** when we choose   as if it were from native stock
a slip for grafting we consider it   12 **express to** show, manifest

God's mercy, maiden, does it curd thy blood
To say I am thy mother? What's the matter
That this distempered messenger of wet,   15
The many-colored Iris, rounds thine eye?
Why, that you are my daughter?

HELENA   That I am not.

COUNTESS
I say I am your mother.

HELENA   Pardon madam;
The Count Rousillon cannot be my brother.
I am from humble, he from honored name;   20
No note upon my parents, his all noble.
My master, my dear lord he is; and I
His servant live and will his vassal die.
He must not be my brother.

COUNTESS   Nor I your mother?

HELENA
You are my mother, madam; would you were—   25
So that my lord, your son, were not my brother—
Indeed my mother! Or were you both our mothers,
I care no more for than I do for heaven
So I were not his sister. Can't no other
But, I your daughter, he must be my brother?   30

COUNTESS
Yes Helen, you might be my daughter-in-law.
God shield you mean it not! "Daughter" and
    "mother"
So strive upon your pulse! What, pale again?
My fear hath catched your fondness! Now I see
The myst'ry of your loneliness and find   35

---

15 **distempered** vexed/inclement
    messenger of wet i.e., precursor
    of many tears
16 **many-colored Iris** i.e., tear-drop
    (Iris was **messenger** of the gods,
    the rainbow her path)
17 **That . . . not** (pun on **daughter-
    in-law**)

21 **note** distinction, honor
23 **vassal** feudal dependent, slave
25 **mother** (in sense of patroness,
    superior)
29 **Can't no other** cannot it be oth-
    erwise
32 **shield** forbid
34 **fondness** foolishness/infatuation

Your salt tears' head. Now to all sense 'tis gross:
You love my son! Invention is ashamed
Against the proclamation of thy passion,
To say thou dost not. Therefore tell me true—
But tell me then 'tis so, for look thy cheeks   40
Confess it t' one to th' other and thine eyes
See it so grossly shown in thy behaviors
That in their kind they speak it. Only sin
And hellish obstinacy tie thy tongue,
That truth should be suspected. Speak, is't so?   45
If it be so, you have wound a goodly clew;
If it be not, forswear't. Howe'er I charge thee,
As heaven shall work in me for thine avail,
To tell me truly.

HELENA   Good madam, pardon me!

COUNTESS
Do you love my son!

HELENA   Your pardon, noble mistress!   50

COUNTESS
Love you my son?

HELENA   Do not you love him, madam?

COUNTESS
Go not about; my love hath in't a bond
Whereof the world takes note. Come, come, disclose
The state of your affection for your passions
Have to the full appeached.

HELENA   Then I confess,   55
Here on my knee before high heaven and you,
That before you and next unto high heaven
I love your son.
My friends were poor but honest; so's my love.
Be not offended for it hurts not him   60
That he is loved of me. I follow him not

---

36 **head** source; **gross** obvious
43 **in their kind** in their own way
   (i.e., with tears)
46 **clew** ball of thread/intricate key
   to a labyrinth

48 **avail** advantage
55 **appeached** accused
59 **friends** relatives

By any token of presumptuous suit
Nor would I have him till I do deserve him—
Yet never know how that desert should be.
I know I love in vain, strive against hope,   65
Yet in this captious and intenable sieve
I still pour in the waters of my love
And lack not to lose still. Thus Indian-like,
Religious in mine error, I adore
The sun that looks upon his worshipper   70
But knows of him no more. My dearest madam
Let not your hate encounter with my love
For loving where you do; but if yourself,
Whose aged honor cites a virtuous youth,
Did ever in so true a flame of liking   75
Wish chastely and love dearly that your Dian
Was both herself and Love, O then give pity
To her whose state is such that cannot choose
But lend and give where she is sure to lose,
That seeks not to find that her search implies   80
But riddle-like lives sweetly where she dies.

COUNTESS

Had you not lately an intent—speak truly—
To go to Paris?

HELENA   Madam, I had.

COUNTESS   Wherefore? Tell true.

HELENA

I will tell truth, by grace itself I swear.
You know my father left me some prescriptions   85
Of rare and proved effects, such as his reading
And manifest experience had collected

---

62 **token** sign, expression
66 **captious** capacious/ensnaring
    intenable unretentive, incapable
    of containing
67 **still** continually
68 **lack . . . still** (1) do not fail to
    lose continually (2) do not lack a
    continuous ability to lose

74 **cites** is evidence of
76 **Dian** (Diana, chaste goddess of
    the hunt)
77 **Love** god of love
80 **that** what
81 **lives . . . dies** (wordplay on **lives**
    = dwells and **dies** = loves)

For general sovereignty, and that he willed me
In heedfull'st reservation to bestow them
As notes whose faculties inclusive were   90
More than they were in note. Amongst the rest
There is a remedy—approved, set down—
To cure the desperate languishings whereof
The king is rendered lost.

COUNTESS   This was your motive
For Paris, was it? Speak.   95

HELENA

My lord your son made me to think of this,
Else Paris and the medicine and the king
Had from the conversation of my thoughts
Haply been absent then.

COUNTESS   But think you Helen,
If you should tender your supposed aid,   100
He would receive it? He and his physicians
Are of a mind: he that they cannot help him,
They that they cannot help. How shall they credit
A poor unlearned virgin when the schools,
Emboweled of their doctrine, have left off   105
The danger to itself?

HELENA   There's something in't
More than my father's skill which was the great'st
Of his profession, that his good receipt
Shall for my legacy be sanctified
By th' luckiest stars in heaven, and would your honor   110
But give me leave to try success, I'd venture
The well-lost life of mine on his grace's cure

---

88 **sovereignty** supreme excellence
89 **heedfull'st reservation** strictest secrecy
90-91 **notes . . . in note** prescriptions (notes) whose inherent effectiveness was greater than was reputed (**in note**)
92 **approved** tested
93 **languishings** lingering disease

94 **rendered** given out to be
104 **schools** medical faculty
105 **Emboweled . . . doctrine** emptied of their learning
  left off abandoned
108 **that** so that
  receipt prescription
111 **try success** test the outcome

By such a day and hour.
COUNTESS   Dost thou believe't?
HELENA
Ay madam, knowingly.
COUNTESS
Why Helen, thou shalt have my leave and love,   115
Means and attendants, and my loving greetings
To those of mine in court. I'll stay at home
And pray God's blessing into thy attempt.
Be gone tomorrow and be sure of this:
What I can help thee to thou shalt not miss.   *Exeunt.*   120

---

114   **knowingly** from experience

✠

Rehearsing the Scene

The Countess wants to confirm that Helena loves her son;
while Helena on the other hand wishes to hide her affections,
not suspecting that her secret has been discovered. At the end tables have been turned: they both want Helena to succeed; but
the Countess can only "pray", whereas Helena has a plan she is
determined to put into action.

Even in sympathetic company Helena is private and secretive
(see the incomplete verse at lines 2 and 58). She tries to ward off
discovery by pretending to misunderstand what is said to her.
But her strategy is not wholly successful. Sudden shifts of syntax
and insistent repetitions betray the tension within her; and even-
tually one tear, followed by many, betrays it openly.

Helena fears her love of Bertram and her love of the Countess
must be mutually exclusive. Her initial struggle in the scene is to
maintain the integrity of her relationship with the Countess.
When her secret passion for Bertram inevitably erupts she naturally fears that she will lose them both. The actress's hardest task
is to give conviction to her long delay before she confesses her
love. Attention to the huge social difference between the Count-

ess and herself will help by suggesting ways in which respect and dependence can be shown. A desperation is also needed, and here the powerful images Helena uses to express her thoughts can be used to create a convincing inner reality. Helena equates her love for Bertram with the images of pouring water into a large sieve (ll. 66-68), adoring the inanimate sun (ll 69-71) and lending money to someone who will never repay (ll 78-79). These images can both provide a sense of painful actuality which the actress can use for "as if"s to enliven her creation of character. The actress can speak of Bertram *as if* he were the sun which she begs for a favor and which can neither hear nor respond to her entreaties. She can speak of her love *as if* it were a gift forced from her against her will to be given to a totally unworthy person. Helena has to be prepared to "live sweetly where she dies" (l. 81): if "sweet" implies pleasure, comfort and pleasing, and if "die" means sexual love (as it often did in Renaissance love poetry), the "riddle" Helena lives with implies an intense mixture of pain and delight. By the end of her confession Helena may speak with hard irony. Having explored the sources of Helena's imagery, an actress should be acquainted with some of the bitterness Helena may feel. There is a strength of mind in her rhythms and in the versification, as well as sensitivity.

At the end of the scene Helena has to believe that she alone possesses a cure for the king's ailment which the greatest medical authorities have been unable to remedy. She is prepared to risk her life to put this plan into effect (see lines 111-13) and silences the Countess's opposition. In the play it becomes clear that she plans to use this seeming miracle to gain authority from the king to choose Bertram as her husband; but here she says nothing about this. She becomes secretive once again at the end of the scene, but she is much stronger than at the beginning.

In coaxing Helena to divulge her secret the Countess uses many strategies: firmness, humor, careful argument, circuitous eloquence, simple assurance of affectionate regard. Perhaps she even laughs at the young girl's attempts to evade truth-telling—see, for example, "Go not about" (l. 52), by which time the most loving "mother" might be excused for showing some impatience. The Countess seems to be a sensitive and resourceful counselor, but other approaches can be effective. Another, and perhaps older, version of the Countess could be a powerful lady used to Helena's flattery, and everyone else's: she is impatient at the world and at this young person's delay. She might be tetchy, curt and loud: certain phrases she uses can, on second thoughts, belong more to Alice in Wonderland and fantasy than to polite and elegant society: "I say I am your mother . . . Nor I your mother . . . What, pale again . . . Speak, is't so? If it be so . . ." It will not be surprising when this countess seems to forget all about her son as soon as Helena starts speaking about curing the king; it might even seem to an audience that she wants Helena to fail in her cure, and so to be rid of her. Such a Countess would be totally different from the one usually presented; but it would be interesting to attempt her, at least in rehearsal. There is something not quite acceptable in the Countess's assurance and the pressure she exerts on the defenseless Helena.

25

Othello

Act IV, Scene iii

EMILIA and DESDEMONA

✠

Othello has just ordered Desdemona to "Get you to bed on th' instant," promising to "be returned forthwith." In the two previous scenes he has struck and humiliated her in public and denounced her as a whore in private. He has appeared so crazed and blinded by jealousy that Lodovico, sent to Cyprus on official business to the Commander of this island outpost, has been shocked and amazed:

> Is this the noble Moor, whom our full senate
> Call all-in-all sufficient? Is this the nature
> Whom passion could not shake?   (IV.i.266-68)

Emilia, who has come from Venice to attend on Othello's new bride, has seen a great deal, but not all, of this violence:

> Hath she forsook so many noble matches,
> Her father and her country, all her friends,
> To be called whore? Would it not make one weep?
>   (IV.ii.124-26)

The two women find themselves alone in the Moor's private apartment.

✠

EMILIA How goes it now? He looks gentler than he did.

DESDEMONA
He says he will return incontinent
And hath commanded me to go to bed
And bade me to dismiss you.

3 **incontinent** immediately

EMILIA   Dismiss me?   5

DESDEMONA

It was his bidding; therefore, good Emilia,
Give me my nightly wearing and adieu.
We must not now displease him.

EMILIA   I would you had never seen him!

DESDEMONA

So would not I. My love doth so approve him   10
That even his stubbornness, his checks, his frowns—
Prithee unpin me—have grace and favor.

EMILIA   I have laid these sheets you bade me on the
bed.

DESDEMONA

All's one. Good Father, how foolish are our minds!   15
If I do die before, prithee shroud me
In one of these same sheets.

EMILIA   Come, come! You talk.

DESDEMONA

My mother had a maid called Barbary.
She was in love and he she loved proved mad
And did forsake her. She had a song of "Willow,"   20
An old thing 'twas but it expressed her fortune
And she died singing it. That song tonight
Will not go from my mind; I have much to do
But to go hang my head all at one side
And sing it like poor Barbary. Prithee dispatch.   25

EMILIA

Shall I go fetch your nightgown?

DESDEMONA

No, unpin me here.
This Lodovico is a proper man.

EMILIA   A very handsome man.

DESDEMONA   He speaks well.   30

---

11 **checks** rebukes
12 **Prithee** I pray thee (colloquial)
15 **All's one** it does not matter
17 **talk** talk nonsense

19 **mad** unstable, faithless
26 **nightgown** dressing gown
28 **proper** fine/attractive/honest

EMILIA I know a lady in Venice would have walked
  barefoot to Palestine for a touch of his nether lip.
DESDEMONA (*Sings.*)
     "The poor soul sat singing by a sycamore tree,
       Sing all a green willow;
     Her hand on her bosom, her head on her knee,
       Sing willow, willow, willow.
     The fresh streams ran by her and murmured her moans,
       Sing willow, willow, willow;
     Her salt tears fell from her, and soft'ned the stones,
       Sing willow, willow, willow—"   40
  Lay by these.   (*Gives* EMILIA *her clothes or jewels.*)
         "Willow, Willow"—
  Prithee hie thee; he'll come anon.
     "Sing all a green willow must be my garland.
     Let nobody blame him; his scorn I approve"—
  Nay, that's not next. Hark! Who is't that knocks?   45
EMILIA It is the wind.
DESDEMONA (*Sings.*)
     "I called my love false love, but what said he then?
       Sing willow, willow, willow;
     If I court moe women, you'll couch with moe men."
  So get thee gone; good night. Mine eyes do itch,   50
  Doth that bode weeping?
EMILIA   'Tis neither here nor there.
DESDEMONA
  I have heard it said so. O these men, these men!
  Dost thou in conscience think, tell me, Emilia,
  That there be women do abuse their husbands
  In such gross kind?
EMILIA   There be some such, no question.   55
DESDEMONA
  Wouldst thou do such a deed for all the world?
EMILIA
  Why, would not you?

42 **hie** hurry; **anon** at once   49 **moe** more
43 **green . . . garland** (emblem of
    forsaken lovers)

DESMEMONA   No, by this heavenly light!

EMILIA
Nor I neither by this heavenly light;
I might do't as well i' th' dark.

DESDEMONA
Wouldst thou do such a deed for all the world?   60

EMILIA The world's a huge thing; it is a great price
for a small vice.

DESDEMONA
In troth, I think thou wouldst not.

EMILIA In troth, I think I should, and undo't when I
had done. Marry, I would not do such a thing for a   65
joint-ring nor for measures of lawn, nor for gowns,
petticoats, nor caps, nor any petty exhibition, but
for all the whole world? Ud's pity, who would not
make her husband a cuckold to make him a
monarch? I should venture purgatory for't.   70

DESDEMONA
Beshrew me if I would do such a wrong
For the whole world.

EMILIA Why the wrong is but a wrong i' th' world; and
having the world for your labor, 'tis a wrong in
your own world and you might quickly make it right.   75

DESDEMONA I do not think there is any such woman.

EMILIA Yes, a dozen, and as many to th' vantage as would
store the world they played for.
But I do think it is their husbands' faults
If wives do fall. Say that they slack their duties   80
And pour our treasures into foreign laps
Or else break out in peevish jealousies,
Throwing restraint upon us; or say they strike us

---

57 **this . . . light** the moon
66 **joint-ring** ring made of two separable halves; **lawn** fine linen
67 **exhibition** gift, allowance
68 **Ud's** God's
71 **Beshrew** curse on

77 **to th' vantage** in addition
78 **store** populate
80 **duties** sexual duties as husbands
81 **foreign** other than their wives'
83 **Throwing** inflicting

Or scant our former having in despite—
Why we have galls; and though we have some grace,   85
Yet have we some revenge. Let husbands know
Their wives have sense like them: they see and smell,
And have their palates both for sweet and sour,
As husbands have. What is it that they do
When they change us for others? Is it sport?   90
I think it is. And doth affection breed it?
I think it doth. Is't frailty that thus errs?
It is so too. And have not we affections,
Desires for sport and frailty, as men have?
Then let them use us well; else let them know,   95
The ills we do, their ills instruct us so.

DESDEMONA
Good night, good night. Heaven me such uses send,
Not to pick bad from bad, but by bad mend.   *Exeunt.*

---

84 **having** allowance (with sexual allusion); **in despite** out of spite
85 **have galls** feel resentment
90 **change** exchange
91 **affection** feeling, desire
96 **so** to do likewise

97 **uses** ways of living. profits
98 **Not . . . mend** not to find occasion for evil-doing in bad fortune, but to learn from it

✠

Rehearsing the Scene

Lines 15-17 show that Desdemona's restrained and loyal words at the beginning of this scene hide other thoughts—of death and of her wedding night. Desdemona goes on, in growing intimacy, to recall the song of a forsaken maid-servant. She sings it clearly at first, but as she prepares for bed she confuses the words. The sad, quiet song, the deliberate undressing and other preparations—perhaps Emilia brushes her hair—together with talk about an attractive man and a stillness which allows the women to hear, or think they hear, the wind outside the door—can all serve to create a sense of calm before a storm; so Desdemona will seem secure in her own generous and committed love for Othello. But alternatively, with hesitant and broken singing, sudden and sharp shifts in voice and quick apprehensive glances, the mood can be tense, nervous and pained; so Desdemona will seem to be struggling to continue loyal in face of her husband's brutality, partly covering her alarm and partly seeking to distract her own thoughts. "O these men, these men" (l. 52) introduces a new tone. Desdemona can be truly in search of answers to her questions, and almost culpably naive; or she can know very well what Emilia will say, and so seem to be trying, gently and reflectively, to understand her own lack of anger against her husband. However Emilia makes sure that, sooner or later, the two women are laughing together in a shared intimacy.

When Desdemona insists on the faithfulness of all women—whether in jest or earnest—Emilia replies with a more sustained speech, remarkable for its vigor and plain speaking at any time but, in Shakespeare's day, wholly exceptional as a claim for women's equal rights with men and as a warning to husbands. Emilia holds attention easily, but the actress can choose one of several interpretations: is Emilia passionate in denunciation, or resentful, or careful, or self-deprecating? Does she pause at all? Syntax and versification offer the best opportunities for doing so only at the very beginning, and towards the end of the speech. And how does Desdemona listen? She will leave the stage at the opposite side, but does she embrace Emilia before doing so?

SCENES
FOR
TWO
ACTORS

26

Henry VI, Part Three

Act V, Scene vi

RICHARD, Duke of Gloucester, and KING HENRY VI

✠

Henry VI became king as a mere child. At once his uncles and other powerful nobles started the remorseless series of intrigues, battles and murders known as the Wars of the Roses, between the two houses of York and Lancaster.

Henry VI, a Lancastrian, had married a French princess, Margaret of Anjou, angering the Yorkists. Later in his reign he tried many times to negotiate a peace with the Yorkists, even by disinheriting his own son, Prince Edward. In the inevitable battles which followed, Henry's army was repeatedly defeated. After the Battle of Towton, he was hounded down, captured and imprisoned.

The Lancastrian struggle was carried on by Margaret on behalf of their son, Prince Edward. After defeat at the Battle of Tewksbury however she was forced to witness the fatal stabbing of her son by the three Yorkist brothers: Edward, now King, George, Duke of Clarence, and Richard, Duke of Gloucester.

The youngest brother Richard, born misshapen, nonetheless dreamed of "sovereignty," deciding:

> My eye's too quick, my heart o'erweens too much,
> Unless my hand and strength could equal them.

(III.ii.144-45)

He takes a leading part in making his elder brother king and then proceeds to strengthen his own position:

> since this earth affords no joy to me
> But to command, to check, to o'erbear such
> As are of better person than myself,
> I'll make my heaven to dream upon the crown,
> And, whiles I live, t' account this world but hell
> Until my misshaped trunk that bears this head

Be round impaled with a glorious crown.   (III.ii.165-71)

In this scene, Richard visits Henry in prison.

✠

RICHARD
Good day, my lord. What, at your book so hard?
KING HENRY
Ay my good lord—"my lord," I should say rather.
'Tis sin to flatter. "Good" was little better.
"Good Gloucester" and "good devil" were alike
And both preposterous, therefore not "good lord."   5
RICHARD
Sirrah leave us to ourselves; we must confer.
KING HENRY
So flies the reckless shepherd from the wolf;
So first the harmless sheep doth yield his fleece
And next his throat unto the butcher's knife.
What scene of death hath Roscius now to act?   10
RICHARD
Suspicion always haunts the guilty mind;
The thief doth fear each bush an officer.
KING HENRY
The bird that hath been limed in a bush,
With trembling wings misdoubteth every bush,
And I, the hapless male to one sweet bird,   15
Have now the fatal object in my eye
Where my poor young was limed, was caught and
    killed.

---

5 **preposterous** against natural order, without sense
6 **Sirrah** (used to address inferiors)
7 **reckless** uncaring
10 **Roscius** renowned Roman actor
13 **limed** caught with birdlime (a sticky substance used to trap birds)
14 **misdoubteth** is suspicious of
15 **hapless . . . bird** i.e., unfortunate father of a young son (whom Richard has already slain)
16 **fatal object** one, particular ominous instrument

RICHARD

    Why what a peevish fool was that of Crete

    That taught his son the office of a fowl!

    And yet for all his wings the fool was drowned.   20

KING HENRY

    I, Daedalus; my poor boy, Icarus;

    Thy father, Minos that denied our course;

    The sun that seared the wings of my sweet boy,

    Thy brother Edward; and thyself the sea

    Whose envious gulf did swallow up his life.   25

    Ah, kill me with thy weapon, not with words!

    My breast can better brook thy dagger's point

    Than can my ears that tragic history.

    But wherefore dost thou come? Is't for my life?

RICHARD

    Think'st thou I am an executioner?   30

KING HENRY

    A persecutor I am sure thou art.

    If murdering innocents be executing,

    Why then thou art an executioner.

RICHARD

    Thy son I killed for his presumption.

KING HENRY

    Hadst thou been killed when first thou didst presume,   35

    Thou hadst not lived to kill a son of mine.

    And thus I prophesy, that many a thousand

    Which now mistrust no parcel of my fear

    And many an old man's sigh and many a widow's,

    And many an orphan's water-standing eye—   40

    Men for their sons, wives for their husbands,

    Orphans for their parents' timeless death—

---

18 **that of Crete** i.e., Daedalus who made wings for himself and his son so that they could escape from King Minos of Crete

19 **office** function

22 **denied our course** refused us permission to go

25 **gulf** i.e., the sea's gullet

27 **brook** endure

38 **parcel** part

40 **water-standing** flooded with water

42 **timeless** premature

Shall rue the hour that ever thou wast born.
The owl shrieked at thy birth, an evil sign;
The night-crow cried, aboding luckless time; 45
Dogs howled and hideous tempest shook down trees;
The raven rooked her on the chimney's top
And chatt'ring pies in dismal discords sung.
Thy mother felt more than a mother's pain
And yet brought forth less than a mother's hope, 50
To wit, an indigested and deformed lump,
Not like the fruit of such a goodly tree.
Teeth hadst thou in thy head when thou wast born
To signify thou cam'st to bite the world;
And if the rest be true which I have heard, 55
Thou cams't—

RICHARD
I'll hear no more. Die prophet, in thy speech.

Stabs him.

For this, amongst the rest, was I ordained.

KING HENRY
Ay, and for much more slaughter after this.
O God forgive my sins and pardon thee! *Dies.* 60

RICHARD
What? Will the aspiring blood of Lancaster
Sink in the ground? I thought it would have mounted.
See how my sword weeps for the poor king's death!
O may such purple tears be always shed
From those that wish the downfall of our house! 65
If any spark of life be yet remaining,
Down, down to hell and say I sent thee thither—

Stabs him again.

I that have neither pity, love nor fear.
Indeed 'tis true that Henry told me of,
For I have often heard my mother say 70
I came into the world with my legs forward.
Had I not reason, think ye, to make haste

45 **aboding** foreboding   48 **pies** magpies
47 **rooked her** crouched

And seek their ruin that usurped our right?
The midwife wondered and the women cried,
"O Jesus bless us, he is born with teeth!"   75
And so I was which plainly signified
That I should snarl and bite and play the dog.
Then since the heavens have shaped my body so,
Let hell make crook'd my mind to answer it.
I have no brother, I am like no brother;   80
And this word "love" which graybeards call divine,
Be resident in men like one another
And not in me. I am myself alone.
Clarence beware: thou keep'st me from the light,
But I will sort a pitchy day for thee   85
For I will buzz abroad such prophecies
That Edward shall be fearful of his life
And then to purge his fear I'll be thy death.
King Henry and the prince his son are gone:
Clarence thy turn is next, and then the rest,   90
Counting myself but bad till I be best.
I'll throw thy body in another room
And triumph Henry, in thy day of doom.

Exit with the body.

79 **answer** correspond, retaliate	86 **buzz abroad** spread news around
	88 **purge** clear, get rid of

☧

Rehearsing the Scene

While the form of this scene appears to depend simply on the two long solo speeches, the action of the scene depends on interaction between them: the killing of a king, without form of justice and without chance of escape.

Henry senses his fate from the very beginning of the scene. Immersed in the moral meditation of his reading, he responds with a polite reflex to Richard's greeting. Once shaken from his reverie and recognizing Richard's blatant villainy, he adjusts his language to reflect his disgust and repugnance. Here his phrasing is short and broken: he is not making a speech but marking fresh discoveries of his feelings as he speaks.

Henry probably speaks compulsively. His imagery suggests how he feels as he faces his executioner: first like a sheep abandoned by its shepherd, then like an actor about to perform. Other images follow that are more strongly developed: a trapped bird, and finally a man at peril who tried to escape by flying up towards the sun. At line 26, Henry changes: as Richard stands waiting, the frightened man is suddenly aware that his verbal thrusts are futile against Richard's determined strength. He now wants to cut short the agony.

Why does Richard delay? Does he enjoy taunting Henry? Does he need time to prepare for the killing? His sword is unlikely to be drawn already, because he dismisses the Lieutenant of the Tower with the excuse of wanting to "confer." (If someone is available to enter with Richard and then leave, as the Lieutenant, his silent obedience can heighten tension; but for working on this scene, or indeed playing it, he can be imagined standing out of sight, beyond the prison door.) The actor playing Richard should be familiar with how he feels justified in promoting the Yorkist cause. By implying that Henry is "guilty" (ll. 11-12), Richard offers justification for his action. Without adequate exploration of Richard's motives he will turn into a very predictable villain.

Provoked by Richard's off-hand justification of the murder of Henry's son, which Richard attributes to Edward's presumption, Henry now begins an eloquent condemnation of Richard. During the prophesy that follows Henry's rhythms become stronger; he now reminds Richard of the omens at the time of his birth, and he finishes by castigating the crookbacked prince for his deformity. It is at this point that Richard strikes, determined to expunge Henry's vulgar interpretation of his providential birth, proud to be what he is. Does Henry speak out of spite to Richard, or with the complete freedom that only a man about to die may enjoy?

Even as he is mortally wounded Henry may feel the satisfaction of having proved, if nothing else, his rhetorical point, as he claims the final prophetical statement: "Ay, and for much more slaughter after this." His final 2 lines do not form a composed couplet, but two contrasted utterances. His second line is a prayer for forgiveness for himself and pardon for Richard. How much does Henry have to struggle to speak and to bear his pain? Clearly blood is spilt and visible (line 63). Does Henry pray truly and compassionately for his murderer, or do his last words express panic, combining denunciation, self-concern and piety in unresolved conflict with each other?

Richard's inelegant "What?" in response to Henry's final speech may show his agitation at Henry's plea for the pardon of his murderer. It may also evidence shock at Henry's brief rally at the end. Even now he seems to endow Henry's blood with a certain vitality as he addresses Henry still: "Down, down to hell and say I sent thee thither." Richard stabs Henry's corpse again perhaps out of a perverse fear of the power which still resides inside it.

Satisfied that his enemy is dispatched, he now passionately puts forth the arguments for his own cause which he had failed to do while Henry lived. Richard's soliloquy has great energy, fired by a sense of himself and sharpened with humor and economy of phrase. Much of it can be said to the audience (see "think ye" of line 72), inviting them to share his vision and his humor, and then separating himself from everybody at "I am myself alone." Or perhaps he is so obsessed with himself that he talks to himself, impressing himself or goading himself forward, because he cannot rest. He retreats towards the close into thoughts about the immediate future.

Before Richard leaves the stage he has to lift Henry's body in order to "throw" it in another room: lifting a dead weight is never easy and yet to drag the body offstage would be against the implication of Richard's words. Some actors will manage the lift with apparent ease, but it can be effective in another way if Richard has to struggle to live up to the aspiration of what he says.

King John
Act IV, Scene ii
HUBERT and KING JOHN

✠

King John had inherited the English throne as the chosen heir of his older brother, the famous hero of the Crusades, Richard Coeur-de-Lion. But his right to do so is uncertain because Richard was survived by his very young son, Prince Arthur. In the play, the King of France fights in support of Arthur, but John gains possession of the young prince, takes him away from his mother and places him in prison.

Hubert, a politician who has given a "voluntary oath" to serve John, is summoned to a private conference by the king, who tells him that Arthur is "a very serpent in my way" (III.iii.61). When Hubert replies that he will keep the boy so that "he shall not offend your Majesty," the following dialogue ensues:

KING JOHN: Death.
HUBERT: My lord?
KING JOHN: A grave.
HUBERT: He shall not live
KING JOHN: Enough . . .
    I could be merry now. Hubert, I love thee . . .

Hubert set about trying to blind Arthur in prison, so to make him incapable of kingship while stopping short of killing him. But then he listened to the boy's pathetic entreaties and spared him entirely. Hubert reports to the king that he has obeyed instructions and killed Arthur. Everyone had expected that John would act against Arthur, and so when he reports his death, the nobles blame the king and walk out.

The king sends messengers to win back the support of his nobles.

It is at this point that Hubert enters.

✠

Enter HUBERT *to* KING JOHN.

HUBERT
My lord, they say five moons were seen tonight:
Four fixèd and the fifth did whirl about
The other four in wondrous motion.

KING JOHN
Five moons?

HUBERT   Old men and beldams in the streets
Do prophesy upon it dangerously;   5
Young Arthur's death is common in their mouths
And, when they talk of him, they shake their heads
And whisper one another in the ear,
And he that speaks doth gripe the hearer's wrist
Whilst he that hears makes fearful action   10
With wrinkled brows, with nods, with rolling eyes.
I saw a smith stand with his hammer, thus,
The whilst his iron did on the anvil cool,
With open mouth swallowing a tailor's news;
Who, with his shears and measure in his hand,   15
Standing on slippers, which his nimble haste
Had falsely thrust upon contrary feet,
Told of a many thousand warlike French
That were embattailèd and ranked in Kent.
Another lean unwashed artificer   20

3 **wondrous** miraculous
4 **beldams** old women
5 **prophesy . . . dangerously** predict disasters from this sign/start politically dangerous rumors from it.
6 **is . . . mouths** is much talked about

10 **makes . . . action** reacts fearfully
12 **thus** (Hubert demonstrates, with hand poised in air)
18 **a . . . thousand** many thousands of
19 **embattailèd** ready for battle
20 **artificer** skilled workman

Cuts off his tale and talks of Arthur's death.

KING JOHN

Why seek'st thou to possess me with these fears?
Why urgest thou so oft young Arthur's death?
Thy hand hath murdered him: I had a mighty cause
To wish him dead but thou hadst none to kill him.   25

HUBERT

No had, my lord? Why, did you not provoke me?

KING JOHN

It is the curse of kings to be attended
By slaves that take their humors for a warrant
To break within the bloody house of life
And on the winking of authority   30
To understand a law, to know the meaning
Of dangerous majesty when perchance it frowns
More upon humor than advised respect.

HUBERT

Here is your hand and seal for what I did.

KING JOHN

O when the last accompt twixt heaven and earth   35
Is to be made, then shall this hand and seal
Witness against us to damnation!
How oft the sight of means to do ill deeds
Make deeds ill done! Hadst not thou been by,
A fellow by the hand of nature marked,   40
Quoted and signed to do a deed of shame,
This murder had not come into my mind;
But taking note of thy abhorred aspect,
Finding thee fit for bloody villainy,

22 **possess me** inform me/fill my mind
24 **cause** matter of dispute, contention
26 **No had** had I not
   provoke urge, incite
28 **humors** whims
29 **bloody . . . life** i.e., the body
30-31 **on . . . law** to take as a law the oversights (or slightest reactions) of powerful people
33 **advised respect** mature reflection, discrimination
34 **hand** signature
35 **last . . . earth** Day of Judgement
39 **deeds ill done** evil deeds done/deeds done badly
   by present
41 **Quoted** noted, marked
   signed significantly marked/assigned

Apt, liable to be employed in danger,   45
I faintly broke with thee of Arthur's death
And thou, to be endearèd to a king,
Made it no conscience to destroy a prince.

HUBERT

My lord.

KING JOHN

Hadst thou but shook thy head or made a pause   50
When I spake darkly what I purposèd,
Or turned an eye of doubt upon my face,
As bid me tell my tale in express words,
Deep shame had struck me dumb, made me break off,
And those thy fears might have wrought fears in me. 55
But thou didst understand me by my signs
And didst in signs again parley with sin;
Yea, without stop, didst let thy heart consent,
And consequently thy rude hand to act
The deed which both our tongues held vile to name. 60
Out of my sight and never see me more!
My nobles leave me and my state is braved,
Even at my gates, with ranks of foreign pow'rs;
Nay, in the body of this fleshly land,
This kingdom, this confine of blood and breath,   65
Hostility and civil tumult reigns
Between my conscience and my cousin's death.

HUBERT

Arm you against your other enemies:
I'll make a peace between your soul and you.
Young Arthur is alive! This hand of mine   70
Is yet a maiden and an innocent hand,
Not painted with the crimson spots of blood.

---

45 **liable** suitable
46 **faintly . . . of** lightly touched on the subject of
48 **Made . . . destroy** showed no scruples about killing
51 **darkly** secretly, obscurely
53 **As** as if to

57 **sin** (wordplay on **sign/sin**)
58 **stop** hesitation
62 **state is braved** power is defied
64 **in . . . land** within my own body
65 **confine** confinement/prison
71 **maiden** unblemished

Within this bosom never entered yet
The dreadful motion of a murderous thought,
And you have slandered nature in my form   75
Which, howsoever rude exteriorly,
Is yet the cover of a fairer mind
Than to be butcher of an innocent child.

KING JOHN

Doth Arthur live? O haste thee to the peers!
Throw this report on their incensèd rage   80
And make them tame to their obedience.
Forgive the comment that my passion made
Upon thy feature, for my rage was blind
And foul imaginary eyes of blood
Presented thee more hideous than thou art.   85
O answer not, but to my closet bring
The angry lords with all expedient haste.
I conjure thee but slowly: run more fast.   *Exeunt.*

74 **motion** impulse
75 **form** appearance
81 **tame...obedience** submit to obeying orders as they should
84 **imaginary...blood** i.e., John's eyes which imagined blood being spilt
86 **closet** private room
88 **conjure** entreat

✠

Rehearsing the Scene

Hubert brings bad news which heightens the king's fear and guilt. John tries to put the blame on Hubert, who then reveals he has not killed Arthur. At once John sees a chance of restoring his fortunes and he sends Hubert off quickly. This drama is simple and comparitively easy to play, but the challenge and interest of the scene lie in the long speeches for both characters. These are sustained by realistic observation and vivid imagery. Hubert can seem to see the five whirling moons as he speaks and transmit the tensions of the people he describes—he may imitate their postures, perhaps gripping the king at line 9. John responds sharply to Hubert's presence, as that of a man marked by shame and cruelty, but then recreates their earlier encounter in his own mind so that the guilt rests on Hubert only. A feverish energy informs both syntax and versification. "Murder" becomes a word he can no longer use, but it haunts his thoughts.

These longer speeches are not solos; the two characters interact all the time. For example, Hubert does not go away when John orders him to do so (l. 61); John does not insist but his thoughts turn inwards again, so that he speaks first of his kingdom and then of his own body which suffers a similar tumult. Hubert listens closely and intervenes using John's imagery; then he, too, reinvents the past—it is true he has not killed Arthur, but untrue to say that he has never had a "murderous thought." He says this so urgently that John cannot respond to "Young Arthur is alive" until Hubert has done speaking nine lines later.

The actor of Hubert will be concerned because the king says he has an "abhorred" appearance and he almost acknowledges as much himself. But no ugly feature is required; indeed any misshaped or disproportioned appearance would lessen the power of this scene. What is required is more interesting: Hubert must show outward signs of involvement with cruelty, lies and subterfuge; he is a committed assassin whose nerve has given way. Besides, John sees Hubert's hideousness more horribly because of his own fears and "foul" imagination.

How Hubert responds to the king's last orders will vary in each performance: how much does Hubert want, genuinely, to help his king? The text shows that he does not leave at once, for John goes on to ask for forgiveness. (Does he stop Hubert leaving, or is Hubert waiting for such a confirmation of trust?) After line 85, Hubert may be about to answer, but if so John will stop him to urge haste once more. Does John wait, still insecure, to watch Hubert leave the stage and then go slowly himself? Or is there a moment of renewed trust between the two? They might embrace in relief; or Hubert could kneel in obedience. Or John could be too anxious to stay any longer than necessary, leaving just as soon as Hubert starts to go.

28

Henry IV, Part One

Act I, Scene ii

PRINCE HENRY and SIR JOHN FALSTAFF

✠

Young Prince Henry of Wales has slipped away from the court of his father, King Henry IV, and visits, as is his custom, a tavern in East-cheap in the City of London.

Sir John Falstaff is among a special group of the prince's friends who are important to Henry outside official duties and away from official territory. Falstaff, an old out-of-work soldier, is also enormously fat. In his youth he had attended the prestigous schools of the Inns of Law in London; now he is reduced to his own peculiar kind of genteel poverty which is neither respectable nor conventional.

✠

FALSTAFF
Now Hal, what time of day is it lad?
PRINCE Thou art so fat-witted with drinking of old sack
and unbuttoning thee after supper and sleeping
upon benches after noon, that thou hast forgotten to
demand that truly which thou wouldest truly know.
What a devil hast thou to do with the time of the   5
day? Unless hours were cups of sack and minutes
capons, and clocks the tongues of bawds and dials the
signs of leaping houses, and the blessed sun himself a
fair hot wench in flame-colored taffeta, I see no reason   10
why thou shouldst be so superfluous to demand the
time of the day.

---

2 **fat-witted** stupid, dull
  sack Spanish white wine
8 **capons** fattened, castrated cocke-
  rels;   **bawds**   procurers
  dials sundials

9 **leaping houses** brothels
10 **taffeta** silk
11 **superfluous** excessive/beside the
  point

FALSTAFF Indeed you come near me now Hal, for we that
take purses go by the moon and the seven stars
and not by Phoebus, he that "wand'ring knight so   15
fair." And I prithee sweet wag, when thou art a king,
as God save thy grace—majesty I should say, for
grace thou wilt have none—

PRINCE What, none?

FALSTAFF No by my troth, not so much as will serve to be   20
prologue to an egg and butter.

PRINCE Well how then? Come roundly, roundly.

FALSTAFF Marry then sweet wag, when thou art king let
not us that are squires of the night's body be called
thieves of the day's beauty. Let us be Diana's   25
foresters, gentlemen of the shade, minions of the
moon, and let men say we be men of good government, being governed as the sea is by our noble and
chaste mistress the moon, under whose countenance
we steal.   30

PRINCE Thou sayest well and it holds well too, for the
fortune of us that are the moon's men doth ebb and
flow like the sea, being governed as the sea is by the
moon. As for proof now: a purse of gold most
resolutely snatched on Monday night and most   35
dissolutely spent on Tuesday morning, got with

13 **near me** close to my point
14 **go by** walk by the light of/tell
  time by; **seven stars** constella-
  tion of Pleiades
15 **Phoebus** the sun
15-16 **wandering . . . fair** (from a lost
  ballad about a "knight errant")
17 **grace** (title for a king: puns follow on **grace** = spiritual quality
  and = prayer before meals)
21 **egg and butter** lenten fare
22 **Come roundly** out with it
23 **Marry** indeed (mild oath: by the
  Virgin Mary)

24 **squires . . . body** personal attendants of a knight's person/night's
  body (i.e., the moon)
25 **beauty** (pun on "booty," and
  perhaps on **body**);
  Diana the moon-goddess
26 **minions** favorites
27-28 **government** conduct
28 **governed** controlled, ruled
29 **under . . . countenance** (1) under whose protection (2) by
  whose light
30 **steal** (1) move silently (2) take
  purses
31 **holds well** can be taken further

swearing "Lay by" and spent with crying "Bring in,"
now in as low an ebb as the foot of the ladder and
by and by in as high a flow as the ridge of the gallows.

FALSTAFF By the Lord, thou say'st true lad—and is not   40
my hostess of the tavern a most sweet wench?

PRINCE As the honey of Hybla, my old lad of the castle,
and is not a buff jerkin a most sweet robe of durance?

FALSTAFF How now, how now mad wag? What, in thy
quips and thy quiddities? What a plague have I to do   45
with a buff jerkin?

PRINCE Why what a pox have I to do with my hostess
of the tavern?

FALSTAFF Well thou hast called her to a reckoning many
a time and oft.   50

PRINCE Did I ever call for thee to pay thy part?

FALSTAFF No; I'll give thee thy due, thou hast paid all
there.

PRINCE Yea and elsewhere, so far as my coin would
stretch; and where it would not, I have used my credit.   55

FALSTAFF Yea and so used it that, were it not here
apparent that thou art heir apparent . . . But I prithee
sweet wag, shall there be gallows standing in England
when thou art king? And resolution thus fubbed as
it is with the rusty curb of old father Antic the law? Do   60
not thou when thou art king, hang a thief.

PRINCE No, thou shalt.

---

37 **Lay by; Bring in** (Highwaymen's calls, to victims and to tavern-keepers)

38 **ebb** low tide (i.e., lowest rank of society)

39 **flow** rise (of a tide; with allusion to excessive drinking in a tavern, see **dissolutely spent**)

42 **Hybla** (Sicilian town famous for honey); **old . . . castle** old rake (puns on Sir John Oldcastle, Falstaff's name in early version of the play, and on "The Castle," a famous London brothel)

43 **buff** oxhide (used for coats of soldiers and Sheriff's officers) **durance** (1) confinement (2) durable cloth

44-45 **in thy . . . quiddities** are you making your usual jibes and quibbles

47 **pox** venereal disease (wordplay on **plague**)

49 **to a reckoning** (1) for the bill (2) to account

59 **resolution** courage; **fubbed** cheated (of its reward

60 **rusty curb** outdated restraint **Antic** buffoon

FALSTAFF Shall I? O rare! By the Lord I'll be a brave
    judge.
PRINCE Thou judgest false already. I mean thou shalt   65
    have the hanging of the thieves and so become a rare
    hangman.
FALSTAFF Well Hal, well; and in some sort it jumps with
    my humor as well as waiting in the court, I can tell
    you.   70
PRINCE For obtaining of suits?
FALSTAFF Yea for obtaining of suits whereof the hangman
    hath no lean wardrobe. 'Sblood, I am as melancholy
    as a gib-cat or a lugged bear.
PRINCE Or an old lion or a lover's lute.   75
FALSTAFF Yea or the drone of a Lincolnshire bagpipe.
PRINCE What sayest thou to a hare or the melancholy
    of Moorditch?
FALSTAFF Thou hast the most unsavory similes and
    art indeed the most comparative, rascalliest, sweet   80
    young prince. But Hal, I prithee trouble me no more
    with vanity. I would to God thou and I knew where
    a commodity of good names were to be bought. An
    old lord of the council rated me the other day in the
    street about you sir; but I marked him not, and yet he   85
    talked very wisely; but I regarded him not, and yet he
    talked wisely and in the street too.
PRINCE Thou didst well, for wisdom cries out in the
    streets and no man regards it.

63 **brave** (1) fine (2) fearless
68 **sort** kind; **jumps** suits (pun on
    hangman making his victims
    jump)
71 **suits** requests
72-73 **obtaining . . . wardrobe** (the
    clothes of a hanged man were
    forfeited to his **hangman**)
73 **'Sblood** By God's blood
74 **gib-cat** tomcat; **lugged** baited
77 **hare** (proverbially melancholy)
78 **Moorditch** (drainage site near
    London)

80 **comparative** full of compari-
    sons, challenging
82 **vanity** worldly concerns (a Puri-
    tan term)
83 **commodity** supply
84 **rated** scolded
85 **marked** heeded
86 **regarded** paid attention/respect
    to
88-89 **wisdom . . . regards it** (from
    Proverbs, I. 20-24)

FALSTAFF O thou hast damnable iteration and art   90
indeed able to corrupt a saint. Thou hast done much
harm upon me Hal, God forgive thee for it! Before
I knew thee Hal, I knew nothing and now am I, if a
man should speak truly, little better than one of the
wicked. I must give over this life and I will give it   95
over! By the Lord, and I do not, I am a villain! I'll be
damned for never a king's son in Christendom.

PRINCE Where shall we take a purse tomorrow Jack?

FALSTAFF Zounds, where thou wilt lad! I'll make one.
An I do not, call me villain and baffle me.   100

PRINCE I see a good amendment of life in thee: from
praying to purse-taking.

FALSTAFF Why Hal, 'tis my vocation Hal. 'Tis no sin
for a man to labor in his vocation.

90 **iteration** trick of repetition (the Devil quoted scripture)	99 **Zounds** by God's wounds
93 **knew nothing** was innocent	99 **make one** be one of the gang
94-95 **one . . . wicked** (Puritan style, again)	100 **An** if
	baffle disgrace publicly
95 **give over** renounce	103 **vocation** calling (Puritan jargon)
96 **and** if	104 **labor . . . vocation** (see I, Corinthians, vii. 20)

✠

Rehearsing the Scene

These characters contest with each other by taking each other's words and retuning them to their own purposes. Their words spring forward, almost as if they had energy within them, fueled by invention, fantasy and intimate knowledge of each other's resources. Words also set traps, create detours and spring surprises. The duologue is a game, played by two experts who enjoy each other's exploits. A sense of display and competition should run throughout.

Actors should not worry unduly about the large number of glossarial notes. Difficulty is part of any good game or contest; besides, once the notes are mastered, the speeches will have more precision and vitality. If the audience doesn't see every blow which lands on an opponent, a fight can still maintain interest. The main thing to achieve is that the actors know why they say every single word. It may be doubted whether even the original audiences would have had the knowledge or quickness of uptake to appreciate every nuance.

Prince Hal can be presented in two distinct ways. He can remain essentially uninvolved, objectively experimenting with a man as corrupt as Falstaff; he can even speak cruelly of hangmen and folly. Or he can be a young man, normally under restraint, who needs to flirt, at least, with illegality, and to grow closer to the expansive, rebellious mind of a substitute father who lives outside the law.

Falstaff, in sober fact, does need to fear the hangman because stealing was punishable by death. At the mere mention of the "gallows" (l. 39) he can be stopped dead in his tracks, until he manages to shift matters onto a quite different subject. On the other hand the same exchange can be played as if Falstaff's good humor renders him fireproof, so that he shakes off unpleasant notions very easily, without a serious thought. Talk of melancholy (l. 73 ff.) may be just another comic pose—pretending to be a fashionable, intellectual young man of high breeding and sophistication, and so mocking Hal for being so far from his natural place at his father's court.

A number of divergent interpretations of character will open up—rather like playing on a seesaw. If Falstaff feels disadvantaged, he can plummet downwards and become someone who thinks seriously of reforming himself. However Falstaff can exalt himself by his extravagant impersonation of puritanism and piety, as well as by running the marathon gamut of puns (here apparent/heir apparent, booty/beauty/body). If Hal becomes disenchanted with the game, he may descend to cruelty and mockery. If he relishes what he hears (Falstaff's journey from "Diana's foresters" to "gentlemen of the shade," to the triumphant and mellifluous "minions of the moon," with its spice of indecency), every joke can be accompanied by laughter. Their joint enterprise can become as pleasurable as a dance.

The seesaw effect starts at the beginning of the scene. Does Falstaff rouse Hal from other deeper thoughts? Or does he speak because Hal has just woken him from a deep and noisy sleep—

perhaps by throwing a bucket of cold water over him? Or do they enter together, drinking and laughing, so that Falstaff is easily offering a new subject for jest, by reminding Hal how time flies when they have fun? So the seesaw can be down at either side at the start, or nicely balanced between the two.

At line 98, however, Hal springs a question of immediate and practical importance which will provide the scene's climax. By proposing a robbery, Hal's irreverent fancy now invites a dangerous tangible consequence. Falstaff either takes it in his stride, the short phrases suggesting vigor and triumph, or he is shaken and has to struggle to live up to a role that is no longer comfortable, the short phrases coming slowly and expressing a troubled mind.

29

Henry IV, Part Two

Act IV, Scene v

KING HENRY IV and PRINCE HENRY

✠

Prince Henry had arrived at his father's deathbed and sat alone
with the king, who was so weak that he seemed to slip irrevocably
into death. The prince then took the crown, symbol of his new responsibilities, and retired into another room to weep and meditate.
Just at this moment the king revived and called for his attendants.
Hearing that Prince Henry was last seen watching by his bed, the king
concludes that his son has taken the crown because he is anxious
only to seize power for himself.

✠

KING
But wherefore did he take away the crown?

Enter PRINCE HENRY.

Lo, here he comes. Come hither to me, Harry.
Depart the chamber, leave us here alone.
PRINCE
I never thought to hear you speak again.
KING
Thy wish was father, Harry, to that thought.   5
I stay too long by thee, I weary thee.
Dost thou so hunger for mine empty chair
That thou wilt needs invest thee with my honors
Before thy hour be ripe? O foolish youth!
Thou seek'st the greatness that will overwhelm thee.   10
Stay but a little for my cloud of dignity

6 **by thee** (1) with thee (2) in your
   opinion

Is held from falling with so weak a wind
That it will quickly drop. My day is dim.
Thou hast stol'n that which after some few hours
Were thine without offense and at my death   15
Thou hast sealed up my expectation:
Thy life did manifest thou lov'dst me not
And thou wilt have me die assured of it.
Thou hid'st a thousand daggers in thy thoughts
Which thou hast whetted on thy stony heart   20
To stab at half an hour of my life.
What, canst thou not forebear me half an hour?
Then get thee gone and dig my grave thyself,
And bid the merry bells ring to thine ear
That thou art crowned, not that I am dead.   25
Let all the tears that should bedew my hearse
Be drops of balm to sanctify thy head.
Only compound me with forgotten dust;
Give that which gave thee life unto the worms.
Pluck down my officers, break my decrees,   30
For now a time is come to mock at form,
Harry the Fifth is crowned. Up, vanity!
Down, royal state! All you sage counselors, hence!
And to the English court assemble now
From every region apes of idleness!   35
Now neighbor confines purge you of your scum:
Have you a ruffian that will swear, drink, dance,
Revel the night, rob, murder and commit
The oldest sins the newest kinds of ways? —
Be happy, he will trouble you no more,   40
England shall double gild his treble guilt,
England shall give him office, honor, might,
For the fifth Harry from curbed license plucks

12 **wind** (alluding to the sick man's breath)
13 **dim** (1) clouded (2) weak
16 **sealed up** confirmed
22 **forebear me** leave me alone
27 **balm** consecrated oil (for annoint-ing the king at his coronation)
28 **compound** mix
30 **Pluck** force
31 **form** law and order
36 **confines** regions
    purge cleanse, empty out

The muzzle of restraint and the wild dog
Shall flesh his tooth on every innocent.   45
O my poor kingdom, sick with civil blows
When that my care could not withhold thy riots,
What wilt thou do when riot is thy care?
O thou wilt be a wilderness again,
Peopled with wolves, thy old inhabitants.   50

PRINCE
O pardon me, my liege! But for my tears,
The moist impediments unto my speech,
I had forestalled this dear and deep rebuke
Ere you with grief had spoke and I had heard
The course of it so far. There is your crown   55
And He that wears the crown immortally
Long guard it yours. If I affect it more
Than as your honor and as your renown,
Let me no more from this obedience rise
Which my most inward true and duteous spirit   60
Teacheth, this prostrate and exterior bending.
God witness with me, when I here came in
And found no course of breath within your majesty,
How cold it struck my heart. If I do feign,
O let me in my present wildness die   65
And never live to show th' incredulous world
The noble change that I have purposed.
Coming to look on you, thinking you dead,
And dead almost my liege to think you were,
I spake unto this crown as having sense   70
And thus upbraided it: "The care on thee depending
Hath fed upon the body of my father,
Therefore thou best of gold art worst of gold;
Other, less fine in carat, is more precious,
Preserving life in medicine potable,   75

45 **flesh** sink into flesh, initiate to
    bloodshed
47 **riots** riotous living
48 **riot . . . care** your responsibility
    is the nation's disorder
53 **dear** grievous, heartfelt

57 **affect** desire
59 **obedience** kneeling
63 **course** movement, process
74 **carat** quality
75 **medicine potable** gold in solu-
    tion (drunk as a medicine)

But thou most fine, most honored, most renowned,
Hast eat thy bearer up." Thus my most royal liege,
Accusing it, I put it on my head
To try with it as with an enemy
That had before my face murdered my father,   80
The quarrel of a true inheritor.
But if it did infect my blood with joy
Or swell my thoughts to any strain of pride,
If any rebel or vain spirit of mine
Did with the least affection of a welcome   85
Give entertainment to the might of it,
Let God forever keep it from my head
And make me as the poorest vassal is
That doth with awe and terror kneel to it.

KING

O my son,   90
God put it in thy mind to take it hence
That thou mightst win the more thy father's love,
Pleading so wisely in excuse of it!
Come hither Harry, sit thou by my bed
And hear, I think, the very latest counsel   95
That ever I shall breathe. God knows my son,
By what bypaths and indirect crooked ways
I met this crown and I myself know well
How troublesome it sat upon my head.
To thee it shall descend with better quiet,   100
Better opinion, better confirmation,
For all the soil of the achievement goes
With me into the earth. It seemed in me
But as an honor snatched with boisterous hand
And I had many living to upbraid   105
My gain of it by their assistances,
Which daily grew to quarrel and to bloodshed

79	**try** prove, test myself	95	**latest** last
83	**strain** impulse, emotion	98	**met** gained
85	**affection of** disposition towards	102	**soil** (1) stain (2) earth, dirt
88	**vassal** feudal tenant, slave	104	**boisterous** rough

Wounding supposed peace. All these bold fears
Thou see'st with peril I have answered
For all my reign hath been but as a scene   110
Acting that argument. And now my death
Changes the mood, for what in me was purchased
Falls upon thee in a more fairer sort,
So thou the garland wear'st successively.
Yet though thou stand'st more sure than I could do,   115
Thou art not firm enough since griefs are green
And all my friends, which thou must make thy friends,
Have but their stings and teeth newly ta'en out,
By whose fell working I was first advanced
And by whose power I well might lodge a fear   120
To be again displaced. Which to avoid,
I cut them off and had a purpose now
To lead out many to the Holy Land,
Lest rest and lying still might make them look
Too near unto my state. Therefore my Harry,   125
Be it thy course to busy giddy minds
With foreign quarrels that action, hence borne out,
May waste the memory of the former days.
More would I but my lungs are wasted so
That strength of speech is utterly denied me.   130
How I came by the crown, O God forgive
And grant it may with thee in true peace live!

PRINCE

My gracious liege,
You won it, wore it, kept it, gave it me:
Then plain and right must my possession be   135
Which I with more than with a common pain
'Gainst all the world will rightfully maintain.

108 **fears** causes of fear	120 **lodge** harbor
111 **argument** theme	122 **cut them off** removed them
112 **mood** mode, style	124 **look** (1) examine (2) aspire
purchased acquired (not inherited; legal term)	127 **hence bourne out** carried on elsewhere
114 **successively** by inheritance	128 **waste** efface
119 **fell** fierce, cruel	136 **pain** effort, pains

✠

Rehearsing the Scene

None of the other duologues in this book is so still and quiet as this, or so unchanging in theme and action. But the dramatic power of the scene shifts between domestic and public focus throughout. At one moment, we witness the transition power from monarch to heir. At the next, we are at the bedside of a dying father and grieving son as they impart to each other their final rites of passage.

Within this basic situation some surprising elements are used to concentrate attention and accentuate the conflict and its eventual resolution. Harry enters with the crown, but this symbol of power is not referred to directly until line 55. The sacred quality of the crown becomes defined by their avoidance of that explosive subject. Although the king mentions the crown at lines 25 and 32, it is only with reference to his son's coronation, not his own possession or loss of it. It may not be until line 55, when he speaks of the crown, that Harry returns the crown to his father's side. Harry's words(see l. 59) indicate that he is kneeling before his father , but until this moment he has probably been standing at some distance to signify the gulf that has grown between them. Instead of going straight to the bedside to sit with his father, as any son might do in such a situation, Harry waits until line 94 when his father specifically asks that he should. During the whole of the king's first speech, still holding the crown, the Prince may be uncertain where to go; he may move across the stage as he tries unsuccessfully to speak, or as he struggles with his tears (see ll. 51-55). Once he has knelt, he may remain on his knees until he speaks of the "poorest vassal" who is inspired by "awe and terror" (ll. 88-89). Until his father asks him to "Come hither," the distance between them has been of Harry's choosing, and the actor must decide what has held him back until now: guilt, awe, terror, sorrow, tact and calculated cunning are some possibilities.

The dying king seems to gain strength and vigor by speaking, as each new thought seems to grow from of the preceding one. The king is unable to sustain any one idea for more than one,

two or three lines until near the end of the speech, when he focuses on a condemnation of his son. This gives an undoubted
power of the king's speech, and a climactic structure, but there
is a question about how it should be spoken: is it unstudied, a
sincere outpouring of a father's feeling (it is very methodical for
that), or is it a carefully calculated attack, each blow judged
nicely to wound?

In contrast, the prince's speech is more sustained, its syntax
holding five and more lines together at each reach, before their
sense is fully achieved; its last sentence is built up over eight
lines. Only when speaking of his own feelings is a single sentence as short as two-and-a-half lines; with simple words, the
contrast gives the effect of a son's sincerity:

> God witness with me, when I here came in
> And found no course of breath within your majesty,
> How cold it struck my heart.   (ll. 62-64)

When Harry chastises the crown (lines 71-77) his speech may
sound particularly artificial or studied, giving credence to the
possibility that Harry is less spontaneous and possibly more
prone to feign than he has claimed at lines 59-64. Is Harry so
very aware of his own shortcomings that he becomes self-
conscious when trying to explain them? Are his arguments so
very complicated and reasonable because he is afraid of breaking
down in tears again?

The single short line, "O my son," marks the emotional center
of the scene and also the major change in its action; nowhere
else is the father so open in addressing the son. From now on
the two are very close; and the king finds new strength for confession and political advice. But his voice may grow quiet with
passion as he nears death. The king's thoughts are now more
sustained. He assures his son that his crime against his predeces-
sor Richard II will go with him "into the earth" (ll. 102-3); later,
however, he seems to indicate that the shadow of his guilt may
stay and still cross Harry's path. As his strength evaporates, his
last words become a prayer, admitting guilt but still avoiding any
mention of the assassination of Richard II. As his father declines
in strength, Harry confidently picks up the reigns of power. He
is more blunt than his father, using simple words "won . . . wore
. . . kept . . . gave" (ll. 133-35). He now asserts his own tough

and independent sense of right, and his unflinching trust in self-determination.

Both characters speak of God, and both actors should consider carefully what they mean by this word. Does either of them truly respect a higher authority and a providential power? Some Elizabethans' view of God was close to what we consider fundamentalism, and so when characters refer to God it can be as to a much more potent, less abstract figure than in modern drama. But then why do these two characters refer to God so infrequently? Do they talk of the deity only when they feel insecure or guilty? Or is God used to account for fortune in war and politics, or as a convenient way of calling for special attention or registering an oath? Why, for example, is "God" on the lips of the king at the end of the scene, whereas his son speaks only of his father's efforts and his own determination to be strong?

While in the play itself the king lingers on, the actors performing the scene in class may elect his demise at line 132, giving the actor playing Harry a chance to explore his feelings towards the crown now that it is his. Will he regard it differently than when he entered with it at the beginning of the scene?

30

Julius Caesar

Act IV, Scene iii

CASSIUS and BRUTUS

✠

Marcus Brutus and Caius Cassius, two principal conspirators in the assassination of Julius Caesar, the Roman Emperor, now meet in Brutus' tent in preparation for their battle against Octavius Caesar and Mark Antony. A guard is set at the entrance to insure their privacy.

✠

CASSIUS
That you have wronged me doth appear in this:
You have condemned and noted Lucius Pella
For taking bribes here of the Sardians,
Wherein my letters, praying on his side
Because I knew the man, was slighted off.   5
BRUTUS
You wronged yourself to write in such a case.
CASSIUS
In such a time as this it is not meet
That every nice offense should bear his comment.
BRUTUS
Let me tell you Cassius, you yourself
Are much condemned to have an itching palm   10
To sell and mart your offices for gold
To undeservers.
CASSIUS   I an itching palm?

---

2 **noted** publicly disgraced
4 **praying . . . side** appealing on his behalf
5 **slighted off** slightingly dismissed
8 **nice** unimportant; **his** its

comment scrutiny
10 **condemned to have** accused of having
itching palm covetous nature
11 **mart** deal in; **offices** official position

You know that you are Brutus that speaks this
Or by the gods this speech were else your last.

BRUTUS

The name of Cassius honors this corruption   15
And chastisement doth therefore hide his head.

CASSIUS

Chastisement!

BRUTUS

Remember March, the ides of March remember.
Did not great Julius bleed for justice' sake?
What villain touched his body that did stab   20
And not for justice? What, shall one of us
That struck the foremost man of all this world
But for supporting robbers, shall we now
Contaminate our fingers with base bribes
And sell the mighty space of our large honors   25
For so much trash as may be grasped thus?
I had rather be a dog and bay the moon
Than such a Roman.

CASSIUS   Brutus bait not me;
I'll not endure it. You forget yourself
To hedge me in. I am a soldier, I,   30
Older in practice, abler than yourself
To make conditions.

BRUTUS   Go to! You are not, Cassius.

CASSIUS I am.

BRUTUS I say you are not.

CASSIUS

Urge me no more, I shall forget myself;   35

---

15 **honors** lends respectability to
18 **ides of March** March 15th (the day Caesar was assassinated)
21 **And not** except
23 **supporting robbers** protecting corrupt officials
25 **mighty . . . honors** great potential of our patronage
26 **trash** rubbish/money (contemptuous)
27 **bay** howl against
28 **bait** harass (bears were **baited** at the stake)
30 **hedge me in** confine, limit me
32 **make conditions** manage business
35 **Urge** incite, press

Have mind upon your health, tempt me no farther.

BRUTUS Away, slight man!

CASSIUS

Is't possible?

BRUTUS   Hear me, for I will speak.

Must I give way and room to your rash choler?

Shall I be frighted when a madman stares?   40

CASSIUS

O ye gods, ye gods! Must I endure all this?

BRUTUS

All this? Ay more: fret till your proud heart break.

Go show your slaves how choleric you are

And make your bondmen tremble. Must I budge?

Must I observe you? Must I stand and crouch   45

Under your testy humor? By the gods

You shall digest the venom of your spleen

Though it do split you, for from this day forth

I'll use you for my mirth, yea for my laughter,

When you are waspish.

CASSIUS   Is it come to this?   50

BRUTUS

You say you are a better soldier:

Let it appear so, make your vaunting true

And it shall please me well. For mine own part,

I shall be glad to learn of noble men.

CASSIUS

You wrong me every way, you wrong me Brutus: 55

I said an elder soldier, not a better.

Did I say, better?

BRUTUS   If you did, I care not.

	crouch i.e., bow
36 **tempt** try, test	46 **testy humor** irritability
37 **slight** insignificant	47 **digest . . . spleen** swallow the
39 **way and room** free course and	poison from your bad temper
scope	49 **for my mirth . . . laughter** as an
rash choler quick temper	object of fun and ridicule
40 **stares** glares	52 **vaunting** boasting
44 **budge** flinch	54 **learn of** be instructed by
45 **observe** humor, pay respect to	

CASSIUS
   When Caesar lived, he durst not thus have moved me.
BRUTUS
   Peace, peace, you durst not so have tempted him.
CASSIUS   I durst not?   60
BRUTUS   No.
CASSIUS
   What? Durst not tempt him?
BRUTUS   For your life you durst not.
CASSIUS
   Do not presume too much upon my love;
   I may do that I shall be sorry for.
BRUTUS
   You have done that you should be sorry for.   65
   There is no terror Cassius, in your threats;
   For I am armed so strong in honesty
   That they pass by me as the idle wind
   Which I respect not. I did send to you
   For certain sums of gold which you denied me;   70
   For I can raise no money by vile means.
   By heaven, I had rather coin my heart
   And drop my blood for drachmas than to wring
   From the hard hands of peasants their vile trash
   By any indirection. I did send   75
   To you for gold to pay my legions
   Which you denied me. Was that done like Cassius?
   Should I have answered Caius Cassius so?
   When Marcus Brutus grows so covetous
   To lock such rascal counters from his friends,   80
   Be ready gods with all your thunderbolts —
   Dash him to pieces!
CASSIUS   I denied you not.
BRUTUS
   You did.

58 **moved** angered   73 **drachmas** i. e., money
59 **tempted** provoked   75 **indirection** devious means
67 **honesty** integrity   80 **rascal counters** worthless coins
69 **respect not** ignore

CASSIUS   I did not. He was but a fool
That brought my answer back. Brutus hath rived my
    heart.
A friend should bear his friend's infirmities   85
But Brutus makes mine greater than they are.

BRUTUS
I do not till you practice them on me.

CASSIUS
You love me not.
BRUTUS   I do not like your faults.

CASSIUS
A friendly eye could never see such faults.

BRUTUS
A flatterer's would not though they do appear   90
As huge as high Olympus.

CASSIUS
Come Antony and young Octavius come,
Revenge yourselves alone on Cassius,
For Cassius is aweary of the world:
Hated by the one he loves, braved by his brother,   95
Checked like a bondman, all his faults observed,
Set in a notebook, learned and conned by rote
To cast into my teeth. O I could weep
My spirit from mine eyes! There is my dagger
And here my naked breast, within a heart   100
Dearer than Pluto's mine, richer than gold:
If that thou be'st a Roman, take it forth.
I that denied thee gold, will give my heart.
Strike as thou didst at Caesar for I know
When thou didst hate him worst, thou lovedst him
    better   105
Than thou ever lovedst Cassius.

---

84 **rived** split
91 **Olympus** (legendary home of
   the Greek gods)
93 **alone** only
95 **braved** challenged, opposed
96 **Checked** rebuked

97 **conned by rote** learned by heart
98 **cast . . . teeth** throw in my face
101 **Dearer** more precious
   Pluto (god of the underworld;
   often confused with Plutus god
   of riches)

BRUTUS   Sheathe your dagger.
Be angry when you will, it shall have scope.
Do what you will, dishonor shall be humor.
O Cassius you are yoked with a lamb
That carries anger as a flint bears fire   110
Who, much enforced, shows a hasty spark
And straight is cold again.
CASSIUS   Hath Cassius lived
To be but mirth and laughter to his Brutus
When grief and blood ill-tempered vexeth him?
BRUTUS
When I spoke that I was ill-tempered too.   115
CASSIUS
Do you confess so much? Give me your hand.
BRUTUS And my heart too.
CASSIUS   O Brutus!
BRUTUS   What's the matter?
CASSIUS
Have not you love enough to bear with me
When that rash humor which my mother gave me
Makes me forgetful?
BRUTUS   Yes Cassius, and from henceforth   120
When you are over-earnest with your Brutus,
He'll think your mother chides and leave you so.

---

107 **scope** free play
108 **dishonor . . . humor** insults will
   be as if a whim, idiosyncracy
111 **Who** which; **much enforced**
   strongly provoked/struck

112 **straight** immediately
114 **ill-tempered** ill-balanced
119 **rash humor** hasty temperament
122 **leave you so** let it go at that

✠

Rehearsing the Scene

This quarrel springs immediately to life. Both characters know they can be overheard by sentries outside the tent, and this knowledge prevents a loud climax from coming too soon.

The characters are clearly and boldly contrasted, each providing a self-portrait which can be used by actors as a point of departure for exploration. Brutus says he is:

> a lamb
> That carries anger as the flint bears fire
> Who, much enforced, shows a hasty spark
> And straight is cold again.   (ll. 109-122)

Brutus' emotion in this scene must burst through a customary self-promotion and discipline in argument and debate. He tries to be self-aware at all times: "Let me tell you . . . Hear me, for I will speak . . . For I am armed so strong in honesty . . . When Marcus Brutus grows so covetous . . ." (ll. 9, 38, 67, and 79). Cassius says about himself:

> . . . that rash humor which my mother gave me
> Makes me forgetful.   (ll. 119-20)

He is naturally quick and passionate; his most sustained argument is laced with exclamations and shows of temperament.

The energy in their conflict will be enhanced by the actors' response to textual variations of tone, pitch, syntax, vocabulary and meter. When the two characters use the same words, picking up ideas from each other, they turn them to their own advantage, changing the implications and rhythms (for Brutus, see lines 6, 42, 51, 59, and 65; for Cassius, lines 12, 17, 56, 60, and 82). Metrical changes define thrusts and parries. When thoughts are most violently opposed, they share a single verse line, so that the second speaker responds to the first by taking over and changing the rhythms already established: see lines 12, 28, 32, 38, 50, 57, 62, 82, 83, 88. On three crucial occasions, a half-line is left uncompleted, so marking a silence and change of mood; so the duelists disengage, following a particularly violent thrust. On two occasions the metrical basis for speech seems to break down entirely, at lines 33-34 and 60-61: perhaps these metrical crises could be taken very quickly, recklessly and instinctively. Or a long silence might be held between the two speeches; or one speaker or both might speak very slowly, weighing each word carefully.

Line 84 is a special metrical problem because it has twelve syllables. Either the actor must pack the long line into the ten-syllable norm, or he should treat the line as two incomplete verse lines so that Cassius takes a pause in the middle of his reply to Brutus. This could be an instance of his "rashness," or a moment when he masters his instinct for a hasty reply.

Immediately after this exceptional metrical crux, Cassius forces an entirely new level of consciousness to the scene by talking of his "heart" and of "friends", and by proceeding to the simple challenge "You love me not" (l. 87). (His earlier mention of "love" at line 63 had been summarily swept aside.) Brutus attempts to deflect Cassius' emotional tone, but Cassius will have none of it as he offers his dagger and sets the emotional stakes even higher. In grappling with Cassius' histrionic action, the actor must well understand the character's motive. Is this a bit of melodramatic bravado? Clearly here Cassius is attempting to regain control of the scene, but resort to such a drastic action may evidence a lack of control. Does Cassius know that it is nearly absurd, in its suddenness and melodramatic impracticality, and does he calculate that this is likely to impress the self-important Brutus? Or is Cassius so "rash" and "over-earnest" that he truly means what he does, and intends it to be taken literally? When he says, with Brutus-like self-awareness, that "Cassius is aweary of the world" (l. 94), is he honestly asking Brutus to kill him? Is he close to tears as lines 98-99 suggest? To act this moment truthfully, the actor will have to sense Cassius' deepest instincts; simple notions of his "rashness" will not be sufficient.

Why does Brutus change at this point? Does Cassius expose himself here in a way that his "friend" finds irresistible? Does Brutus *need* friendship, love and trust, despite his talk about justice, honor and his ability as a soldier? Is he able to dismiss Cassius to dishonor among "slaves" and "bondmen" (ll. 43-44), but unable to face him on his own without reconciliation of their differences? Do Cassius' emotional appeals bring out a different side of Brutus?

This quarrel scene is justly famous: it has both fire and mystery.

31

Hamlet

Act V, Scene i

Two CLOWNS

✠

Both the good texts of *Hamlet*, the second Quarto and the first Folio, name these two persons engaged in preparing for a funeral as Clowns. This implies that they are rustic or foolish persons and also theatrical entertainers; and both meanings are appropriate.

The one called "Clown" in the prefixes to the speeches is identified as "Goodman Delver," and later in the play he says he has been digging graves in Denmark for thirty years. The "Other" clown may be a parish clerk or an unskilled laborer; probably he is a much younger man.

A trapdoor is the usual theatrical means for providing a grave on stage, but a few low platforms arranged with a space between them will suffice. Alternatively this duologue can be played as if all the digging takes place subsequently, with a few preparatory actions accompanying the song; in this case, a bare stage will serve.

It is early morning, and the clowns know that they are preparing for the burial of the young daughter of the king's chief counselor, who has died by drowning.

✠

CLOWN   Is she to be buried in Christian burial when she
willfully seeks her own salvation?
OTHER   I tell thee she is. Therefore make her grave
straight. The crowner hath sate on her and finds it
Christian burial.   5

1 **Christian burial** (suicides were buried in unconsecrated ground)
2 **salvation** (mistake for "damnation")
4 **straight** at once
crowner coroner (variant form)
4-5 **finds . . . burial** i. e., judges that it was not suicide

258 HAMLET

CLOWN How can that be unless she drowned herself in her own defense?

OTHER Why 'tis found so.

CLOWN It must be *se offendendo*; it cannot be else. For here lies the point: if I drown myself wittingly, it argues an act and an act hath three branches—it is to act, to do, to perform. Argal she drowned herself wittingly. 10

OTHER Nay but hear you, Goodman Delver.

CLOWN Give me leave. Here lies the water—good. Here stands the man—good. If the man go to this water and drown himself, it is, will he nill he, he goes—mark you that. But if the water come to him and drown him, he drowns not himself. Argal he that is not guilty of his own death, shortens not his own life. 15

OTHER But is this law? 20

CLOWN Ay marry is't , crowner's quest law.

OTHER Will you ha' the truth on't? If this had not been a gentlewoman, she should have been buried out o' Christian burial.

CLOWN Why there thou say'st. And the more pity that great folk should have count'nance in this world to drown or hang themselves more than their even-Christen. Come, my spade. There is no ancient gentlemen but gard'ners, ditchers and gravemakers: they hold up Adam's profession. 25 30

OTHER Was he a gentleman?

CLOWN 'A was the first that ever bore arms.

6 **in . . . defense** (a plea relevant to homicide, not for suicide)
9 *se offendendo* (mistake for *se defendendo*—another confusion of opposites)
12 **Argal** (mistake for (Latin) *Ergo* = therefore)
14 **Goodman** (prefix used for addressing a man by his profession)

17 **will he nill he** whether he will or not
22 **marry** indeed; **quest** inquest
27 **count'nance** privilege
28-29 **even-Christen** fellow Christians
29 **ancient** going back to earliest times
31 **hold up** keep going
33 **bore arms** had a coat of arms (sign of a gentleman)

OTHER Why he had none.

CLOWN What, art a heathen? How dost thou understand 35
the Scripture? The Scripture says Adam digged. Could
he dig without arms? I'll put another question to
thee. If thou answerest me not to the purpose, confess
thyself—

OTHER Go to. 40

CLOWN What is he that builds stronger than either the
mason, the shipwright or the carpenter?

OTHER The gallowsmaker for that frame outlives a
thousand tenants.

CLOWN I like thy wit well in good faith. The gallows 45
does well. But how does it well? It does well to those
that do ill. Now thou dost ill to say the gallows is built
stronger than the church. Argal the gallows may do
well to thee. To't again, come.

OTHER Who builds stronger than a mason, a shipwright 50
or a carpenter?

CLOWN Ay tell me that and unyoke.

OTHER Marry now I can tell.

CLOWN To't.

OTHER Mass, I cannot tell. 55

CLOWN Cudgel thy brains no more about it, for your
dull ass will not mend his pace with beating. And
when you are asked this question next, say "a grave-
maker." The houses he makes last till doomsday. Go
get thee in and fetch me a stoup of liquor. 60

(*Exit* OTHER CLOWN.)

(*Song.*)

In youth when I did love, did love,
Methought it was very sweet
To contract—O—the time for—a—my behove,

---

43 **frame** (1) gallows (2) timber
frame of a building
46 **does well** is a good answer
52 **unyoke** give over (as oxen at the
end of a day's work)
55 **Mass** by the mass
60 **stoup** tankard

63 **contract** shorten
O . . . a (probably exclamations
or grunts as breath is taken during the singing)
behove advantage

O, methought there—a—was nothing—a—meet.

But age with his stealing steps   65
Hath clawed me in his clutch,
And hath shipped me into the land
As if I had never been such.

✠

Rehearsing the Scene

These two characters seem to do little more than argue and
tell jokes, but they have a task to accomplish. A grave has to be
"prepared" and that involves the business of digging or of re-
moving the covers from a grave almost ready for use. If there is a
trapdoor or other access to a small space at a lower level, the
Clown can start the scene alone and already digging; this is the
usual way in modern productions, and has the advantage of providing him with the comic possibilities of disappearing from
view at points in the scene. If the "Other" clown is a parish clerk,
he can hold a paper on which their orders have been written;
the scene may then start with the entry of them both, in the middle of an argument.

Clown gets much of what he says muddled, starting off by
confusing such a basic matter as "salvation" and "damnation". Of
course he must be untroubled by the absurdity; rather he should
be pleased to be handling such important matters decisively—he
might smile or even laugh at each misused word. But yet there is
a perverse sense in what he says, and he should perhaps speak
with the weight of sober experience: a person comitting suicide
may, in his or her view, be finding a better alternative to life, and
does in one sense kill in "defense" of self.

His song is very garbled as well. The original by Thomas Lord
Vaux was printed under the title "The aged lover renounceth
love." Lines from several stanzas are brought together in the
clown's version; and the idea of "contracting" time for youthful
desire is the Clown's invention, where the original has "requires." Again there is some sense in his muddling: for the
youthful lover, time may indeed contract because the moments
of pleasure are fleeting. In almost all he says Clown is concerned

with time, referring back to the creation of the world and forward to doomsday. When he considers one particular action in time, he splinters it into three identical procedures and then goes on to demand enough time to show, physically, the simplest possible distinction. He can use various objects for the "man" and the "water" (ll. 15-19); for the latter a spade or plank, for the former a skull (taken from the grave) or his own hand, using two fingers for legs so that "he" may be shown walking.

Clown's concern with time and his methodical presentation of simple ideas do not necessarily mean that he speaks very slowly and deliberately. That is one way of playing him, but he might also speak very briskly and humorlessly about all this, being so at home in considering life-and-death matters that he refers to the passing of time and human deliberations as a matter of course, eerily comfortable with what is imponderable and awesome to other people.

The "Other" clown seems bent on thinking about crime, adding hangings to the immediate concern of suicide; and in his mind a "gallows" has a great deal of work to do. He may also be something of a know-it-all, an upstart intellectual: he tells "the truth on't," asks about the value of statements, and perhaps is seen "cudgelling" his brains (ll. 56-7).

This duologue is a lot more than a collection of jokes because both clowns have fixed ideas in their heads which can be used by actors to create contrasting characters with distinct rhythms of talk and behavior. Their tensions can establish an uneasy or doomed mood. As usual in Shakespeare's duologues, the two characters become progressively more open to the audience's understanding and the scene moves towards a fully developed confrontation between them.

Another way of approaching the scene is for the "Other" clown to press all the time for action, against a rock-like calm in the elder Clown. "Make her grave straight" (ll. 3-4) sets up this intention, and it can be developed in "Why 'tis found so" (as if cutting off talk) and in "Nay but hear you." He will get deflected by questions of law and talk of Adam's arms: perhaps the Gravedigger senses the young man's impatience as well as his air of superiority, and so deliberately taunts him with delaying tactics. When he is defeated to the satisfaction of his mate, the "Other" gets ordered off to fetch some liquor, and time is about to be wasted again.

The call for liquor places Clown in position of master, and this follows a conversation about the privilege of gentlefolk. So perhaps Clown is a natural bully: it is noteworthy that he tells his junior to "unyoke" (l. 52), using the image of a beast of burden. The "Other" starts by being in charge because he knows more about the matter in hand than his senior; and he maintains some advantage by having a good first answer to the riddle. But when he confesses himself beaten, he has lost his initial authority, and could start to leave the stage even before Clown tells him to fetch the liquor.

Whether the Gravedigger has to assert himself in their last moments together, or whether the "Other" admits his defeat, there is no doubt who is left in possession of the stage. But that lasts only for a moment: as the song holds attention, it is time and age which are acknowledged to be in charge; the singer is their servant, and master no more.

32

King Lear

Act IV , Scene vi

The DUKE OF GLOUCESTER and EDGAR

✠

The eighty-year-old King Lear has been turned out of doors into a great storm by his two elder daughters. For attempting to help his king, the Duke of Gloucester has had his two eyes torn out and his own house closed to him.

Gloucester pleaded with a near-naked madman called Tom O'Bedlam to lead him to Dover Cliff where the blinded man plans to take his own life. As this scene begins, they arrive together, after a long journey, at what the madman claims is the clifftop.

Mad Tom is, in fact, his own son Edgar in disguise, whom he had earlier disowned because his other son, the illegitimate Edmund, had tricked him into believing that his brother was trying to kill their father. By this scene Gloucester has learned that he was unwarranted in his rejection of Edgar. But, of course, he does not realize he is accompanied by the son with whom he would most like to be reunited. Edgar has been given clothes to cover his nakedness.

✠

GLOUCESTER
When shall I come to th' top of that same hill?
EDGAR
You do climb up it now. Look how we labor.
GLOUCESTER
Methinks the ground is even.
EDGAR   Horrible steep.
Hark, do you hear the sea?
GLOUCESTER   No, truly.

---

1 **that same hill** the hill we talked
about

EDGAR

Why then your other senses grow imperfect   5
By your eyes' anquish.

GLOUCESTER   So may it be indeed;
Methinks thy voice is altered and thou speak'st
In better phrase and matter than thou didst.

EDGAR

Y' are much deceived: in nothing am I changed
But in my garments.

GLOUCESTER   Methinks y' are better spoken.   10

EDGAR

Come on sir, here's the place: stand still. How fearful
And dizzy 'tis to cast one's eyes so low!
The crows and choughs that wing the midway air
Show scarce so gross as beetles. Half way down
Hangs one that gathers samphire, dreadful trade—   15
Methinks he seems no bigger than his head.
The fishermen that walk upon the beach
Appear like mice and yond tall anchoring bark
Diminished to her cock, her cock a buoy
Almost too small for sight. The murmuring surge   20
That on th' unnumb'red idle pebble chafes
Cannot be heard so high. I'll look no more
Lest my brain turn and the deficient sight
Topple down headlong.

GLOUCESTER   Set me where you stand.

EDGAR

Give me your hand: you are now within a foot   25
Of th' extreme verge. For all beneath the moon
Would I not leap upright.

GLOUCESTER   Let go my hand.

---

6 **By** because of
13 **choughs** jackdaws
    midway air i. e., halfway down
    the cliff
14 **gross** large
15 **samphire** (herb growing on
    cliffs)
18 **anchoring bark** ship at anchor

19 **cock** cockboat, dinghy
21 **unnumb'red idle pebble** innu-
    merable, shifting pebbles
23 **turn** reel
24 **Topple** topple me
27 **upright** upward (any other jump
    would be plainly disastrous and
    foolish)

Here friend 's another purse; in it a jewel
Well worth a poor man's taking. Fairies and gods
Prosper it with thee! Go thou further off,   30
Bid me farewell and let me hear thee going.

EDGAR
Now fare ye well good sir.

GLOUCESTER   With all my heart.

EDGAR
Why I do trifle thus with his despair
Is done to cure it.

GLOUCESTER   O you mighty gods   (*He kneels.*)
This world I do renounce and in your sights   35
Shake patiently my great affliction off.
If I could bear it longer and not fall
To quarrel with your great opposeless wills,
My snuff and loathèd part of nature should
Burn itself out. If Edgar live, O bless him!   40
Now fellow, fare thee well.

EDGAR   Gone sir, farewell.   (*He falls.*)
And yet I know not how conceit may rob
The treasury of life when life itself
Yields to the theft. Had he been where he thought,
By this had thought been past. Alive or dead?   45
Ho, you sir! friend! Hear you sir! speak!
Thus might he pass indeed: yet he revives.
What are you, sir?

GLOUCESTER   Away and let me die.

EDGAR
Hadst thou been aught but gossamer, feathers, air,

29 **Fairies** (supposed to guard and multiply hidden treasure)
33-34 **Why . . . cure it** I play upon his despair in this way in order to cure it
36 **Shake . . . off** deliberately and submissively end my painful life
38 **quarrel with** rebel against; **opposeless** irresistible
39 **snuff** burnt-out (useless and stinking) remains of a candle's wick
42 **how** but what; **conceit** imagination
43 **treasury** treasure
44 **Yields** surrenders
47 **pass** die

So many fathom down precipitating,   50
Thou'dst shivered like an egg, but thou dost breathe,
Hast heavy substance, bleed'st not, speak'st, art sound.
Ten masts at each make not the altitude
Which thou hast perpendicularly fell:
Thy life's a miracle. Speak yet again.   55

GLOUCESTER

But have I fall'n or no?

EDGAR

From the dread summit of this chalky bourn.
Look up a-height: the shrill-gorged lark so far
Cannot be seen or heard. Do but look up.

GLOUCESTER

Alack I have no eyes.   60
Is wretchedness deprived that benefit,
To end itself by death? 'Twas yet some comfort
When misery could beguile the tyrant's rage
And frustrate his proud will.

EDGAR   Give me your arm.

Up, so. How is't? Feel you your legs? You stand.   65

GLOUCESTER

Too well, too well.

EDGAR   This is above all strangeness.

Upon the crown o' th' cliff, what thing was that
Which parted from you?

GLOUCESTER   A poor unfortunate beggar.

EDGAR

As I stood here below, methought his eyes
Were two full moons; he had a thousand noses,   70
Horns whelked and waved like the enridged sea.
It was some fiend; therefore, thou happy father,
Think that the clearest gods, who make them honors

---

50 **precipitating** hurtling down
51 **shivered** shattered
52 **Hast . . . substance** art made of flesh, art not a ghost
53 **at each** on top of each other
57 **bourn** boundary (i. e., Dover Cliff)
58 **a-height** on high

shrill-gorged high-voiced
63 **beguile** cheat, rob (i. e., by suicide)
64 **frustrate** annul
65 **Feel you** have you any feeling in
71 **whelked** twisted
enridged furrowed (with waves)

Of men's impossibilities, have preserved thee.

GLOUCESTER
    I do remember now. Henceforth I'll bear   75
    Affliction till it do cry out itself,
    "Enough, enough," and die. That thing you speak of,
    I took it for a man; often 'twould say,
    "The fiend, the fiend." He led me to that place.

EDGAR
    Bear free and patient thoughts.   80

---

72 **happy father** fortunate old man
73 **clearest** most glorious, most
    pure

73-74 **make them . . . impossibilities**
    make themselves honored be-
    cause they do what men cannot
80 **free** i. e., free from despair which
    fetters the soul

✠

Rehearsing the Scene

In a very deep sense, the play is about endurance; by the time
that the fourth Act is reached every principal character has travelled a long way, carrying very particular burdens. When rehearsing and playing this scene on its own, it is not possible to reproduce that grueling preparation, but both actors need to
approach it as people at the end of long and testing journeys. It
might be helpful to think of being in the last stages of some interrogation and torture, or of being cornered by some all-
powerful gangsters or by sleuths in the service of some super-
power in space. These characters are at the end of their ropes:
one is blind and old, and weakened by suffering; the other has
been feigning madness and has little other resource whereby to
help himself or his father.

    Given this basis, the actors should play a few intentions very
strongly, rather than worry about deeper implications or twists
in the plot; such is the reverbatory power of the words and the

subtlety and variety of the interplay, that the scene will grow in strength almost of its own accord. An audience will not know all that is false or incomplete in the minds and beings of the two persons presented, but such ignorance is like the ignorance of each character and is no impediment to the scene's impact. In some ways a limited knowledge in both audience and actors is entirely appropriate to the characters, who can grasp only one moment at a time; it may help to heighten a sense of reality and of the "mystery of things" (V. iii.16).

Edgar must be presented in three ways: as Mad Tom, as Edgar himself and, towards the end of the scene, as a newcomer who speaks authoritatively of the "clearest gods" who interest themselves in man's preservation (see ll. 73-74). This third person may also give a glimpse of how Edgar feels now about Mad Tom—as a fiend who is troubled and inhuman (see ll. 69-72)—and his advice to Gloucester at the close can also be advice to himself as Edgar, as they prepare to move offstage: "Bear free and patient thoughts."

Earlier in the scene Edgar can be seen beneath his disguise in several ways, as if the covering he had assumed has become thin and torn with use. References to Gloucester's "eyes of anguish," a "fearful And dizzy" depth, and a sea which "chafes" every small pebble, together with a reluctance to "leap upright," culminate in an aside, lines 33-34, which speaks directly for Edgar. The actor must choose whether this discloses a continuing doubt about the right course to take (the structure of the sentence has a suggestion of a query) or whether it affirms a clear and tried perception about the right way to give his father freedom to survive in his own right. (There can be little doubt that Edgar knew that the purpose of their journey together was for his father to end his life.) The actor's choice between uncertainty and faith will affect a choice to be made later: does Edgar panic when he realizes that his father may be dead, or is that momentary fear put to rest easily, without loss of confidence? Some Edgars live on the edge of failure; others discover, progressively, an inner strength and a belief that the gods help those who help themselves.

The chief challenge to the actor of Gloucester is to establish his weary but resolved despair at the beginning—his prayer of ll. 35-40 has a patient dignity at odds with any feverish desperation—and then to move on, through the thwarted suicide, to a submissive patience or a more active acceptance of suffering. The moment of this change seems to follow Edgar's suggestion that a "fiend" has been thwarted by the gods. But Gloucester's "I do remember now" does not lead on to an affirmation of Edgar's belief; instead, he continues to think of the "man" who had led him and had shared his suffering. So it may be Edgar's love which enables his father to "bear" affliction: at the end of this scene, Gloucester and Edgar may be close together, comforting each other in ways beyond their powers to express or perhaps even recognize.

33

Coriolanus

Act IV, Scene v

AUFIDIUS and CORIOLANUS

✠

Tullus Aufidius, General of the Volscians, has led his country's forces against Rome and been defeated twelve times. Victory in repeated engagements has belonged always to Caius Marcius, a young Roman patrician; in the last conflict, the personal valor and leadership of Marcius had turned Rome's ignominious defeat into the amazing capture of the Volscian city of Corioli.

Returned to Rome, Marcius had been given the new name of Coriolanus and persuaded to stand for election as Consul. The popular vote for this political office was at first granted to him, but then established politicians persuaded the people to change their vote and denounce Coriolanus as

> a traitorous innovator.
> A foe to th' public weal. (III.i.174-75)

He was banished from his own country and arrived dressed in "mean apparel" (IV.iv. stage direction) at Antium, the Volscian capital. Here he calls on Aufidius who is feasting "the nobles of the state." He makes such trouble with servants when he tries to enter the house that Aufidius leaves his guests to question the intruder.

✠

AUFIDIUS Where is this fellow?
　　Whence com'st thou? What would'st thou? Thy name?
　　Why speak'st not? Speak man, what's thy name?
CORIOLANUS   If Tullus
　　Not yet thou know'st me and, seeing me, dost not

Think me for the man I am, necessity   5
Commands me name myself.

AUFIDIUS   What is thy name?

CORIOLANUS

A name unmusical to the Volscians' ears
And harsh in sound to thine.

AUFIDIUS   Say what's thy name?

Thou hast a grim appearance and thy face
Bears a command in't. Though thy tackle's torn,   10
Thou show'st a noble vessel. What's thy name?

CORIOLANUS

Prepare thy brow to frown. Know'st thou me yet?

AUFIDIUS

I know thee not. Thy name!

CORIOLANUS

My name is Caius Marcius who hath done
To thee particularly and to all the Volsces   15
Great hurt and mischief, thereto witness may
My surname Coriolanus. The painful service,
The extreme dangers and the drops of blood
Shed for my thankless country are requited
But with that surname—a good memory   20
And witness of the malice and displeasure
Which thou shouldst bear me. Only that name
  remains.
The cruelty and envy of the people,
Permitted by our dastard nobles who
Have all forsook me, hath devoured the rest   25
And suffered me by th' voice of slaves to be
Whooped out of Rome. Now this extremity
Hath brought me to thy hearth, not out of hope
(Mistake me not) to save my life for if

---

5 **Think** take
10 **command** authority;
    tackle rigging of a ship (referring
    to Coriolanus's "poor" attire)
11 **show'st** appear'st

16 **mischief** misfortune
17 **painful** arduous
20 **memory** memorial
26 **voice** vote, judgement
27 **Whooped** hooted, jeered

I had feared death of all the men i' th' world   30
I would have 'voided thee, but in mere spite
To be full quit of those my banishers,
Stand I before thee here. Then if thou hast
A heart of wreak in thee that wilt revenge
Thine own particular wrongs and stop those maims   35
Of shame seen through thy country, speed thee
    straight
And make my misery serve thy turn. So use it
That my revengeful services may prove
As benefits to thee for I will fight
Against my cank'red country with the spleen   40
Of all the under fiends. But if so be
Thou dar'st not this and that to prove more fortunes
Thou'rt tired then, in a word, I also am
Longer to live most weary and present
My throat to thee and to thy ancient malice,   45
Which not to cut would show thee but a fool
Since I have ever followed thee with hate,
Drawn tuns of blood out of thy country's breast
And cannot live but to thy shame, unless
It be to do thee service.

AUFIDIUS   O Marcius, Marcius!   50
Each word thou hast spoke hath weeded from my
    heart
A root of ancient envy. If Jupiter
Should from yond cloud speak divine things
And say, "Tis true," I'd not believe them more
Than thee, all noble Marcius. Let me twine   55
Mine arms about that body where against
My grained ash an hundred times hath broke
And scarred the moon with splinters. Here I clip

31 **in mere spite** out of pure spite	40 **cank'red** corrupted
32 **be full quit of** settle my account	**spleen** hatred
with	41 **under fiends** devils of hell
34 **of wreak** ready for revenge	42 **prove** try
35 **stop those maims** close up, heal	48 **tuns** casks
those wounds	57 **grained ash** straight-grained spear
36 **through** throughout	58 **clip** embrace
straight immediately	

The anvil of my sword and do contest
As hotly and as nobly with thy love   60
As ever in ambitious strength I did
Contend against thy valor. Know thou first,
I loved the maid I married, never man
Sighed truer breath, but that I see thee here,
Thou noble thing, more dances my rapt heart   65
Than when I first my wedded mistress saw
Beside my threshold. Why thou Mars, I tell thee,
We have a power on foot and I had purpose
Once more to hew thy target from thy brawn
Or lose mine arm for't. Thou hast beat me out   70
Twelve several times and I have nightly since
Dreamt of encounters 'twixt thyself and me:
We have been down together in my sleep,
Unbuckling helms, fisting each other's throat,
And waked half dead with nothing. Worthy Marcius,   75
Had we no quarrel else to Rome but that
Thou art thence banished, we would muster all
From twelve to seventy and pouring war
Into the bowels of ungrateful Rome
Like a bold flood o'erbeat. O come, go in   80
And take our friendly senators by th' hands,
Who now are here taking their leaves of me
Who am prepared against your territories,
Though not for Rome itself.

CORIOLANUS   You bless me, gods!

AUFIDIUS

Therefore most absolute sir, if thou wilt have   85
The leading of thine own revenges, take
Th' one half of my commission and set down—
As best thou art experienced since thou know'st

64 **that** because
65 **rapt** enraptured
67 **Mars** god of war
68 **power on foot** army in the field
69 **target** shield;
   brawn strong arm
70 **out** outright

71 **several** separate, different
75 **waked** have awakened
80 **o'erbeat** flow over and subdue
   (the land)
85 **absolute** perfect
87 **commission** command
   set down decide

Thy country's strength and weakness—thine own
  ways,
Whether to knock against the gates of Rome   90
Or rudely visit them in parts remote
To fright them ere destroy. But come in.
Let me commend thee first to those that shall
Say yea to thy desires. A thousand welcomes!
And more a friend than e'er an enemy;   95
Yet Marcius that was much. Your hand: most
  welcome!
                                                    Exeunt.

✠

Rehearsing the Scene

Does Coriolanus expect to be recognized at once or does he
make sure that Aufidius has to wait before he reveals himself
openly? Has Aufidius drunk a great deal at the feast (his servants
had entered calling for "Wine, wine, wine!") or is he fully in
command so that only a very stubborn visitor would not answer
his first challenge? After five specific demands for his name, Coriolanus still pauses before answering directly: by now, however
the introduction is played, there is a strong tension between the
two men. Perhaps Aufidius threatens him physically, but he is
unlikely to be provided with a sword at this feast among friends.

Coriolanus has a shocking message to deliver—that he wants
to turn traitor and fight against his own country—and he prepares slowly before naming it. The actor must decide whether it
is Coriolanus's pride which makes him delay or his astute knowledge of his enemy's mind which enables him to lead Aufidius
step by step into acceptance of whatever he proposes. Either
way, an incisive eloquence, in imagery, syntax and occasional
verbal simplicity, should express a complete, unquestionable
conviction and a mind packed with memory and plans for future
action. Coriolanus will watch Aufidius very closely as he stands
defenseless before him, and as he dares him to follow his advice.
By the time he offers his "throat" to be cut (l. 45), he may know
that he has won and that his adversary is ready to do as he wish-

es: if he does not, he is being very provocative when, in the very next moment and in the same sentence, he speaks of the "tuns of blood" he has shed "out of thy country's breast." This encounter can have the danger of a meeting between a lion seeking its prey and a tiger defending its lair; but there is a choice between a proud courage as its controlling force, or an astute cunning which has been learned from recent defeat in public and political life.

Aufidius breaks the tension with "O Marcius, Marcius!" and soon the two generals embrace in friendship. Again there is a major choice for the actor. Has Aufidius been drinking so heavily that he is ready to enjoy the thrill of this meeting and to accept almost any proposal? Or is he silent so long because he is calculating his own advantage, and does he accept the proposal in a way which he knows will render Coriolanus unsuspecting of further treachery? A third way to present Aufidius is to make him totally obsessed with his enemy, so that their meeting does become for him a "contest" in "love" (ll. 58-62), one which brings emotional excitement and physical satisfaction.

Verbally the end of the scene belongs almost entirely to Aufidius. His imagery and comparisons are often both personal and vast in reference—the splinters from his spear "scarring the moon," his heart dancing as never before, his army ready to serve the god of war, his quarrel flooding through the bowels of Rome—yet the syntax retains strict control, each idea contained tightly and efficiently. When Aufidius moves on to consider immediate action, he is swift and impressive, keeping alternatives in mind and taking care of several consequences of his personal decision.

The difficulty at the close of the scene is that Coriolanus has only one half-line to speak and that is addressed to the gods, not to the man who offers him all that he has asked. Is this a conscious or unconscious affront to Aufidius? Or does Coriolanus imply that Aufidius is acting like a god? Or is it an expression of personal satisfaction, in which the whole world, Aufidius included, is drawn together in Coriolanus's mind? Or, yet again, is it a form of words to cover the careful calculation which the sober man is making as he watches the enemy who must now be his helper? It is also possible that Coriolanus's main response is silent and that he has responded to the physical embrace of his enemy in a way that transports him, as it does his assailant, with instinctive physical pleasure. With so few words as guide, the actor should experiment widely, making sure that each choice grows truly out of the earlier part of the scene; then a clear decision should be made before preparing for performance.

34

The Winter's Tale

Act IV, Scene i

AUTOLYCUS and the YOUNG SHEPHERD

✠

Autolycus tells his own version of his life story and Clown, the young shepherd, enters talking to himself about his immediate task. Sixteen years ago, when he was very young, Clown and his father had had a very strange adventure. In a great storm by the sea coast of Bohemia, the Old Shepherd had discovered a baby abandoned in a cradle, and Clown had seen a ship wrecked at sea and an old man devoured by a bear. Money found in the cradle had meant that these shepherds had prospered while the infant had grown up to be the "mistress" of their summer feast.

The setting is the countryside and the time a morning in June.

✠

Enter AUTOLYCUS, *singing.*
When daffodils begin to peer,
With heigh the doxy over the dale,
Why then comes in the sweet o' the year,
For the red blood reigns in the winter's pale.

The white sheet bleaching on the hedge,   5
With heigh the sweet birds, O how they sing!
Doth set my pugging tooth an edge,
For a quart of ale is a dish for a king.

The lark that tirra-lirra chants,
With heigh, with heigh, the thrush and the jay!   10
Are summer songs for me and my aunts

---

1 **peer** appear/peep above ground
2 **doxy** beggar's mistress (slang)
4 **pale** (1) enclosure (2) paleness

7 **pugging** thieving
11 **aunts** women (slang)

While we lie tumbling in the hay.
I have served Prince Florizel and in my time wore
three-pile but now I am out of service.

But shall I go mourn for that, my dear?   15
  The pale moon shines by night
And when I wander here and there
  I do then most go right.
If tinkers may have leave to live
  And bear the sow-skin budget,   20
Then my account I well may give
  And in the stocks avouch it.

My traffic is sheets; when the kite builds, look to
lesser linen. My father named me Autolycus, who
being, as I am, littered under Mercury, was likewise a   25
snapper-up of unconsidered trifles. With die and drab
I purchased this caparison and my revenue is the silly
cheat. Gallows and knock are too powerful on the
highway. Beating and hanging are terrors to me; for
the life to come, I sleep out the thought of it. A prize,   30
a prize.

Enter CLOWN, *a young shepherd.*

CLOWN Let me see, every 'leven wether tods, every tod

---

14 **three-pile** thick, costly velvet
20 **sow-skin budget** pigskin toolbag
22 **avouch** affirm
23 **traffic** speciality, wares
23-24 **when the kite . . . linen** (a
warning: a kite snatches scraps of
household goods for building its
nest)
24 **Autolycus** (son of Hermes and
grandfather of Odysseus; Homer
and Ovid both identified him
with thieving);
who i. e., his father
25 **littered under Mercury** born
when the planet Mercury was in

the ascendant (the god Mercury was pa-
tron of thieves)
26-27 **With die . . . caparison** I
aquired these clothes by gaming
and whoring
27-28 **silly cheat** petty theft
28 **Gallows** (highwaymen were punished by hanging);
knock beating (from intended
victims)
30 **life to come** life in the next
world
32 **every . . . tods** every eleven
sheep yield a **tod** (28 lb.) of wool

yields pound and odd shilling; fifteen hundred shorn,
what comes the wool to?

AUTOLYCUS (*Aside.*) If the springe hold, the cock's   35
mine.

CLOWN I cannot do't without counters. Let me see, what
am I to buy for our sheep-shearing feast? Three
pound of sugar, five pound of currants, rice—What
will this sister of mine do with rice? But my father   40
hath made her mistress of the feast and she lays it on.
She hath made me four-and-twenty nosegays for the
shearers (three-man-song men all and very good
ones, but they are most of them means and basses,
but one Puritan amongst them and he sings psalms to   45
hornpipes). I must have saffron to color the warden
pies, mace—dates none, that's out of my note—
nutmegs seven, a race or two of ginger—but that I
may beg—four pound of prunes and as many of raisins
o' th' sun.   50

AUTOLYCUS Oh that ever I was born!

CLOWN I' th' name of me!

AUTOLYCUS Oh help me, help me; pluck off these rags
and then death, death!

CLOWN Alack poor soul, thou hast need of more rags   55
to lay on thee, rather than have these off.

AUTOLYCUS Oh sir the loathsomeness of them offends
me more than the stripes I have received which are
mighty ones and millions.

CLOWN Alas poor man, a million of beating may come to a   60
great matter.

AUTOLYCUS I am robbed sir, and beaten, my money and
apparel ta'en from me and these detestable things put

---

35 **springe** trap
    cock woodcock/fool
43 **three-man-song** men singers of
    songs in three parts
44 **means** tenors
45-46 **sings . . . hornpipes** (i. e., is un-
    usually cheerful for a Puritan:

hornpipes = lively dance-tunes)
46-47 **warden pies** pies made with
    warden, or cooking, pears
47 **out . . . note** not on my list
48 **race** root
50 **o' th' sun** sun-dried

upon me.

CLOWN What, by a horseman or a footman?   65

AUTOLYCUS A footman sweet sir, a footman.

CLOWN Indeed he should be a footman by the garments
he has left with thee; if this be a horseman's coat,
it hath seen very hot service. Lend me thy hand, I'll
help thee. Come lend me thy hand.   70

AUTOLYCUS Oh good sir tenderly, oh!

CLOWN Alas poor soul!

AUTOLYCUS Oh good sir, softly good sir; I fear sir, my
shoulder blade is out.

CLOWN How now? Canst stand?   75

AUTOLYCUS Softly dear sir; good sir softly. You ha' done
me a charitable office.   (*Picks his pocket.*)

CLOWN Dost lack any money? I have a little money
for thee.

AUTOLYCUS No good sweet sir; no, I beseech you sir. I   80
have a kinsman not past three-quarters of a mile hence
unto whom I was going; I shall there have money
or anything I want. Offer me no money I pray you;
that kills my heart.

CLOWN What manner of fellow was he that robbed   85
you?

AUTOLYCUS A fellow sir, that I have known to go about
with troll-my-dames. I knew him once a servant of
the prince: I cannot tell good sir, for which of his
virtues it was, but he was certainly whipped out of   90
the court.

CLOWN His vices, you would say; there's no virtue
whipped out of the court. They cherish it to make it
stay there, and yet it will no more but abide.

AUTOLYCUS Vices, I would say sir. I know this man   95
well; he hath been since an ape-bearer, then a process-

---

65 **horseman or a footman** high-
   wayman or a footpad
88 **troll-my-dames** game in which
   balls were rolled through hoops
   (possibly used here = "aunts",
   whores)

94 **abide** pause, stay briefly
96 **ape-bearer** showman with a performing monkey
96-97 **process-server** sheriff's man
   who serves summonses

server, a bailiff; then he compassed a motion of the
Prodigal Son and married a tinker's wife within a
mile where my land and living lies and, having flown
over many knavish professions, he settled only in   100
rogue. Some call him Autolycus.

CLOWN Out upon him! Prig, for my life, prig! He haunts
wakes, fairs and bear-baitings.

AUTOLYCUS Very true sir. He sir, he! That's the rogue
that put me into this apparel.   105

CLOWN Not a more cowardly rogue in all Bohemia;
if you had but looked big and spit at him, he'd have
run.

AUTOLYCUS I must confess to you sir, I am no fighter;
I am false of heart that way and that he knew, I   110
warrant him.

CLOWN How do you now?

AUTOLYCUS Sweet sir, much better than I was. I can stand
and walk. I will even take leave of you and pace softly
towards my kinsman's.   115

CLOWN Shall I bring thee on the way?

AUTOLYCUS No good-faced sir, no sweet sir.

CLOWN Then fare thee well, I must go buy spices for
our sheep-shearing.   *Exit.*

AUTOLYCUS Prosper you, sweet sir! Your purse is not   120
hot enough to purchase your spice. I'll be with you
at your sheep-shearing too. If I make not this cheat
bring out another and the shearers prove sheep, let
me be unrolled and my name put in the book of
virtue!   *(Song.)*
　　　　　Jog on, jog on, the footpath way,
　　　　　And merrily hent the stile-a;
　　　　　A merry heart goes all the day,
　　　　　Your sad tires in a mile-a.   *Exit.*

97 **compassed a motion** acquired a puppet-show
98 **Prodigal Son** (Biblical themes were common)
99 **living** property, estate
102 **Prig** thief
110 **I am false . . . way** my heart fails me in that sort of business
122 **cheat** rogue's trick
124 **unrolled** struck off the official list (of rogues)
127 **hent** take hold of (to leap over)

✠

Rehearsing the Scene

Ale, women and birdsong, enjoyed in summer sunshine, and the delight of singing about them to an appreciative audience, start this scene; and it concludes with a song for the foot traveller who has a whole day for his journey and a fence to leap over. These songs set the mood: both can be entirely merry and openhearted, but both allude to a darker side of life—winter when there is little pleasure for the wanderer, and a sad heart which will burden a lonely traveller. Clown also has two aspects: he has enough money in his purse for the feast, but he is a prey for the most obvious con artist.

The actors must choose how much to play the dark side of their lives. Either they can be two feeble optimists, unaware of danger or of anything beyond the pleasures of the moment (even Autolycus's fear of hanging may be kept in check by the thought of his own ability to escape), or their present good spirits can be precarious, and misadventure has clearly left its mark on them, so that a certain desperation, forcefulness or fear is evident, even on this sunny occasion.

Does Autolycus overact his agony so grossly that the Clown is shown as a complete fool, or does he act it surprisingly well because it is informed by a genuine terror (see ll. 28-29)?

Does Clown have true difficulty with his accounting, or does his delight in feasting and singing so preoccupy his mind that the counting becomes a festival game in itself?

However dark or light the playing, there is a touch of magic in the events. As soon as Autolycus speaks of "beating and hanging" (l. 29), whether this is in jest or earnest, a shepherd does enter on cue ready to be fleeced. When Clown is troubled by having to keep track of his purchases, the pickpocket is at hand to relieve him of his cash. When Clown is ready to be generous, he has already lost his money, and Autolycus only just escapes discovery.

A number of issues need to be considered carefully. Is Autolycus by any standard dressed in genuinely ragged clothes or does his attire appear ragged only in the context of his service to Prince Florizel (ll. 13-14)? Does Clown enter practicing his figures to prove to himself that he can do the shopping, or because is he amazed at how much he has to spend on the feast? Is Clown so pleased with his joke about a "horseman's coat" (ll. 67-9) that he does not suspect the pretended pain of Autolycus, or does he barely notice that he has made a joke because he is intent on helping Autolycus to understand his predicament? His inability to see Autolycus's joke about "virtue" at court (ll. 89-95) might favor the second interpretation and suggest that Clown is very sober throughout the scene, despite all his excitement—or because of it.

When Autolycus describes himself as the thief who has robbed himself, is he enjoying the extra risk that he will be recognized? Or is he so pleased with his pickpocketing that he says what comes most readily to mind and then gets alarmed when he has said too much?

Does Clown become bellicose himself as he tells Autolycus to look "big and spit"? Now that he has set the stranger on his feet, the good shepherd may have become more confident, forgetting his own troubles and behaving as if he were totally in charge of events; so his last speeches will be almost boasts, an assumption of great generosity. But Clown might just as well fear Autolycus and issue his last speeches as attempts at bravado as he returns to the same problems with which he entered the scene. Either way, Clown will shape the scene and provide its concluding climax: Autolycus has a very rewarding part, but Clown can, and should, pull attention away from him and control the balance of the scene without seeming to do so.

35

The Tempest

Act II, Scene i

SEBASTIAN and ANTONIO

✠

After attending the wedding of his daughter in Tunis, Alonso, King of Naples, has been shipwrecked together with his entire court. Only his son and heir, Ferdinand, is missing and the others, keeping together for safety's sake, have been searching for him. They have become increasingly aware that something very unusual is happening, for they are all entirely unscathed by their adventure and their clothes look, if anything, "fresher than before." Moreover they have felt, quite suddenly, very tired and all at the same time have fallen asleep on the ground—all except Sebastian and Antonio.

These two are both younger brothers. Antonio had usurped the power of his elder brother years ago, and had set him adrift at sea accompanied by his infant daughter; since then he has reigned as Duke of Milan. Sebastian's older brother is Alonso, who is the king sleeping at his feet.

For this scene, four or more sleeping bodies are required but these can be supplied by pillows, boxes, rolls of material, whatever is conveniently at hand. One such "body" should be identified as the king's, and another as Gonzalo's—he is a very senior court politician.

Swords are needed for this scene, in scabbards.

✠

SEBASTIAN
What a strange drowsiness possesses them!
ANTONIO
It is the quality o' th' climate.
SEBASTIAN   Why
Doth it not then our eyelids sink? I find not
Myself disposed to sleep.

ANTONIO   Nor I: my spirits are nimble.
They fell together all, as by consent;   5
They dropped as by a thunderstroke. What might
Worthy Sebastian? O what might!—No more!—
And yet methinks I see it in thy face,
What thou shouldst be. Th' occasion speaks thee and
My strong imagination sees a crown   10
Dropping upon thy head.
SEBASTIAN   What? Art thou waking?
ANTONIO
Do you not hear me speak?
SEBASTIAN   I do and surely
It is a sleepy language and thou speak'st
Out of thy sleep. What is it thou didst say?
This is a strange repose, to be asleep   15
With eyes wide open, standing, speaking, moving
And yet so fast asleep.
ANTONIO   Noble Sebastian,
Thou let'st thy fortune sleep—die rather—wink'st
While thou art waking.
SEBASTIAN   Thou dost snore distinctly;
There's meaning in thy snores.   20
ANTONIO
I am more serious than my custom. You
Must be so too, if heed me; which to do
Trebles thee o'er.
SEBASTIAN   Well I am standing water.
ANTONIO
I'll teach you how to flow.
SEBASTIAN   Do so. To ebb
Hereditary sloth instructs me.
ANTONIO   O   25
If you but knew how you the purpose cherish

---

5 **consent** agreement
9 **speaks** calls to action/ testifies to
18 **wink'st** hast thine eyes closed
22 **if heed** if you heed
23 **Trebles thee o'er** increases your

fortunes threefold
25 **hereditary sloth** inherited laziness/being born a younger son
26 **purpose** proposal

Whiles thus you mock it, how, in stripping it,
You more invest it! Ebbing men indeed
Must often do so near the bottom run
By their own fear or sloth.

SEBASTIAN   Prithee say on.   30
The setting of thine eye and cheek proclaim
A matter from thee and a birth indeed
Which throes thee much to yield.

ANTONIO   Thus sir:
Although this lord of weak remembrance, this
Who shall be of as little memory   35
When he is earthed, hath here almost persuaded
(For he's a spirit of persuasion, only
Professes to persuade) the king his son's alive,
'Tis as impossible that he's undrowned
As he that sleeps here swims.

SEBASTIAN   I have no hope   40
That he's undrowned.

ANTONIO   O out of that "no hope"
What great hope have you! No hope that way is
Another way so high a hope that even
Ambition cannot pierce a wink beyond
But doubt discovery there. Will you grant with me   45
That Ferdinand is drowned?

SEBASTIAN   He's gone.

ANTONIO   Then tell me
Who's the next heir of Naples?

SEBASTIAN   Claribel.

ANTONIO
She that is Queen of Tunis, she that dwells

---

28 **invest** (1) clothe (2) give (royal) power to
29 **so near . . . run** i. e., their fortunes touch rock bottom
30 **Prithee** pray, please
31 **setting** fixed expression
32 **matter** theme of importance
33 **throes** pains (pun on **matter** = pus)

34 **weak remembrance** failing memory
36 **earthed** buried
38 **Profess to persuade** (1) has the profession of councilor (2) argues to argue
44 **wink** glimpse
45 **doubt discovery** distrust what it sees

Ten leagues beyond a man's life, she that from Naples
Can have no note—unless the sun were post;   50
The man i' th' moon's too slow—till newborn chins
Be rough and razorable; she that from whom
We all were sea-swallowed, though some cast again,
And by that destiny to perform an act
Whereof what's past is prologue, what to come   55
In yours and my discharge.

SEBASTIAN   What stuff is this? How say you?
'Tis true my brother's daughter 's Queen of Tunis,
So is she heir of Naples; twixt which regions
There is some space.

ANTONIO   A space whose ev'ry cubit
Seems to cry out, "How shall that Claribel   60
Measure us back to Naples? Keep in Tunis
And let Sebastian wake!" Say this were death
That now hath seized them, why they were no worse
Than now they are. There be that can rule Naples
As well as he that sleeps, lords that can prate   65
As amply and unecessarily
As this Gonzalo—I myself could make
A chough of as deep chat. O that you bore
The mind that I do, what a sleep were this
For your advancement! Do you understand me?   70

SEBASTIAN
Methinks I do.

ANTONIO   And how does your content
Tender your own good fortune?

SEBASTIAN   I remember

---

49 **man's life** i. e., a lifetime's journey
50 **note** information;
post messenger
53 **sea-swallowed** drowned;
cast thrown on shore (pun on **cast** = throw of dice)
54 **perform** (pun on **cast**ing a play; see l. 53)

56 **discharge** (1) execution (2) performance
59 **cubit** (about twenty inches)
61 **Measure us** travel to us
68 **chough . . . chat** jackdaw to chatter as gravely as he
71 **content** understanding
72 **Tender** regard, take care of

You did supplant your brother Prospero.

ANTONIO   True.
And look how well my garments sit upon me
Much feater than before. My brother's servants   75
Were then my fellows, now they are my men.

SEBASTIAN
But for your conscience—

ANTONIO
Ay sir, where lies that? If 'twere a kibe,
'Twould put me to my slipper, but I feel not
This diety in my bosom. Twenty consciences   80
That stand 'twixt me and Milan, candied be they
And melt, ere they molest! Here lies your brother,
No better than the earth he lies upon—
If he were that which now he's like, that's dead—
Whom I with this obedient steel (three inches of it)   85
Can lay to bed forever; whiles you, doing thus,
To the perpetual wink for aye might put
This ancient morsel, this Sir Prudence, who
Should not upbraid our course. For all the rest,
They'll take suggestion as a cat laps milk;   90
They'll tell the clock to any business that
We say befits the hour.

SEBASTIAN   Thy case, dear friend,
Shall be my precedent. As thou got'st Milan,
I'll come by Naples. Draw thy sword. One stroke
Shall free thee from the tribute which thou payest   95
And I the king shall love thee.

ANTONIO   Draw together
And when I rear my hand, do you the like
To fall it on Gonzalo.

SEBASTIAN   O but one word!

---

75 **feater** more trimly
78 **kibe** blister on the heel
81 **candied** sugared, flattered
82 **molest** cause trouble
87 **wink** closed eye (i. e., sleep)

90 **suggestion** temptation
91 **tell the clock** (1) count the
    strokes of the clock (2) agree
98 **one word** i. e., one thing more

✠

Rehearsing the Scene

Although Antonio takes the initiative, it would be a mistake to assume that he alone drives the scene forward. Sebastian is a practiced politician and knows how to play the waiting game to his own advantage; he is also the first one to look carefully at the sleeping bodies.

Antonio is very careful in raising the subject of assassination: see, for example, the complicated syntax and active wit of his speech, once Sebastian has indicated he is ready to listen (ll. 33-40). It is quite possible for Sebastian to be the one in control, his reference to his own "sloth" (l. 25) being only a pretense at aristocratic laziness and self-deprecation, designed to insure that Antonio commits himself first.

Antonio speaks of his own "strong imagination" (l. 10) and this can be a useful clue for the actor. However concerned Antonio may be not to wake the sleepers and not to speak before time, Sebastian can see by the "setting" of his eye that he is in the grip of some idea that matters a great deal to him (ll. 31-33). When Antonio alludes for the first time to what must be done, his theatrical and godlike summons (ll. 54-56), springing out of a sharper, more everyday wit, can resound with imaginative power. Sebastian remains cool, and perhaps critical of this excess, but Antonio's mind is now racing ahead. The actor should resist making the proposal of murder too simple and enthusiastic: Antonio is able at this crisis to manage neat mimicry as a preface for his first use of the word "death," which is slipped in and then followed by a judicious touch of flattery (ll. 62-65). In contrast, Sebastian answers the summons carefully and briefly, "Methinks I do" (l. 71); and, when pressed to be more specific, challenges Antonio to commit himself. Probably this is the point where Antonio knows he has won, for he answers briskly and confidently (ll. 73-77).

But here is a critical juncture for both actors and an indication of how much can be presented subtextually in this scene. Having both played a very clever game of probing and concealment, searching behind words and appearances, now they may confront a major issue with the minimum of fuss, perhaps in a silence. As at lines 54-56, Antonio's reassuring words (ll. 74-76) echo now some words from *Macbeth* (I.iii and V.ii) concerned with the murder of Duncan: are these men, like Macbeth, responding to fear as well as to ambition? "But for your conscience" (l. 77) is an incomplete verse line and in the silence which follows the two may face the full consequences of murder. Antonio continues in a lighter vein, perhaps a sign that he fights to put fear behind him.

At this time the bodies should be very real to both characters. And a strange delay occurs, for although Sebastian says "Draw thy sword" (l. 94), Antonio's "Draw together" two lines later shows that neither acts at once. The scene will be very, very quiet; perhaps the breathing of the sleepers becomes audible. They have indeed been "snoring," according to Ariel who will enter later to waken them(see II.i. 304). Perhaps neither of them has drawn before Sebastian's "O but one word!".

Sebastian's last words seem to come from nowhere, and that might be intentional: perhaps they should be a response to strange and harsh sounds accompanying the arrival of the spirit Ariel who has been sent by Prospero, the lord of the island, a magician andthe former Duke of Milan, and who will wake the sleepers immediately after Sebastian has spoken. But Sebastian may well have questions to raise: Why does Antonio leave to him the secondary job of killing Gonzalo? How can Sebastian be sure he will not be blackmailed? Why not at least try to kill all the courtiers? If a strong subtextual energy has been created earlier, the actor should be able to find plenty of motive for a last-minute stall.

On a verbal level this scene is straightforward and intermittently witty, but to play the reality of two men preparing to murder and—perhaps more difficult—to trust each other, is not at all easy.

SHAKESPEARE'S PLAYS IN PERFORMANCE by John Russell Brown

In this volume, John Russell Brown snatches Shakespeare from the clutches of dusty academics and thrusts him centerstage where he belongs—in performance.

Brown's thorough analysis of the theatrical experience of Shakespeare forcibly demonstrates how the text is brought to life: awakened, colored, emphasized, and extended by actors and audiences, designers and directors.

"A knowledge of what precisely can and should happen when a play is performed is, for me, the essential first step towards an understanding of Shakespeare."
—*from the Introduction by John Russell Brown*

paper•ISBN 1-55783-136-X•$14.95

SOLILOQUY!

The Shakespeare Monologues
Edited by Michael Earley and Philippa Keil

At last, over 175 of Shakespeare's finest and most
performable monologues taken from all 37 plays are
here in two easy-to-use volumes (MEN and WOMEN).
Selections travel the entire spectrum of the great
dramatist's vision, from comedies and romances to
tragedies, pathos and histories.

*"Soliloquy is an excellent and comprehensive collec-
tion of Shakespeare's speeches. Not only are the monologues wide-ranging and varied, but they are superbly
annotated. Each volume is prefaced by an informative and
reassuring introduction, which explains the signals and
signposts by which Shakespeare helps an actor on his journey through the text. It includes a very good explanation of
blank verse, with excellent examples of irregularities which
are specifically related to character and acting intentions.
These two books are a must for any actor in search of a
'classical' audition piece."*

ELIZABETH SMITH
Head of Voice & Speech
The Juilliard School

paper•MEN: ISBN 0-936839-78-3 • WOMEN: ISBN 0936839-79-1

APPLAUSE

THE ACTOR AND THE TEXT
by Cicely Berry

As voice director of the Royal Shakespeare
Company, Cicely Berry has worked with actors such
as Jeremy Irons, Derek Jacobi, Jonathan Pryce, Sinead
Cusack and Antony Sher. The Actor and The Text
brings Ms. Berry's methods of applying vocal production skills within a text to the general public.

While this book focuses primarily on speaking
Shakespeare, Ms. Berry also includes the speaking of
some modern playwrights, such as Edward Bond.

As Ms. Berry describes her own volume in the
introduction:

" ... this book is not simply about making the
voice sound more interesting. It is about getting
inside the words we use ...It is about making the language organic, so that the words act as a spur to the
sound ..."

paper•ISBN 1-155783-138-6

MONOLOGUE WORKSHOP

From Search to Discovery
in Audition and Performance
by Jack Poggi

To those for whom the monologue has always been synonymous with terror, *The Monologue Workshop* will prove an indispensable ally. Jack Poggi's new book answers the long-felt need among actors for top-notch guidance in finding, rehearsing and performing monologues. For those who find themselves groping for speech just hours before their "big break," this book is their guide to salvation.

The Monologue Workshop supplies the tools to discover new pieces before they become over-familiar, excavate older material that has been neglected, and adapt material from non-dramatic sources (novels, short stories, letters, diaries, autobiographies, even newspaper columns). There are also chapters on writing original monologues and creating solo performances in the style of Lily Tomlin and Eric Bogosian.

Besides the wealth of practical advice he offers, Poggi transforms the monologue experience from a terrifying ordeal into an exhilarating opportunity. Jack Poggi, as many working actors will attest, is the actor's partner in a process they had always thought was without one.

paper•ISBN 1-55783-031-2

STANISLAVSKI REVEALED
by Sonia Moore

Other than Stanislavski's own published work, the most widely read interpretation of his techniques remains Sonia Moore's pioneering study, The Stanislavski System. Sonia Moore is on the frontier again now as she reveals the subtle tissue of ideas behind what Stanislavski regarded as his "major breakthrough," the Method of Physical Actions. Moore has devoted the last decade in her world-famous studio to an investigation of Stanislavski's final technique. The result is the first detailed discussion of Moore's own theory of psychophysical unity which she has based on her intensive practical meditation on Stanislavski's consummate conclusions about acting.

Demolishing the popular notion that his methods depend on private—self-centered—expression, Moore now reveals Stanislavski as the advocate of deliberate, controlled, conscious technique—internal and external at the same time—a technique that makes tremendous demands on actors but that rewards them with the priceless gift of creative life.

paper • ISBN: 1-55783-103-3

ACTING IN RESTORATION COMEDY

Based on the BBC Master Class Series
By Simon Callow

The art of acting in Restoration Comedy, the buoyant, often bawdy romps which celebrated the reopening of the English theatres after Cromwell's dour reign, is the subject of Simon Callow's bold new investigation. There is cause again to celebrate as Callow, one of Britain's foremost actors, aims to restore the form to all its original voluptuous vigor. Callow shows the way to attain clarity and hilarity in some of the most delightful roles ever conceived for the theatre.

Simon Callow is the author of *Being an Actor* and *Charles Laughton: A Difficult Actor*. He has won critical acclaim for his performances in numerous productions including *Faust*, *The Relapse*, and *Titus Andronicus*.

paper • ISBN: 1-55783-119-X